LEADING FROM
BEHIND

THE OBAMA DOCTRINE AND THE U.S.
RETREAT FROM INTERNATIONAL AFFAIRS.

LEADING FROM
BEHIND

THE OBAMA DOCTRINE AND THE U.S. RETREAT FROM INTERNATIONAL AFFAIRS.

HERBERT I. LONDON
WITH BRYAN GRIFFIN

LONDON CENTER
FOR POLICY RESEARCH

The London Center for Policy Research

New York, New York

www.londoncenter.org

© 2017 The London Center for Policy Research

Book design by Logotecture

ISBN-13: 978-0692839218
ISBN-10: 0692839216

Contents

Author's Note

Foreign policy, to the extent it is discernable, often hides behind a man—e.g., the Monroe Doctrine, the Bush Doctrine, Wilsonian policy. Since the president is commander in chief, his prerogatives and decisions constitute the nature of international affairs for the nation.

When President Obama said he was intent on "change," scarcely anyone imagined the magnitude of that change. There have been changes on the domestic front, but even the Affordable Care Act does not measure up in scope and influence to the change that has occurred in foreign policy.

President Obama's decisions on Iran, Syria and the Islamic State fit a strict, even unbending, ideological pattern. His animating motivation has been to retract American power from the Middle East and establish a new national consensus for a policy based on an accommodationist foreign policy.

The ostensible purpose of this new policy stance was to create a post-American world that includes pockets of influence that in the aggregate create a balance of power. Rather than have a great power (read: United States) that serves as a balance wheel, international affairs would, in the president's mind, revert to a Congress of

Vienna stance, in which many nations would vie with one another for global stability.

Assuming the best possible motive for his position, President Obama reflects a belief that American military action in far-off lands tends to do more harm than good, sowing resentment abroad and cynicism at home. Hence the president's "apologia" peregrinations, all the while calculating for a physical and emotional withdrawal from global affairs.

Whether intended or not, the president's view about world affairs has led many international leaders to assume the United States could no longer be counted on as an ally and an "insurance policy," even with mutual defense pacts signed and sealed. In the post-American world, the U.S. is either irrelevant, as is the case in the recent Syrian peace negotiations, or an ally that is unreliable, as is the case after the International Court of Justice ruled against China and for the Philippines in the Spratly Islands case.

As the papers in this book contend, when a president fails to balance his outlook with intelligence on the ground, principle becomes theology. This theology is often expressed as the "undo" Bush Doctrine—a reflexive opposition to President Obama's predecessor and a knee-jerk response to Bush supporters. President Obama's overarching position, implicit in his 2009 Cairo speech and explicit in press conferences throughout his presidency, is: What Bush has accomplished, he will oppose.

In a February 2015 address, President Obama derided the Islamic State (IS) as a brutal, vicious death cult that, in the name of religion, carries out unspeakable acts of barbarism. Yet he cautioned against blanket judgment, arguing, "Lest we get onto our high horse and think this is unique to some other place, remember that during the Crusades and the Inquisitions, people committed terrible deeds in the name of Christ."

This remarkable statement provided an opening into the mindset of the president. Not merely is this anachronistic analogy inappropriate, but it reveals a view of policy that glosses over American interests and behavior. It also tellingly confuses the atrocities committed in the name of Christianity centuries ago with acts that are contemporaneous. And surely the president had to realize that Christian acts of violence in the past were antithetical to the faith's precepts, while Islam has been inexorably linked with violence, as Koranic verses attest. The prophet Mohammed devised a concept of jihad, "execution is the path of Allah," as a means of converting brutal practice into religious duty. As he noted, "I was ordered to fight all men until they say, 'There is no god but Allah.'"

For reasons known only to him, President Obama refuses to acknowledge this doctrinal issue, even though President el-Sisi of Egypt, a pious Muslim, has described "the violence within our faith" and called for "a revolution from within." The belief in many Islamic quarters that this is a coercive religion that aims to bring its message to all corners of the earth has been ignored by the leader of the free world. When the militant dimensions of the religion were verified in Paris, San Bernardino and Orlando, the president tended to euphemize these acts as violent extremism, bending over backward to avoid saying these actions conform to certain elements of the faith. Yet to deny this reality, to imagine that this flame within Islam can be extinguished through investment in education and skills training, is the height of folly. President Obama has appeared as a man apart, an intractable force unwilling to accept the irreconcilable nature of the militant Islamic challenge.

Not only has President Obama turned Middle East policy upside down, but his policy perspective has had as disastrous an influence on the geopolitics of North Africa and South Asia. The president is bluntly critical of traditional U.S. allies as well as advice from the Washington foreign policy establishment. In the case of this president, the appellation that foreign policy is a one-man show applies. He ardently believes that U.S. involvement in Vietnam left behind chaos, slaughter and an authoritarian government. He does not believe that Reagan influenced the release of American hostages in Iran. Most significantly, he seems to believe that he has a superior ability to deal with foreign policy matters than his predecessors had.

Even when it can be presented as an unequivocal failure, the president defends his Syria policy of non-intervention by noting that he avoided the deployment of American forces in an enlarged war and resisted the pressure from his advisors to intervene. His own "red line" in the use of chemical weapons turned out to be ephemeral. Yet, pulling back from immediate pressures and thinking it "through in my own mind was in America's interest...was as tough a decision as I've made." Here is the presidential "stranger," a man who believes he can make decisions without the guidance of others and, as President Obama put it, avoid the "playbook that comes out of the foreign policy establishment."

In one instance President Obama told Russian president Putin that if Russia could force Syrian president Bashar al-Assad to get rid of chemical weapons, a U.S. military strike against al-Assad would be unnecessary. In one bold stroke President Obama invited Russia to be a principal in Middle East policy, a shift of 180 degrees from the 1975 position that Russia should be kept out of regional affairs.

President Obama rationalized this decision and many others by arguing that "the arc of history" is moving toward a more tolerant and peaceful world. One might even describe this (trend) as the Marxist view of inevitable historic evolution. The problem, of course, is that human intervention alters the arc and changes the history.

Because of President Obama's fanatical adherence to this belief, the Islamic State is not a major threat and the Chinese assertions of territorial claims over the South China Sea and the contested islands within their unilaterally defined air perimeter are not major issues. As a consequence, precipitous action of any kind is unwarranted.

Since World War II the Chinese leadership from Mao to Xi remembered the U.S. role in forcing the Japanese out of China. Until recently the Chinese admired American military strength and its technological advantages. Chinese goals on the technical front are organized around U.S. achievements. However, in the past eight years admiration has been converted into cynicism, and fear of American military superiority in the Pacific basin has been converted to assertiveness. For the Chinese, the U.S. is not what it once was, and China is on the pathway to being the hegemon in Asia.

In eight years of presidential authority, President Obama's grand strategy of avoidance and retreat has not resulted in a more stable world than the one President Bush passed on to his successor. The Iran deal merely delays and does not prevent the Iranian acquisition of nuclear weapons. Even the so-called achievements of the Obama years—the opening to Cuba, the Paris climate-change accord, the Trans-Pacific Partnership trade agreement and the Iran nuclear deal—depend on the "potential" of future action. None of the "achievements" have achieved anything in actuality, a point the administration will concede; but spokespeople nonetheless refer to what will happen. That, as I see it, is a wager, not a policy.

Although theories on foreign policy vanish like soap bubbles, there are four general categories that seemingly characterize the present debate and limn President Obama's stance on international affairs.

Liberal internationalism is predicated on the belief that intervention on a military scale and for humanitarian purposes may be necessary to preserve order. As the liberal internationalists see it, liberal states founded on individual rights, free speech, private property and the rule of law do not engage in war. Hence, as President Reagan, among others, noted, we need a "campaign for democratic developments." The essence of this position is that stability and democracy go hand in glove.

Realism in international affairs emerged from the "realpolitik" statesmanship of early modern Europe. It is based on the foundational belief that world politics is a continuing and unending field of conflicts with various actors pursuing power. Realism assumes no actor exists above states, and states will inevitably pursue their own interests. In realist tradition, security is based on the principle of a balance of power and on the assumption that moral absolutes such as right and wrong are impractical.

The nationalist school of thought, most recently advocated by Donald Trump, is that one's own nation state comes first, a reflection of a distinct and idiosyncratic grouping that must be protected against opposing interests. Hence, the nationalist opposes liberal immigration policy and entangling foreign alliances.

President Obama's foreign policy—to the extent there is one—is based on less foreign and less policy. The president's view is "rejectionist—i.e., reject the interventions arranged by President Bush and reject the idea that the U.S. has the power (and the assumed burden) to be the guarantor of global equilibrium. The primary position is that previous alliances and bilateral defense pacts are less significant than bringing enemies into the vast arms of the international community so that their hostility can be modified. Consistent with the president's position is his conviction that he is not an advocate for narrowly defined American interests, but is more a "citizen of the world," to use his own phase.

In affirming a non-interventionist stance, the president also displayed a hard-left position on some matters, such as the closing of Guantanamo and the dramatic reduction of nuclear weapons as a deterrent. On December 21, 2016, President Obama ordered an American abstention on a United Nations Security Council vote condemning Israeli settlements in the West Bank. The 14-0 vote accedes to the Palestinian demand for a return to the 1967 borders and by "international law" forbids any development in contiguous Israeli territory. This swan song by President Obama was intended as an anti-Israeli slight—some have called it a betrayal—that was intended to legitimatize the establishment of a Palestinian state by decree. Moreover, any attempt to undo this decision in the Trump administration will undoubtedly face a Russian or Chinese veto in the Security Council. Evidence exists to contend that the Obama administration actually orchestrated the resolution and was responsible for its wording. This decision represents a historic break in diplomatic relations between Israel and the United States, a position consistent with leftist advocacy and President Obama's antipathy to the state of Israel.

As President Obama noted in a 2009 U.N. speech, "It is my deeply held belief that in the year 2009—more than at any point in human history—the interest of nations and people are shared.... In an era when our destiny is shared, power is no longer a zero-sum game. No one nation can or should try to dominate another nation. No world order that elevates one nation or group of people over another will succeed. No balance of power among nations will hold."

What patrons of foreign policy want to know is—whatever the orientation—whether the policy position has been successful. By that one asks, are the nations of the globe reasonably stable? Some contend that President Obama's position offers a respite from international obligations the U.S. cannot afford and encourages other states to fill the power vacuum. Most critics, however, would deem President Obama to have been a failure.

Russia has a new and influential platform in the Middle East. China has converted itself into the neo-Middle Kingdom of the Pacific, with U.S. weakness complicit in the power grab. The Islamic State has marched through Iraq and Syria with little opposition and created the first caliphate in modern times, spreading death and destruction in its wake. Iran's imperial ambitions have been reinforced by an administration that believes the Shia Muslims can be a regional, stabilizing influence. And from Japan to Egypt, from Saudi Arabia to Pakistan, there is the widely accepted notion that the U.S. cannot be counted on. "A loss of confidence" is the way many foreign leaders describe their attitude to the United States.

In a curious way, the dispersal of power has led to a scenario similar to that of 1914, when there was confusion about global leadership and a relatively minor event, the assassination of Archduke Franz Ferdinand, set the world aflame. What holds the globe in check from the escalation of animosities is the fear of nuclear exchange and a possible Armageddon. But, of course, there is the chance a rogue government or non-government actor could use a nuclear device, setting the world on an irreversible course.

Offsetting the legacy of President Obama is the challenge of the next administration, the Trump administration. Whether Obama policy can be undone remains to be seen, but the path to resolution has many hazards along the way, and the lights on this road are not synchronized in green. Moreover, Donald Trump, an inexperienced hand on foreign policy, must assume responsibility for many of the policy decisions during the Obama years. On the one hand, he is constrained by the past; on the other hand, he has to try to undo the past by restoring U.S. leadership in global matters. This is a difference in positions even Solomon could not possibly reconcile.

To judge from the presidential campaign, Donald Trump is likely to move away from defense alliances and trade agreements, disengaging from nation building and moving incrementally for China and Russia to have influence over their respective regions— without calling them spheres of influence. But this assumes that President Trump will act like candidate Trump. Very often events take hold of stated goals. As a non-ideological personality, he might end up as an interventionist should Russian and Chinese imperial goals interfere with or overstep American global interests. His pragmatism might emerge as existential interventionism. History has many examples that confirm this outcome.

Herbert I. London

Editor's Note

I want to thank my friend, Herb London, for asking me to be a part of this project. It was an honor to be asked to compile his anthology. Dr. London's voice is an important current of clarity in the groundswell of modern punditry. In his writing, as I know him to act in life, Dr. London emphasizes the importance of a strong moral compass. I know America possesses such a foundation. I hope, in part through this anthology, that the importance of America's leadership by this compass on the world stage is reaffirmed.

President Obama's foreign policy has lessened American influence abroad. Like many swept up in the popular trend of American self-flagellation, it is easy to write off American international leadership as egotistical or elitist. It is nothing of the sort, and extraordinarily more important than that. America is a loud, clear, constant advocate for freedom, equality, mutual human respect and—by a superior military—peace. America may not be perfect, but in that which it does abroad it strives to uphold these virtues.

The difficult choices that must be made for peace, often at odds with the easy or even non-confrontational choices, are the choices that America does not shy away from making. The oppressors, the violent and the authoritarian shroud themselves in the free passes granted by the current zeitgeist of moral relativism. The world is at a critical juncture. A nuclear Iran, an emboldened China, a volatile Russia and a feckless international body define our time. It is my sincerest hope that U.S. presidents to come will face these challenges with the unyielding resolve that America is a force for good.

Bryan Griffin

Introduction

The articles in this book are an attempt to make sense of the evolving foreign policy of President Obama during the eight years of his presidency, and of the changing conditions of world affairs during this same period.

In many cases, they responded in real time to certain events, or were timely articles as segues to larger critiques of President Obama's habitual foreign policy offenses.

We leave it to the reader to discern the many currents of policy that emerged during that time, but on one matter there cannot be any doubt: the Obama years ushered in great change on the world stage.

What part of that change is due to the president, and what part can be attributed to world conditions over which he had little control, remain as subjects for future scholarship.

Examining foreign policy through lengthy, philosophical analysis is an exercise for the academic. Instead, we have compiled Dr. London's original articles, with brief contextual information, for the reader to experience President Obama's decisions on the world stage as we all observed them.

The Obama Doctrine

Blind Faith in Diplomacy

President Obama's foreign policy was defined by the use of "soft power." In January of 2009, **New York Times** *columnist Roger Cohen wrote an op-ed praising President Obama's marked shift away from President Bush's active approach to defeating terrorism. A proven orator on the campaign trail, President Obama sought to use his skill on behalf of America's foreign interests. However earnest President Obama may have been in declaring the war on terror over, saying it didn't make it so.*

The Obama Doctrine (2009)
Originally published on Family Security Matters

"The war on terror is over" declared *International Herald Tribune* columnist Roger Cohen, celebrating on behalf of the collected eminences of the official and unofficial foreign policy establishment.

As he notes, "the with-us-or-against-us global struggle…in which a freedom-loving West confronts the undifferentiated forces of darkness…has been terminated."

The presumption is that we are not fighting a war—which we refuse to acknowledge; we are merely engaged in "a strategic challenge." Goodbye, Bush Doctrine; hello Obama rapprochement with the Muslim world.

President Obama argues that "the language we use matters." Of course it does, but action speaks louder than words. If the recent language of respect is to be taken seriously, arms will be converted into plowshares and goodwill may seize the globe. The only problem with this analysis is al Qaeda doesn't buy into President Obama's rhetoric and most in the organization don't read the *Herald Tribune*.

Mr. Cohen, caught up in celebratory notions, tells us President Obama understands the need for respect and self-critical analysis, something omitted from Bush speeches, despite scant evidence provided for this claim. Now that President Obama says, "Americans are not your enemy," there is little to fear from the Muslim world.

Mr. Cohen is convinced President Obama is inclusive, as opposed to Bush's supremacist views, clearly a move in a realistic direction.

According to Mr. Cohen, "Bush had the ideological framework wrong. President Obama has transformed it by ending the war on terror." Alas, one side may declare a war over, but that declaration hasn't any bearing on those who choose to continue fighting. Words may influence a policy, but they rarely influence what happens on the ground.

Clearly President Bush made tactical errors, but he did understand there is a global struggle with radical Islam that will test our mettle. His strategic vision included the use of forceful opposition where it will make a difference internationally, the use of democracy as an instrument for stabilization and the use of preemption in order to avoid a catastrophic loss of life.

When President Obama said he would turn the clock back 20 or 30 years in examining our relationship with the Muslim world, what could he possibly have been thinking? Was it the orchestrated violence of Muammar Qaddafi that we should want to revisit? Or perhaps the kidnapping of American diplomats in Tehran?

Does President Obama actually believe that "soft power," namely his persuasive arguments, will substitute for battleships or fighter jets? Has a new age commenced because he wills it? Will Osama bin Laden or Mahmoud Ahmadinejad accept his well-meaning rhetoric as signs of an accommodating America? And even if we are accommodative, why should our enemies adapt a similar stance? What would they gain in doing so?

President Bush didn't disrespect Iran; he merely recognized the imperial aspirations of the mullahs—a point often made by Arab leaders in the Middle East. Perhaps the new approach President Obama has adopted, and people like Mr. Cohen countenance, will work. I certainly hope so.

But common sense suggests the Obama overtures are naïve and troublesome. They foreshadow a United States unwilling to stand by its commitments and foreign interests. As everyone knows, talk is cheap. It is even discounted in diplomatic channels. If negotiation serves as cover for the Iranian pursuit of nuclear weapons, it is also dangerous.

As Vice President Joe Biden indicated during the campaign season, this president will be tested. Well, the tests have begun. Mr. Cohen may believe President Obama has started down the track of a new paradigm. But there are others—and I fall into this category—who believe we are on the road to appeasement and accommodation that failed us in the past and led to the dislocation and death of millions in the last century.

Words can soothe and they can harm. If the Obama Doctrine is "speak softly and don't carry a stick," I'm afraid it cannot be effective. Evil hasn't disappeared from world affairs because President Obama has willed it. If anything, his rhetoric suggests the triumph of belief over reality or the naïve notion that hope and truth are interchangeable.

Obama's Deal Depends on Rational Actors (2015)
Originally published on Newsmax

President Obama and Secretary of State John Kerry have conceded that some portion of the money released to Iran through the lifting of sanctions will result in "bad behavior," a euphemism for terrorism. The supposition of the president's team is that despite the bad behavior, Iran, unconstrained by sanctions, will in time join the community of responsible nations. In other words, our concessions will yield a positive response from Supreme Leader Ali Khamenei and his acolytes.

What is evidenced in these negotiations is the implicit Western belief in rationalism, a stance that suggests our enemies, with the appropriate incentives, will act just as we would. "Trust but verify" is the qualifier President Reagan used in his negotiations with the Soviets. President Obama, on the other hand, has resorted to trust and having faith in rational expectations. What happens when the adversary is irrational remains unclear. A theological belief system and acceptance of taqiyya, or a religious lie to promote the interests of Islam, challenge assumptions of rationality.

Nonetheless, rationalists persist. At a recent meeting a discussion took place on ways to combat the Islamic State's influence in the Middle East. The intelligent and well-meaning host argued that a campaign designed to show the unspeakable and monstrous crimes of ISIL combatants might discourage many from joining this poisonous group. Here was the rationalist worldview on display— clear, hopeful and seemingly sensible. Yet the one point rationalists cannot seem to comprehend is that rationalism doesn't defeat irrationalism. At some point, even if it isn't in his nature and even if there is a recalcitrance to embrace this position, the rationalist must be as ruthless as his enemy.

The only way to defeat the dragon is to deliver enough heat to counter his fire. President Lincoln had to send a message to Generals Grant, Sherman and Sheridan—destroy the enemy. General Patton wasn't loved by Eisenhower or FDR, but he could be as ruthless in war as the Nazi forces. Victory against relentless enemies doesn't occur because of films and conferences, it occurs because of sacrifice and bloodshed. That is the axiom of war.

For those who want to avoid war at all costs, there is talk, negotiation and concession. But this is merely a delaying tactic until that moment when the enemy feels sufficient strength or recognizes weakness in his opponent to attack. History speaks volumes on this point.

Yet the same mistake will be made in the West as it was made in the past, because we are constrained by an unwillingness to recognize evil. For us, there is always a rationalization, a belief that there must be a reason for "bad behavior." When the 9/11 attack occurred, there were rationalists publishing articles about American misdeeds in the Middle East and a host of explanations, each having some scintilla of evidence behind it. But it would not be said that this attack was an act of evil and, in order to correct it, we must stamp out that evil using every means available to us.

As a consequence we negotiate, hoping that enemies who say "death to America" don't really mean it. President Obama rationalizes by saying, "That's politics." Too bad no one from the press asks if his political statements should be put under the same lens.

Goethe's Mephistopheles tells Faust, "I am the spirit that denies! And justly so, for all that time creates, He does well who annihilates!" Alas, we deny those who wish to annihilate. We assume that we are immune, that history—this time—will not repeat itself, that the beast who wants to destroy will betray his instincts and act as we would like. Unfortunately the enemy of the West isn't only found in the desert of the Middle East or the steppes of Russia, but within ourselves and a rationalist view that is unwilling to recognize evil.

Shrinking the Military

The soft power approach came at the cost of physical military assets under the Obama administration. Substantial cuts were made to U.S. naval forces. In his reelection bid, President Obama mocked Republican candidate Mitt Romney in a presidential debate when Romney brought up the shrinking naval fleet as a point of concern. "You mentioned the Navy, for example, and that we have fewer ships than we did in 1916," President Obama said. "Well, governor, we also have fewer horses and bayonets because the nature of our military's changed."

Hollowing Out the U.S. Navy (2013)
Originally published on Family Security Matters

From the time Alfred Mahan wrote his classic work on naval power at the beginning of the 20th century to the present, this two-ocean nation relied on sea power to protect its territory at home and its interests abroad. In fact, it was axiomatic to suggest that the hegemonic role the United States played in maintaining global equilibrium was directly related to its ability to project naval power.

Clearly this wasn't always the case. In the World War I period from 1914 to 1918, the United States had a fleet of 363, a fleet smaller than those of Germany, the United Kingdom and France. It remained at that level in the 1920s (an average of 376) and during the '30s till 1938 (an average of 339 ships). Needless to remind anyone about the onset of WWII, there was a slight increase in new vessels from '39 to '41, during the Lend Lease period (a total of 394), but by 1942, with the war in full swing, there were 1,782 ships in the Navy, and by 1945 at the end of the war, the U.S. had 6,768 vessels.

This force level was not sustainable. With retrenchment very much in the air after the war, naval forces were reduced to 634 in 1950. However, Cold War saber rattling as a function of Stalinist diplomacy led to an increase in ships in the U.S. to 1,030 by 1955, a high point from '55 to the present.

In the 1960s naval forces averaged 878 during the decade, and in the 1970s they averaged a reduced 606. In fact, President Reagan, who often discussed the need for a 600-ship navy, never reached that goal in his eight years in office, the highest level being 594 in 1987 and the average being 561 during his tenure.

Now the U.S. Navy is a mere shadow of itself. During the recent presidential debate, candidate Mitt Romney noted that naval capability had shrunk to a level lower than during World War I. Technically he was correct, since naval forces are now at 287. President Obama glibly responded by suggesting this is irrelevant; after all, we don't rely on bayonets or horses either. His implication is that our ships are more sophisticated than their predecessors at sea, so the numbers do not carry the same logistical weight they once did.

By any standard, this is questionable. Numbers matter. If one-third of our ships are in repair and one-third are in port for the rest and relaxation of sailors, there are approximately 90 vessels available to patrol the seven seas protecting American interests. This is not only a historical record, it is a number inadequate for the task at hand.

An active and assertive blue-water Chinese navy is intent on challenging U.S. naval superiority in the Pacific. In the past, challenges of this kind were met by a show of force, an aircraft carrier force or joint military maneuvers with an allied nation. At the moment, we do not have the fleet strength for a symbolic act or to engage in joint training with, say, Japan. The Obama administration has simply hollowed out U.S. capabilities.

The argument for this decision is that we cannot afford to be a supreme military force. It was revealing that administration officials said recently the U.S. would not be a superpower by 2030. Based on the possibility of sequestration and further military retrenchment, that date may be an exaggeration. Decline is a choice, and it appears as if the Obama team has opted to embrace it based on the goal of additional domestic spending.

Military spending is four and a half percent of the GDP, a far cry from World War II levels and a fraction of domestic spending on Medicare, Medicaid and Social Security. What the Obama team does not seem to realize is that a hollow military capability puts at risk everything this nation has accomplished. Domestic spending clearly has its place, but defense spending refers to our very existence. If we insist on underwriting so-called entitlements at the expense of our naval assets, we will relinquish the future and put ourselves in the position of arranging deck chairs on the *Titanic*. When that ship went down and when the ship of state goes down, it didn't and won't matter who has the best view of the horizon.

America's shrinking military was also a product of President Obama's proclivity to spend. With over $9 trillion of debt racked up by President Obama's administration, large domestic entitlement programs took priority over military spending and upkeep.

Underreach: Tightening the Noose on Foreign Policy (2010)
Originally published on the Gatestone Institute

As the plans for American foreign policy are being debated in the White House and the corridors of Congress, it is increasingly apparent that the options are limited.

It is not that options are limited by the lack of imagination, albeit that is a factor. The overarching concern is that foreign policy options are limited by the lack of resources.

The Obama initiatives to stimulate the economy and insinuate the government into the banking, financial services, automobile, insurance and healthcare industries are tied inextricably to the decisions on the foreign policy front.

It would appear that intentionally or inadvertently, domestic decisions are driving national security and foreign policy goals. How can you build a 300-ship navy when you require resources for universal healthcare? And how can you pay for sustained military deployments when the deficit is 40 percent of the GDP?

It may be convenient for this administration to have an aggressive domestic stance, one that devours the bulk of the budget so that the president can pursue his desire for the incremental withdrawal of forces abroad and the cessation of new military hardware. Why even consider the F22, for example, when there are insufficient funds for the construction of this aircraft?

This is the pursuit of a global strategy using capital limitation as its justification. Just as it was fashionable in the 1990s to discuss overreach—the worldwide deployment of troops that drained our resources—it is now appropriate to describe present policy as underreach—the belief that any deployment is beyond our present resource capability.

Where this strategy leads is obvious. The United States is on the highway to the Great Britain of 1990, a once-great power that ruled the seas but is relegated to marginal military status in the present. Should the U.S. pursue this goal to its logical conclusion, there will no longer be a global hegemon capable of shaping world affairs; there will only be regional powers and international instability.

Of course it should be noted that all foreign policy decisions are constrained by available capital. A nation incapable of generating wealth can only be a military power if it impoverishes its people. For democracies this tactic is unacceptable. If we have guns, we insist on butter as well. Hence an Obama plan that promises a lot of butter, limits and eliminates guns.

What differentiates President Obama from his predecessors is that domestic spending drives his agenda and offers a rationale for international timidity and conciliation. He embraces a view of U.S. imperial impulses that must be subdued, and he seeks to do so by spending on the domestic front, thereby forcing decisions on the international stage.

As the president has noted, "We have run out of money." But we have only run out of money for defense preparations. The domestic agenda proceeds in an unrelenting fashion, oblivious to asymptotes. One Obama aide noted the only limit to our spending is in our imagination. Presumably that imagination has the dollar printing presses working overtime.

This condition has alarmed our putative allies and given comfort to our enemies. The president may appear as a sensible man doing only what the budget dictates. But in truth, the budget is a political instrument that can be used to drive policy decisions. The nexus between domestic and foreign spending is palpable. In the Obama age only the former counts; it is the manifestation of his philosophical underpinnings and the rationale for his foreign policy decisions.

Transnationalism

A push for globalism was a priority for the Obama administration. Decisive American action in response to global crises was often abdicated for international consensus and approval, which diluted success and delayed help to those in need abroad.

Bush v. Obama Doctrines (2010)
Originally published on the Gatestone Institute

President George W. Bush's foreign policy doctrine was predicated on three principles outlined in a host of speeches from 2002 to 2008. These included: challenging radical Islamist havens abroad (what Vice President Dick Cheney called "draining the swamp"); building democratic institutions as a moderating influence in tyrannical states that harbor radical Islamic factions; and preemption (attacking those intent on doing harm to us before that harm is inflicted).

Whether one agrees with these principles or not, they were the guiding light for the president's foreign policy. What is most notable, however, is the dramatic shift from the Bush to the Obama Doctrine. If Bush placed an unyielding faith in democracy as a source of conversion, President Obama relies instead on transnational associations, what some have described as the end of national sovereignty.

As I see it the Obama doctrine has four central themes, each in its way related to diminished national sovereignty.

The first is a reliance on multilateral organizations such as the United Nations. Elevating the UN ambassador's role to a cabinet position was a telltale sign. Most significantly, channeling U.S. goals through the Security Council, notwithstanding the veto of any one nation, has been a central focus of this administration. This is the case in the Israeli-Palestinian negotiations, as well as in the attempt to prevent the nuclear ambition of Iran.

Second is the Human Rights Commission. Despite the fact that the commission is populated by the most egregious abusers of human rights, the Obama administration reversed the decision of previous presidents and joined this organization, claiming it was in the national interest to monitor cases the commission is considering.

Third, the Obama team believes it must apologize for America's previous foreign policy decisions. From Berlin to Cairo, President Obama has made it clear a new dawn is rising in which the mistakes of the past will be redressed. Instead of an unequivocal defense of the national interest, the administration offers mea culpas. The assertion of American power and its stabilizing influence has been subordinated to multilateral understanding and the appeasement of self-declared enemies.

Fourth, the government's suit against Arizona legislation that calls for the enforcement of the law against illegal aliens is a demonstration of the belief that borders do not matter and sovereignty is in the eye of the beholder. If a state is unable to secure its border against illegal entrants because of a federal lawsuit, the message is unalloyed: this administration will not support state efforts to defend its borders.

The impetus for these positions is the belief that globalization— i.e., a reliance on multilateral arrangements—will provide greater security for the U.S. than the unilateral assertion of American will. That there isn't a shred of evidence to support the theory is irrelevant, since true believers on the Obama team are pursuing this agenda relentlessly.

For those of us who believe only American influence can serve as a stabilizing international force, these are tenebrific days. The sovereignty Americans fought and died for is now held hostage to the Obama Doctrine.

Of course, supporters of this doctrine will argue America does not have the resources to be "the world's policeman." Alas, it is not the lack of resources, but the lack of will that ultimately determines policy directions. We cannot do everything, but we can surely do something.

The ultimate foundation of a free society is a binding cohesive sentiment. But the difference between the Bush Doctrine and the Obama Doctrine suggests a people divided and a foreign policy in disarray. José Ortega y Gasset once noted, "To create a concept is to leave reality behind." As I see it our foreign policymakers need a dose of reality and the suppression of theory. Doctrines should be based on something more than what you would like to see happen. That may be the most important lesson of this moment.

Wilsonian Internationalism Reborn (2010)
Originally published on PJ Media

There is a toxin coursing through the international body politic that resembles Woodrow Wilson's commitment to a world order based on global government. Among contemporary Wilsonians, like Ann-Marie Slaughter and Harold Koh, to mention two State Department spokespeople, there is a belief that international law and a web of common enforcement mechanisms will enhance order and stability in a world fraught with chaos and violence. As was the case with President Wilson's naïve conception of the League of Nations as a body that can maintain international stability, the present-day Wilsonians hold out the hope that global linkages will inspire cooperation and rational decision making among nations. Presumably national interest, even sovereignty, will be subordinated to international councils.

Aligned with this Wilsonian conception is a declinist perception, a belief that the United States must shift from its hegemonic global role to being a member of the international institutions designed to promote world order. Presumably a less robust economy than the U.S. has experienced and fatigue with the unilateral maintenance of global equilibrium have been the catalysts for this transition.

But in every essential way, this conception is faulty.

To cite one example, the Security Council of the United Nations invariably frustrates directions in American foreign policy. Whether it is "sanctions with teeth" directed at Iran's nuclear program or issues related to Taiwanese security, Russian and Chinese vetoes militate against the realization of U.S. interests. Moreover, even though the United States provides 22 percent of the expenditures at the United Nations, it is isolated by voting blocs such as the 57 Muslim nations, the European Union and the Non-Aligned Nations (usually aligned against the U.S.).

It is also the case that the traction gained by Muslim extremists represents a new and insidious challenge to the very existence of Western civilization. It seems obvious that a religion with imperial goals that denies individual rights and recognition of other faiths is in inevitable conflict with the presumptive principles of the West.

On the economic front, China is in competition with the United States and Europe and appears to be unwilling to foster international rules of commerce, much less regional cooperation. While the World Trade Organization is designed to foster common understanding about trade, the body is adhered to selectively by the Chinese when it is in their interest to do so. At the Copenhagen Climate Summit the Chinese made it crystal clear that they would not agree to carbon dioxide reduction that diminished economic growth, whatever the rest of the world thought or confirmed.

Meanwhile U.S. policy makers ignore the obvious as they continue to plow ahead with their quixotic dreams of global cooperation. However, as I see it, this pursuit will only lead to the waste of resources, undermining our standing and challenging U.S. legitimacy. Of course, there are Europeans with visions of sugarplums dancing in their imagination who embrace this

Wilsonian romance. But each day that passes, Islamists, Chinese leaders, Latin American dictators and African potentates act to undermine faith in the dream. The Wilsonian vision died in the '20s and '30s and was interred in World War II, but like a phoenix it has risen with a new generation of internationalists as devoted to the idea as their ancestors were and just as naïve.

Where this internationalist surge will ultimately take us in not clear. But on one point there cannot be any confusion: contemporary Wilsonianism is undermining our national sovereignty. From accounting rules to the Law of the Sea, from trade agreements to nuclear arms agreements, the U.S. is losing control of its own destiny. This is the Brave New World where naiveté runs headlong into national ambition, a place where American dreams turn into a recurring nightmare.

Global Citizenship (2014)
Originally published on Accuracy in Media

When President Obama visited Berlin a couple of years ago he raised the prospect of an idea that circulated throughout the 20th century: world citizenship. Eminentos such as H.G. Wells and Bertrand Russell contended that unless humanity embraced this notion, it is doomed.

Whether this idea has veracity or not is beside the point, since the president believes that transnational progressivism, a form of world government, is the impetus for his foreign policy positions. It explains in part why he has channeled key foreign policy matters through the United Nations and why he maintains the U.S. is neither more nor less exceptional than any other nation.

Universities have climbed aboard this ideological bandwagon, arguing that the world's great challenges demand a global perspective (read: world citizenship). What these programs do not answer is the obvious question: As a global citizen, to whom do I pledge allegiance? Moreover, as a global citizen, what entity protects my rights? From whom do I obtain a passport? And on whose laws should I depend?

If a national allegiance is eliminated, how is one identified in this global melting pot? Clearly this is one of those utopian ideas that only a group of scholars can take seriously. However, in Washington circles it has gained traction through the voices of Dean Koh, Amy Gutman and Ann-Marie Slaughter, among others. There is a well-entrenched belief that American interest should be subordinate to an abstract international interest. The discussion of the Treaty of the Seas, to cite one example, falls into this category since our rivals, in this case Russia and China, pursue their national goals and the U.S. reiterates global goals.

This mindset reminds me of Samuel Butler's novel *Erehwon* ("nowhere" spelled backward). It is the name of a country discovered by the novel's protagonist. But in essence, it is a utopia—a place that exists solely in the human imagination. In most respects, it is very much like "the citizen of the world," an idea that sounds reasonable but is utterly absurd and unworkable.

For advocates of this viewpoint, global citizenship is a way to transform America, to change the idiosyncratic idea of this republic into an amalgam of ideas borrowing from variegated sources. The curriculum in most colleges is moving in this direction. NYU, for example, contends that the "traditional state-to-state mindset may be at odds with the realities of our increasingly globalized planet."

A case can be made for economic issues that transcend geographic boundaries. Pneumonia in Europe causes a cold in North America. However, social and political matters are largely national, and those attempts at post-national enterprises such as the European Union have a dubious history and an uncertain future.

There is little doubt a world government will not soon be upon us unless, of course, Islam conquers the world or China's notion of the Middle Kingdom gains ascendency. But there is a valid concern about procedural policy issues that rely on global principles. To cite yet another example: a recent Supreme Court decision, presumably guided by the U.S. Constitution, relied on a precedent in Zimbabwe's courts. Even if the precedent is useful, this globalized viewpoint has serious implications for the future of American jurisprudence.

One need not be narrowly nationalistic to assume world government and its global citizens are a fantasy most likely realized as dystopia. Unfortunately the advocates of this notion have penetrated the porous walls of the academy and have even influenced those in the corridors of influence and power.

A World Without Borders (2014)
Originally published in Townhall magazine

Policies emerging from the Obama administration are often perplexing. Why did he give the Islamic State a virtual free hand in destroying Iraqi and Syrian borders? Why does the administration support a European Union that is gasping for political breath? Why has the Obama team allowed Latin American youths to cross our border in violation of national sovereignty?

Suppose President Obama has a vision of a world without borders, a one-world government. This is hardly a new idea, nor is it a vision of the hard left that has departed from its historic ambitions. In some respects, it is not dissimilar from the radical Muslim goal of a global caliphate. The difference, of course, is that it won't be achieved through a shared humanity and common purpose.

How this happens is anyone's guess. Presumably rationality—unknown till then—penetrates the forces of darkness with the emergence of a Brave New World. Yet the current world scene doesn't offer much encouragement. The Sykes-Picot lines drawn in the sand after the fall of the Ottoman empire are evaporating before our eyes, but what will be left in their wake isn't encouraging. These are likely to be tribal, narrowly denominational states. Moreover, since the president has vowed not to intervene, we are obliged to sit on the sidelines as dangerous actors influence the fate of the Middle East.

A Europe that since German unification has harbored a dream of continental unity is in the throes of dissolution, due to economic woe and the inability to withstand nationalistic antecedents. What finally precipitates a breakup is hard to reckon, but fiscal policy controlled by states and regulatory policy controlled by a continental bureaucracy are a formula for political tension.

The massive flow of youngsters crossing the Mexican border into the United States with the active duplicity of drug cartels and the seeming acquiescence of the U.S. government has reduced sovereignty to a concept of yesteryear. This policy, or lack thereof, may suit President Obama's dream of a permanent Democratic majority when "illegals" are given amnesty and the consequent right to vote, but it is yielding a backlash in border states that may turn around normal Democratic districts. To understand what a world without borders would resemble, all one has to do is visit the Texas towns on the U.S. side of the Rio Grande. It isn't a pretty picture.

President Obama has noted that these conditions are unpleasant, but a new order based on a "different set of principles," a "sense of common humanity," is just over the horizon. For him, "no world order that elevates one nation or group of people over another will succeed. No balance of power among nations will hold." These comments are nothing short of ahistorical nonsense. Some nations have dominated other nations. All one has to do is observe Putin's actions in Crimea, in defiance of the Budapest accord with guaranteed Ukrainian sovereignty including Crimea, to understand the absurdity of the claim. Balance-of-power politics hasn't been removed from international politics whatever the president's wish may be. It is precisely this balance that the U.S. helped to establish across the globe since the end of World War II, and a balance many allies continue to rely on.

A desire to relinquish American power and influence doesn't lead to the sharing of principles and a common humanity; it promotes chaos. The estimable political philosopher Leo Strauss wrote of

Weimar Germany, it is "the sorry spectacle of justice without a sword or of justice unable to use a sword," conditions that led to the barbarism and savagery that followed in Nazi Germany.

Alas, President Obama's utopia is filled with idealism and promise. What it lacks is realism and a basic appreciation of world history. It is one thing to regard history as a dream from which we should awaken. It is quite another thing to ignore it completely and assume a world without borders is possible.

In Libya, Muammar Qaddafi's cruelty sunk to new lows that garnered international attention in 2011. President Obama used the opportunity to test out his transnational approach to foreign policy. America's role in the Libyan intervention, together with an alliance of NATO forces, was dictated by a UN resolution. The result was a slow, inefficient campaign that met few of its objectives, along with a further destabilized Libya and an alarming precedent of allowing the international community to define the terms of American engagement abroad.

*In an article published in the **New Yorker** in 2011, it was reported that an adviser to President Obama characterized the U.S. strategy in Libya as 'leading from behind.' Obama later distanced himself from the characterization, but the phrase stuck in the public's mind.*

Libya and the Abdication of American Sovereignty (2011)
Originally published on the Gatestone Institute

For many, the American engagement in Libya is an enigma. Was the use of American aircraft a humanitarian mission to prevent a bloodbath; were these planes deployed to assist the so-called rebels; were they called on to send a message to Muammar Qaddafi— perhaps even oust him?

There has been speculation about all of these objectives. To complicate matters, President Obama's speech about Libya was filled with clichés and was sufficiently ambiguous to have the public arrive at any conclusion. (We want Colonel Qaddafi deposed, but that is not a policy objective.)

But now that the dust is settling even as the battles continue, it is increasingly clear, based on commentary from Samantha Powers and Ann-Marie Slaughter, foreign policy advisers, that the objective was different from those widely considered. The Libyan exercise was a test case for transnational progressism. It was predicated from the start on multilateral cooperation and building consensus within the United Nations. How else could one explain the president's consultation with the Security Council rather than the House of Representatives?

This limited action, what the president described amusingly as a "kinetic military operation," was based on British, French and U.S. cooperation and a green light from the Security Council nations. Now there is nothing new about multilateralism. Surely the war in Afghanistan and even Iraq demonstrate this point. What is new is the seeming willingness of this government to abandon national sovereignty, to allow the U.N. to determine how American forces would be deployed.

While one-world advocates have argued for the abandonment of nation states, they have finally found a president who agrees with their goals—President Obama once described himself as a "citizen of the world," but at the time the remark was considered rhetorical hyperbole. Little did anyone know that this was a serious definition of his role.

For acolytes of this position, such as Fareed Zakaria, among others, the declining economic and military strength of the United States warrants multilateral action. However, once this view is adopted as policy there is little turning back. Declinism has its own set of policy options.

That transnationalism was the objective in Libya above all other objectives is manifest in the failure to achieve any other goals. Colonel Qaddafi appears ensconced in Tripoli. The rebels are still on the defensive. Lives of civilians remain at risk. And if humanitarian impulses are driving policy, why not intervene in the

Sudan or the Ivory Coast, where thousands have been and continue to be slaughtered?

If the U.S. is headed down the path of transnationalism, Americans ought to debate this matter. Should American treasure and blood be sacrificed under a UN banner by a multinational body that invariably displays anti-American sentiment? Even if the U.S. is losing the dominant global position it once had, it is the only nation possessing the weapons and logistics to be an international balance wheel.

As I see it, rather than a loss of resources that is driving policy, it is a loss of will, an emotional fatigue. The consequence is that many former internationalists eager to retain their stance have turned to transnationalism as an alternative. In doing so, however, policymakers cede control and independent action. They cede sovereign rights as well.

It is hard to imagine how destabilized the world will be with the draw-down of U.S. global forces and political vacuums filled by the Chinese, Russians and Iranians. With all of the imperfections in American policy, no nation in this century and the last has been more generous in coming to the aid of others in war and peace than the United States. If the Libyan action is a foreshadowing of a new American stance, the world will be a much more dangerous place than it is at the moment and U.S. sovereignty will clearly be called into question.

In a 2012 Congressional hearing on U.S. involvement in Libya, Defense Secretary Leon Panetta revealed the administration's priorities when it came to acting abroad.

Progressives See Constitution as Impediment (2012)
Originally published on Newsmax

In testimony given to Congress, Defense Secretary Leon Panetta asserted that Congress' war powers authority is irrelevant. As he described it, U.S. intervention in Libya, Syria or elsewhere would be justified by permission from "relevant" international tribunals, such as the UN Security Council and NATO—the approval of the congressional representatives being unnecessary.

Presumably the Constitution that vests Congress with the power to declare war as well as deprive presidential warmaking of necessary funding is null and void. It is instructive that President Obama did not consult Congress before intervening in Libya. Based on recent experiences and Secretary Panetta's testimony, what is emerging in this administration is the belief that the United States needs permission from foreign tribunals to use military force. This may be in keeping with the transnational impulses of Dean Koh and other State Department spokespeople, but it is certainly not consistent with the Constitution, national traditions and independence.

Even Senator Carl Levin, a liberal to his core, tried to save Secretary Panetta from the implications in his testimony, but the secretary persisted. For transnationals and progressives, the 18th-century Constitution is an impediment to their goals. The promotion of global norms on human rights, the environment and economic regulation takes precedence over all other considerations. As a strategy for altering the Constitution, transnationalists contend international law should be incorporated into American jurisprudence.

This philosophical stance is not merely legalistic; it goes to the very essence of national sovereignty. Are we an independent nation, relying on self-government and the will of the American people, or are we to be seen as a centrifugal force rotating as one of many states around a global sun, dependent on our relationship with other states and on "permission" for our actions?

For those who see the world as increasingly interdependent, the answer is obvious. What is not so obvious is that many states regard globalization and international law as a way to harness U.S. influence. If unilateral action by the American government is restrained, if Gulliver is tied down, the "malevolent" action of

Americans—as the internationalists see it—would be in retreat, if not nonexistent.

As a consequence, transnationalism is an expression of distrust—distrust in prior government engagements, distrust in the artificial limits imposed by the Constitution and distrust in the projection of American power. That this position has been embraced by national elites is startling. However, the impulse for acceptance is a belief the United States is in decline. According to this scenario we cannot afford our foreign adventures and will no longer have the will to defend our interests. The default position is progressive internationalism. It takes us off the hook. You don't have to put your economic house in order, and we don't have to worry about national interests abroad.

Of course, if we went down this road the U.S. would be a different country—a position radicals would embrace. But most Americans do not buy into the transnational position. In fact, poll after poll suggests the American people do not want American soldiers wearing a United Nations insignia on their uniforms. Whether this transnational position is adopted may have more to do with the subtle manner in which elite opinion insinuates its agenda into daily government decisions than with some plebiscite on the nation's future. In the process of managing details a lot of damage can occur.

For example, Secretary Panetta, managing the largest bureaucracy in government, offers daily signals to his staff and associates. What does he say to engender a belief in transnational defense decisions? What precisely does cooperation with Russia mean? Who will be invited to review defense installations? The future of defense decisions has arrived. Anticipated cuts in the defense budget over the next decade total a trillion dollars. The net result is apparent—a hollowing of military capacity and an inability to act unilaterally.

President Obama promised to change America, and change he has brought. The question that remains is whether this is the change Americans wanted and whether this is the change with which we can live.

President Obama's insistence on soft power was often met with blatant contempt from rival nations. China, Russia and Iran frequently acted with disregard for diplomatic arrangements made by the Obama administration. As other countries knew any red line could be trampled without consequence, agreements on President Obama's watch were worth little more than the paper they were written on.

The U.S. Is the UN (2015)

In 1922 Antonio Gramsci, one of the founders of the Italian Communist party, argued that the major impediment standing in the way of a Marxist revolution in Italy was nationalism. So he attempted to insert Italy in the firmament of the Communist International. Since that time there have been many activists who have campaigned for a one-world government, contending that nationalism is the catalyst for war. Foremost among those "strategists" was Saul Alinsky, who maintained the belief that a pathway to socialism is only possible through deracinating national fervor.

Since President Obama acknowledges his debt to Alinsky, it is instructive that the deal with Iran is the full amplification of this international perspective. When Senator Obama was running for office in 2008 he made it clear that U.S. unilateralism was the factor that militated against global stability. He and his aides, Samantha Powers being a key example, believed we should channel American foreign policy through the United Nations. Rather than the dog that wags the tail, the U.S. would be like any other state; in fact, the president's equivocal stance on American exceptionalism was a manifestation of this policy perspective.

The P5+1 negotiations over Iran's nuclear program held in Vienna and Geneva suggest the U.S. interests in the Middle East are united in some fashion with Russia, China, Germany, France and England. But as events have evolved from the Chinese air perimeter in the South China Sea to the Russian invasion in eastern Ukraine, our national interests are not harmonious with theirs.

Yet for the first time in American history this government has willingly delegated the fate of our security to others. Here is my point.

For the sake of argument, assume Congress disapproves of the president's proposal and even manages to override a presidential veto. The fact is, the proposal will have been approved by the Security Council even with congressional dissent. If at some point Congress votes for sanctions—the proverbial "snap back"—the U.S. would be isolated, without the support of either China or Russia. In other words, the decision regarding Iranian nuclear weapons has been internationalized.

Most significantly, while the U.S. has moved inexorably in this multilateral direction realizing an Obama quest, the Russians and Chinese have been ignoring dictates from the UN. For example, United Nations condemnation of Russia when its missiles downed a Malaysian civilian airliner is now a distant memory. Where is the penalty? What is meant by the stigma of international disapproval?

One assumption of the Obama foreign policy team is that an era of global stability will emerge from the acquiescence of the U.S. to international norms. However, the withdrawal of the U.S. from the international stage and its substitution by multilateral influence have had the opposite effect. The world is destabilized from the Levant to the Far East. Believing, as President Obama does, that Iran will assume a responsible role in the Middle East—withholding its support for terrorism and the expansion of Shia influence—is like believing the leopard will give up its spots if meat is provided on a daily basis.

The accord with Iran is an expression of the politics of hope. In 159 pages the P5+1 express intention, not reality. There isn't any mention of the previous uranium enrichment program, which might serve as a baseline for future evaluations of cheating. Most significantly, there is conspicuous silence about Iranian terrorism, from the Khobar Towers to the Jewish community center bombing in Buenos Aires. In the politics of hope, these historical events simply vanish. Four Americans sitting in Iranian prisons are ostensibly non-persons. The leopard will relieve itself of spots because we say so. Here is Orwellian doublespeak with a vengeance.

It is notable that the Obama influences from the past have been rewarded. The United States is ensconced in the United Nations, an organization that is a metaphorical tar baby. We are like any other nation now, and the rejoicing in the White House has been greeted with lamentation from the remaining freedom-loving people on the globe.

Preemptive Declinism

Hand-in-hand with the ideology of transnationalism comes that of 'preemptive declinism'. In Obama's case, this is the apparent belief, evident from his foreign policy priorities, that America is not an exceptional nation. Despite the country's record of observing and defending human rights worldwide—of preserving peace and defeating evil in the many forms it has taken throughout the twentieth century—Obama acted as if America deserves no more of a role on the world stage than any other nation, conceding to a world choked by moral relativism.

Preemptive Declinism and the "Unexceptional" America (2009)
Originally published on Pundicity

In his negotiation with Russian leader Dmitry Medvedev, President Obama mentioned a position of mutual respect and admiration, a perfectly sensible diplomatic stance. What was unsaid may be even more important.

A concession to reduce the size and scope of our deliverable nuclear capacity in submarines and bombers puts the United States in the odd position of giving away a great deal and receiving very little in return. Russian leaders agreed to comparable numerical arrangements even though much of the country's force is antiquated and will soon be mothballed. The equation assumes comparable strength and delivery capacity, which on its face is wildly inaccurate.

Moreover, the overarching Russian concern is the recognition of influence over those nations in the "near abroad" or what was once the Soviet empire. Should the Obama administration abandon its plan for anti-missile systems in Poland and the Czech Republic, it would be a symbolic gesture that Russian influence in this East European neighborhood cannot be denied. This decision—if enacted—would send reverberations through the Ukraine to the Baltic States and beyond.

It is also instructive that the Obama administration was conspicuously quiescent during the street demonstrations in Iran, suggesting at first that we had no right to interfere in the internal affairs of another nation. When the president did speak he argued that the U.S. would serve as a witness to historical events. This is quite a contrast from a Kennedy generation that would "bear any burden" for the furtherance of freedom.

When North Korea launched its missiles in tests over the Japanese archipelago, President Obama said he was "upset" and that this matter would be addressed in the United Nations. Yet any action has been stalled by a Chinese veto in the Security Council, and the president has yet to complain about the matter.

A decision by the Honduran government, in concert with the army, to oust President Manuel Zelaya precipitated a prompt and critical response from the Obama administration. However, U.S. officials seemed to be unaware of the fact that President Zelaya had violated his nation's constitution in an attempt to extend his authority in true *caudillo* style. In the end, the U.S. has ended up supporting the very forces in South America—e.g., Hugo Chávez and Fidel Castro—intent on undermining American interests.

One might argue that President Obama, lacking foreign policy experience, is learning on the job. Presumably there is much to learn and many challenges ahead.

But there is an underlying philosophical view that has become alarmingly apparent: preemptive declinism, a belief that the United States is not an exceptional nation and is not entitled by virtue of history to play a role on the world stage different from other nations. As President Obama sees it, America is merely one of many.

That America is the balance wheel in an unstable world, creating equilibrium out of chaos, is an anachronistic position for this administration. It would seem that it is more desirable to envision a political vacuum or other world powers emerging than assert American influence.

Therefore the Obama administration acts as if it has less leverage in international affairs than it actually has. It appears timorous and fearful, sending a signal, willy-nilly, that the United States cannot be depended on.

Yet despite setbacks and many worldwide commitments, the U.S. still possesses extraordinary power and influence on the global stage. Of course as with a muscle, if this power isn't used, it will atrophy. At the moment, the rise of declinism is having its effect.

The Pakistani government is not sure it can count on American support over the long term. Prime Minster Nouri al-Maliki in Iraq is visiting Iran on a regular basis because he too is unsure of the American commitment to his country. In fact, all through the Middle East and other foreign capitals, leaders are hedging their bets, unsure of America's role and in some instances positive the U.S. is not a dependable ally.

Declinism also vitiates every aspect of negotiation with allies as well as enemies. Our foes believe they can take advantage of apparent weakness and may overreach and miscalculate. Our friends may grow to distrust us, seeking to go it alone, or worse, enlisting assistance from others.

While President Roosevelt advised Americans to speak softly but carry a big stick, President Obama seems to suggest we should bury the stick and keep on talking. Unfortunately the talk itself has dangerous implications, and the world is not waiting for the United States to undo its present infatuation with declinism.

Obama the Apologist

President Obama spent much of his time in office apologizing for American actions under previous administrations. On what was dubbed his "apology tour," President Obama circled the globe offering America's regrets for taking action in the War on Terror, its military prison in Guantanamo and even for dropping the bomb to end World War II, among other things.

A Man Apart (2009)
Originally published on the Gatestone Institute

Albert Camus was expert at describing a man apart, an existential man called *The Stranger*, who didn't belong in the society in which he found himself. He didn't have emotional roots; in fact, this character was haunted by shadows—the real and the metaphorical. He was the quintessential rebel challenging normative standards.

At the risk of drawing literary comparisons, I am persuaded based on his performance that President Obama is a man apart. He seems to equate power with arrogance; pride with willfulness and exceptionalism with dominance. As a consequence, he has changed foreign policy perceptions. The America he leads is a nation like any other—no more, no less. In fact, as a Nobel laureate, he is considered by the Europeans as a man of the world, not merely a citizen of the United States.

When asked if the United States is exceptional, President Obama said America is exceptional and England is exceptional and Greece is exceptional. That the United States is sui generis didn't cross his mind. How could it? He is pledged to a scenario in which America opts out of its traditional role as peacekeeper, the balance wheel in maintaining international equilibrium. The war against terrorists is over, along with the nation's hegemonic role.

Unfortunately the war fatigue President Obama embodies is not embraced by our global enemies, who see this shift in his policy attitude as a sign of weakness and retreat. I believe President Obama actually thinks that unilateral concessions to our real and putative enemies will result in reciprocal responses. But as his bizarre overtures to the Olympic Committee demonstrated, gestures directed at multilateralism and celebrity status do not result in favorable results. Real power as opposed to soft power still has meaning on the world stage.

A man with roots would know that wild policy swings of the kind that we've experienced with healthcare, cap and trade and education proposals cannot possibly fly with the American people, even with those who voted for President Obama in the last election. Despite cultural shifts in the nation, the United States still fashions itself as a conservative nation. Only a man apart cannot sense that condition.

My contention is not that the president is devoid of conviction. In fact, his political tilt is decidedly to the left, the hardcore left. My assertion is different. I believe this president doesn't understand the rhythms, the pulse of the American people. He is not merely outside the mainstream. He doesn't even recognize it. He is a basketball player who has been asked to bat.

At first I thought his initial popularity would carry him through to a second term. But as each day passes and the false, almost inappropriate, gestures register, Americans are beginning to recognize this man apart. He is our stranger in a land he doesn't understand.

Americans are not war-like, nor does imperial ambition fill their soul. They have done almost nothing for which daily apologies are necessary. Their blood soaks the beaches of Normandy; their graves litter European towns. And their fortune saved millions from the plight of destitution. Americans do not appreciate a man so removed from their history, so out of tune with the American experience, that he reflexively expresses regret for the very conditions that should engender pride.

Perhaps this president will learn. But I am not confident that can happen. His life experience without a father in his home and a mother seeking adventure abroad is unstable. His closest associates vilified the nation he now leads. Is it any wonder his wife said she could take no pride in America till now? The past is to be rejected. Milestones in history are erased from memory as storage cast aside as unnecessary.

This is a unique moment in our history. It is certainly the only time in my life when our national instincts are being reconditioned. From a nation that was a model to the world, we are now told that superiority is unbecoming, a hindrance for the emergence of global egalitarianism.

President Obama, as a man apart, may attempt this recasting of America, but as I see it, America is not yet ready for his experimentation and, most likely, never will be.

The Isolationist President

Obama's reluctance to act decisively with the U.S. military led to an unchecked and massively ballooned Islamic State, a fumbled Libyan intervention, and a Syria that has descended into chaos. Isolationism had its dire consequences.

The Isolationist Impulse and Its Implications (2011)
Originally published on BestThinking: Society & Humanities

Like a recurrent tide that ebbs and flows, isolationism—what some have called Fortress America—arrives at water's edge each generation. War fatigue, monstrous expenditures, casualties and the *cri de coeur* that we cannot be the world's policeman contribute to the belief from the left and the right that we should turn inward, concentrating on building America instead of nation building abroad. Robert Taft lives in 2011.

This clarion call does not make political distinctions. It can be heard from the Ron Paul wing of the Republican party and from the acolytes of Barack Obama, if not President Obama himself. Prompted by the belief that our goal in Afghanistan is vague and an appropriate exit strategy non-existent, and that the Libyan operation violates the War Powers Resolution and remains an ill-advised venture, an anti-war cry across the country is gaining currency.

As I see it the two cases in point provide plenty of ammunition for the anti-war critics. Whatever modest success U.S. forces have had in stabilizing areas of Afghanistan, stabilization is fragile and many of the Afghani forces fight with us during the day and join the enemy at night. The draw-down of troops (10,000) the President is requesting may further jeopardize the modest success we've had; at least that is what General David Petraeus and other military officials have hinted.

The Libyan invasion is a classic example of the disharmony between goals and tactics and the absurdity of delegating any military task to NATO without direct U.S. control. For a two-week period, we bombed Muammar Qaddafi's forces in an effort to assist the so-called rebels. After this fortnight, we simply passed the baton to the NATO generals, who now claim they are running out of ammunition. President Obama said our goal is not to kill Colonel Qaddafi, but to encourage him to step down. Obviously he hasn't gotten the message. He is fighting for his life and we are fighting for…precisely what are we fighting for?

Yet despite my criticism, which runs deep, my fear is that so many have converted these two misadventures into a generalized policy stance. Even former Secretary of Defense Robert Gates has indicated "we will not be fighting major land wars anytime soon." Surely we can choose not to fight any war, but history has a way of intruding on this decision. We may choose to appease or avert our gaze or even accept defeat, but there will be enemies intent on destroying the United States, and they may not have any compunctions about fighting a land war.

The danger of isolationism is that it encourages complacency. Presumably if there aren't any interests abroad, there isn't a need to maintain an active military force. History doesn't repeat itself exactly, but its broad outlines are often duplicated. It now appears as if the scenario unfolding at this time resembles that of the 1930s, a period when the U.S. opted out of worldwide commitments. One can only hope that an attack like the one at Pearl Harbor isn't necessary to awaken the sleeping giant.

As our history has shown, building military readiness after dramatic retrenchment is painful. Far better to add on to existing resources than starting anew. But President Obama seemingly has convinced himself that American interests can be channeled through multilateral organizations, as the Libyan venture suggests. The upshot of this position is to spend less on military matters than we do at the moment and hope that others will fill the vacuum left by our withdrawal. This is a hope and prayer strategy that serves as a gateway for our enemies.

The signal we send through emergent isolationism is that we do not possess the will to stand by commitments to our allies or defend our interests abroad.

Whether this mood is transitory remains to be seen. Americans invariably surprise with their resilience. But have we been worn down by fatigue? Is America different from its past? Will the sentiment of decline dominate the culture? Will this century witness an American withdrawal from global affairs? Will the isolationists ascend to foreign policy leadership?

Despite all the mistakes made by the policy experts, my hope is that the tide of isolationism cascades far into distant seas.

Still No Strategy to Deal With ISIS (2015)
Originally published on Newsmax

It is increasingly the case that foreign policy discussions result in bipolar viewpoints, characterized by those who contend why should we get involved in the affairs of others and those who believe the United States should deploy large forces with massive lethality to contend with enemies.

Each of these opinions has some validity. The trope that we cannot be the world's policeman is somewhat accurate, since we should not and cannot insinuate ourselves in every battle across the globe. Libertarians would contend that the limits of our capability have been reached, perhaps overreached.

Those who believe in a muscular foreign policy argue that our troops represent the only method to truly defend American interests abroad. Former Secretary of State Colin Powell indicated that when troops are deployed, it should be in the form of overwhelming force. While neo-cons would be inclined to deploy troops, it is instructive that the controversial invasion of Iraq was not initially intended to be an exercise in nation building. If toppling Saddam Hussein was the goal, this invasion force was successful.

Hence America is appropriately split between ostensibly international and isolationist positions, with each having ascendency depending on historical circumstances. The U.S. is not an imperial nation seeking neither territory nor colonies, but there are times when military deployment promotes global equilibrium. Conversely, there are times when the U.S. may overreach. The U.S. cannot be a world policeman, but it cannot overlook the fact that a world without a policeman is a very dangerous place.

These choices, however, are not dispositive. In the Middle East, for example, there are nations that would willingly take the fight to enemies like IS, al Qaeda and Iran. In collaboration these states form a formidable fighting force, but they require leadership, intelligence, logistics and special forces. Egypt, Saudi Arabia, Kuwait, Jordan and the UAE are prepared to do the fighting. These nations are imperiled and they realize it.

The Obama administration has not recognized the danger facing these Sunni state allies. A tilt to Iran as regional stabilizer has complicated and destabilized the foreign policy stance of the Sunni nations. Instead of leading from behind, there is simply no evidence of leadership at all. Yet this defense condominium is a position between isolationism and internationalist sentiments that could win widespread support and achieve the goal of regional stability. However one feels about foreign policy, this strategic position is in the arsenal of potential assets we wish to deploy.

Similarly, the competition for harmony in the Pacific between China and the U.S. could be offset by a defense pact of nations that fear Chinese ambitions. These would include Japan, the Philippines, Indonesia, Malaysia, Vietnam, South Korea, India, Australia and New Zealand, among others. What is lacking in this prospective alliance is American leadership that can subdue historical enmity and distrust. Aside from the declaration of a pivot to Asia, there has been no evidence of a substantive change in policy.

When President Obama said he was working on a strategy to cope with the Islamic State, he seemed confused and surprised by the progress of this rogue terrorist organization. Yet even at this time, a real strategy has not been forthcoming for either side of the globe. American foreign policy is adrift and the tides of time do not appear to be on our side, even though answers to what ails us are readily apparent.

Obama's Policy on Radical Islam Failing (2016)
Originally published on Newsmax

Deployments of U.S. forces continue despite the claims of draw-down and withdrawal. The numbers may be on the decline and the use of Special Forces may be on the rise, but the issue that is emerging is why are our military forces in harm's way at all? From Rand Paul to President Obama, from Donald Trump to Mr. and Mrs. John Q. Public, many are asking a fundamental question: What is the benefit to the United States of overseas deployments? It was once a question easily addressed within the context of the Cold War. But at a time when there is a quagmire in the Middle East and European expenditures for self-defense are modest, the question emerging directly, and often inadvertently, is why the U.S. is burdened with defending the civilization. Why is President Obama now sending an additional 250 troops into Syria?

Isolationists from Robert Taft to Charles Lindbergh have asked the question, and their answer came in Nazi jackbooted invasions across Europe and the attack on Pearl Harbor. Today the threat is more complicated and subtle. It does not necessarily rely on nation states. There is also a backdrop of weapons of mass destruction. And much of the enemy's imperial drive is promoted through religious prescriptions. Hence conventional war may have its place, but it is not likely to be dispositive.

Moreover, the internationalists are also in an odd position. Former Vice President Dick Cheney said we should clean out the "swamp" to prevent attacks here in the United States. The problem, of course, is that attacks have already occurred, "sleepers" are probably in our midst and whatever we do in the Middle East may not forestall future violence at home. The threat has metastasized, making it far more difficult to confront. It is also a threat that manifests itself on and off the battlefield. Radicalization of individuals is often as notable a challenge as those firing AK-47s.

What has emerged is a void, a giant whole in the foreign policy apparatus. Military officials deploy their troops efficiently and effectively, but they are not engaged in the making of policy. Policy is in the realm of an uninvited guest at a dinner party.

President Obama leads the way in formulating this position. His stance is "less policy" as policy. Hence military officials do their appointed tactical roles, but without clear, defining goals in mind. We may engage in air assaults, but the end game is elusive.

Richard Weaver, the eminent philosopher, argued that "every man participating in a culture has three levels of conscious reflection: his specific ideas about things, his general beliefs or convictions and his metaphorical dreams." At the moment, "the void" suggests we are only pursuing dreams. The belief the nations of the world will unite and act responsibly to fight militant Islam is a dream. It is this metaphorical dream that President Obama often cites. But it is a dream from which we must awaken if we are to defeat a fanatical foe that wants to destroy us.

The "void" is the impediment that holds the U.S. back from appropriate action. But as Tennyson said, "'Tis not too late to seek a newer world." That would be a world with clearly defined strategic goals and a method for achieving them.

"The true discovery of America is still before us," maintained Thomas Wolfe. It would be a discovery that emerges from the nadir of policy formulation or the lack thereof. The "void" is our dark hole—orbidding, relentless and pushing forward. It is time to push back.

In 2010, the Obama administration led negotiations of a new Strategic Arms Reduction Treaty (START), wherein the number of U.S. and Russian nuclear warheads was to be reduced by half. A 2016 inspection found multiple violations of the terms of the treaty by Russia.

Obama's Foreign Policy in 2011: Not "Hope" But Hopeless (2011)
Originally published on Breitbart

The new START embodies, in my judgment, the emerging mood in American security policy circa 2011. As the preamble to the treaty indicates, the Russians will have a veto over the deployment of anti-missile systems. Despite President Obama's assurance to the Senate that this will not be a unilateral concession, the Russian diplomats see it differently. After all, this is not a treaty between the United States Senate and the president.

Since the Reagan negotiations in Iceland, missile defense has been a U.S. trump card in all strategic discussions. Defense changes the correlation of forces, a point made axiomatic by the Russian unwillingness to accept deployment. But Reagan remained steadfast, as did his successors—until now. The preemptive capitulation on radars in Poland and the Czech Republic was the first sign of a new strategic direction, and the resistance to force modernization is confirmation of the president's tack.

On a larger global stage these decisions suggest American withdrawal, both a physical withdrawal from international commitments and a psychological withdrawal from the U.S. role as world policeman. It is already clear that the withdrawal from Iraq will soon be completed and the withdrawal from Afghanistan will be accelerated this year. What this military vacuum creates may be in the realm of speculation at this point, but surely Iran, as the region's "strong horse," will gain advantage at our expense.

While a butterfly fluttering its wings in one part of the globe may not affect events in another region, this can, and often does, occur. You can be sure that the Chinese, who have developed a formidable blue-water navy, have been biding their time, waiting for a downgrade in U.S. capability and our willingness to influence Asian affairs.

In an effort to compensate for the lack of U.S. assertiveness, the Obama administration—inclined to a form of transnational progressivism—has relied more heavily than was previously the case on UN intervention. Yet it is clear from the use of the veto in the Security Council to an air of anti-Americanism in the General Assembly that U.S. interests cannot be promoted in this multilateral body. The consequence, of course, is that a new world order is emerging without American leadership or a clear design.

This is most effectively seen in American paralysis over prospective Iranian nuclear weapons. Torn between roll-back and deterrence, confused over sanctions and negotiations, the U.S. seems unsure of its position. Moreover, this Obama administration has convinced itself and several Arab states that a peace treaty between the Palestinian territory and Israel will make it easier to clamp down on Iranian nuclear ambitions. Of course, this is fatuous on several levels. Iran's surrogates Hezbollah and Hamas do not want peace with Israel, and Iran can use this anti-Zionist sentiment to foster alliances within radical political groups in the region.

While I am both perplexed and pessimistic about directions in American foreign policy, the hearings announced with the new Republican House leadership are a welcome addition to the national debate. It is doubtful the Obama administration will adopt a new course of action, but it is noteworthy that the American people will have the opportunity to consider alternative tactics.

Foreign policy may not be the bread-and-butter issue that determines campaign success. However, it is the matter that can determine the triumph of nations and international stability. This is a moment to revisit the deployments that served American interests with an honest discussion of pros and cons. In an atmosphere uniformly bleak, this may be all that passes for a ray of sunshine.

At the very beginning of his presidency President Obama was awarded the Nobel Peace Prize for "extraordinary efforts to strengthen international diplomacy and cooperation between peoples." Five years later, a world without resolute American leadership demonstrated just how little peace President Obama's soft power could produce.

The Fifth Anniversary of Obama's Nobel Peace Prize (2014)

October 9 is the fifth-year anniversary of the awarding of President Obama's Nobel Peace Prize. The Nobel Committee conferred this honor because of "his [President Obama's] extraordinary efforts to strengthen international diplomacy and cooperation between [sic] peoples. The Committee has attached special importance to Obama's vision of and work for a world without nuclear weapons."

Furthermore, it was noted that "Obama has as President created a new climate in international politics. Multilateral diplomacy has regained a central position, with emphasis on the role that the United Nations and other international institutions can play. Dialogue and negotiations are preferred as instruments for resolving even the most difficult international conflicts."

In his acceptance speech President Obama did note a "hard truth: We will not eradicate violent conflict in our lifetimes. There will be times when nations—acting individually or in concert—will find the use of force not only necessary but morally justified." He went on to note that the U.S. must uphold the standards of "just war," "prevent the spread of nuclear weapons and maintain international law." He also maintained "that peace is unstable when citizens are denied the right to speak freely or worship as they please…"

Reading the justification for the prize and the president's speech is an exercise in moral confusion. It is the confusion between intent—appeals to the moral high ground—and a reality that suggests the obverse.

For example the committee commends the president for his efforts to strengthen international diplomacy. Yet it is obvious that our allies distrust the president and our enemies disregard him. The so-called coalition of nations "to degrade and destroy" the Islamic State is composed of nine nations, none of whom will commit more than token military assets to the battlefield. In fact, the president cannot cite one example on the world stage where his diplomatic efforts enhanced our interests or those of our allies.

The committee believed that the president would emphasize dialogue and negotiations as the preferred instruments for the resolution of conflict. This belief is an accurate portrayal of the president's impulses, but where has it gotten him? Negotiations over Iran's uranium enrichment program have not led, and in my judgment will not lead, to an accord that prevents the development of nuclear weapons, a point about which most analysts agree.

Five years after the conferring of this prize, the Middle East is aflame; Russian troops have violated Ukrainian sovereignty and returned Crimea to mother Russia; Iran, as the sanctuary for terrorist activity worldwide, is now looked to as the stabilizing force in neighboring Iraq; and, for all the words exchanged in UN councils, the veto power of Russia and China forestalls the adoption of any U.S. initiatives.

The implicit belief that Barack Obama was a shining knight prepared to reshape the world in an image deeply embraced by the Nobel Committee is a chimera. In fact, his pursuit of his own brand of U.S. withdrawal emotionally and militarily from international conflicts has produced a vacuum filled by enemy nations and stateless terrorists. When there isn't anyone to uphold the international law to which the president referred, it is a meaningless concept. Similarly, when the president contends people should be able to worship as they please, does that include religious Americans who do not embrace his campaign to force the use of abortifacients?

Samuel Johnson maintained that "men more frequently have to be reminded than informed." We should be reminded that platitudes do not influence those intent on evil deeds. We have to be reminded that, whether we like it or not, the U.S. is the only nation that can restore stability in the Levant and Asia. And we should remind ourselves without arrogance that the United States carries the banner of liberty. The torch that the Statue of Liberty carries is a light in the heart of all people who wish to be free. But that light burns because the United States was willing to commit blood and treasure to it.

It should be clear even to the Nobel Committee that its commitment to a world reliant on diplomacy has been shattered by events over the last five years. President Obama has his prize, but the world has moved a long distance from peace.

Hypocrisy as Policy

Hypocrisy as Policy (2013)
Originally published on Accuracy in Media

Rarely in the history of this republic has hypocrisy been a public policy position. As Rochefoucauld noted, hypocrisy is the tribute vice pays virtue. But suppose virtue has nothing to do with it. Suppose hypocrisy becomes a way to deceive and deflect criticism.

Two recent examples prove this point.

Recently President Obama argued that there was confusion surrounding the events in Benghazi that led to the death of four Americans, including the ambassador. He contends that every effort would have been made to save Americans if we had known the extent of their parlous state.

However, we did know something about conditions in Libya, since a request was made for reinforcements in the embassy months before the actual attack.

The president also indicated he was aware of the terrorist nature of the assault and acknowledged it as a terrorist-orchestrated event. Yet when UN ambassador Susan Rice spoke about the matter with the approval of the White House, she referred to it as an incident inspired by a film (aka trailer) dealing with the Prophet Mohammed. In fact, this was the standard line from the White House for several weeks until this position was thoroughly discredited.

President Obama said every effort will be made to get to the bottom of this incident. Yet the memos describing the events in Benghazi were altered. Former CIA director Petraeus expressed frustration at the new, scrubbed talking points, noting that they had been stripped of much of the content his agency had provided.

Secretary of State Hillary Clinton, during her testimony, said, "What difference does it make?" Presumably the testimony will not bring those Americans back to life. But it makes a difference for those who believe in the truth and the manner in which government conducts its affairs. Igor Stravinsky once noted that "the old original sin was one of knowledge; the new original sin is one of non-acknowledgement." Alas the new sin surrounds us.

In a similar vein, President Obama claims to be outraged over revelations that the Internal Revenue Service (IRS) used its coercive power to penalize conservative and Tea Party groups. The president went on to say an investigation was underway to ferret out those responsible for these actions at this "independent agency."

What the president failed to note is that the IRS is not an independent agency. It is under the control of the same president who claims to be outraged by its practices. This is a little like a baseball manager saying he is outraged by the fact that his players are using corked bats to gain a hitting advantage even though it is against baseball rules. Doesn't he have to assume responsibility for this violation?

Already there are calls from Secretary of State John Kerry to "move on" from Benghazi. More recently, Democratic leaders said now that the president has acknowledged the unfair practices at the IRS, it is time to put that matter to bed. However, many Americans cannot move on until outstanding matters on both fronts are addressed.

Hypocrisy will not disappear from public life with both parties often culpable, but rarely do we find ourselves in a position where hypocrisy *is* the policy. The truth is a casualty of casuistry and double-talk is the language of politics. Now we see that through this shell game lives can be lost and institutions can be damaged.

Politics may not be beanball, but it should be more than sophistry. At the moment, however, that does not appear to be the case.

Disavowing Nuclear Superiority

A shrunken military and President Obama's isolationist policies met at a most detrimental apex for the U.S.'s nuclear stockpile. Under the Obama administration, America saw an accelerated American disarmament campaign, unmatched by nuclear rivals.

Is President Obama in Touch With Reality? (2014)
Originally published on Family Security Matters

Critics have suggested that President Obama's foreign policy is "feckless." Some have argued the president is insouciant, a relative innocent, incapable of responding to the challenges that confront him. I see it somewhat differently.

In April 2009 in Prague, President Obama promised to lead a crusade to rid the world of nuclear weapons with treaties and the power of America's moral example. This is a position he has long held. As a Columbia student, he wrote a piece in the *Spectator* in which he called for unilateral disarmament, noting that the American example would precipitate a dramatic shift to denuclearization. It was a sophomoric article in my judgment, lacking any historical context, but then again it was written by a 20-year-old with limited experience.

However, the Obama position hasn't been altered. His belief that documents, assurances, negotiations and speeches can maintain stability is without historic precedent. "Soft power" of the kind he espouses works when military power stands behind it. When assurances are called into question by hostile forces and a military reaction—either threat or deployment—is unavailable, the world is put at risk.

In fact, the president's denuclearized dream is likely to result in the very proliferation he opposes. Why? If the nuclear umbrella of the United States is unreliable, nations will seek their own nuclear deterrent. It is not surprising that Saudi Arabia has been in discussion with Pakistan for the purchase of nuclear weapons as a direct reaction to the U.S. rapprochement with Iran over its enrichment of uranium and pursuit of its own bomb.

A bipartisan consensus in Washington has agreed to reduce the U.S. defense budget to its smallest size since the demobilization after World War II. Will this reduction in military assets allow the government to project power if necessary? Of course, it is impossible to answer the question without knowing the mission. However, weakness, or perceived weakness, comes with a price.

Russia has taken Crimea and is on the urge of moving into eastern Ukraine. The president has protested and remonstrated, and it has only made him look ineffectual on the global stage.

With Russian initiative, Syria agreed to dismantle its chemical weapons in order to avoid a U.S. airstrike last September. Now the chemical weapons are intact; the rebel strongholds have fallen; and Bashar al-Assad is ensconced in Syrian leadership. He has effectively won the Civil War at the cost of several hundred thousand lives—in part because of the chemical weapons—and we look hapless as a nation. Moreover, we are dependent on the same Russian president Vladimir Putin who invaded Crimea to bail us out of this embarrassing morass in Syria.

The U.S. continues to engage in talks with Iran on its nuclear programs even after a senior State Department official told Reuters recently that Iran is "very actively trying to procure items for their nuclear program and missile program and other programs"—a violation of the agreement that started the talks in the first place. But so intent is the U.S. on a deal that negotiators simply avert their gaze to present conditions.

There you have it; the president has lost touch with reality—youthful idealism has been wedded to an arrogance that his personal magnetism can change the course of history. The Columbia student has evolved into a president who cannot see the world as it is. A world he wants is the world he sees. If he believes it to be true, it must be so.

When the president speaks at The Hague on the virtues of non-proliferation at the third global Nuclear Security Summit, it would be wise for him to review events of the last six months and perhaps keep a map of the world available for easy reference.

We Cannot Risk Obama's Nuclear Weapons Vision (2015)
Originally published on Newsmax

When President Obama was a student at Columbia University he wrote a paper calling for the "end of nuclear weapons." It was a time when there were similar calls for the elimination of these weapons of mass destruction; this was ostensibly an idealistic *cri de coeur*. Unilateral disarmament of the kind this movement demanded was seen as playing directly into the hands of a Soviet rival expanding its nuclear weapons capability.

The emergence of a multipolar nuclear world has made the once-idealistic call seem polyannaish. A unilateral reduction in U.S. nuclear forces, without a reciprocal response from other nuclear powers, only weakens the deterrent effect of our arsenal.

Yet remarkably, in comments made before the 2015 Nuclear Nonproliferation Treaty Review Conference in New York City, Secretary of State John Kerry stated U.S. "willingness" and "readiness" to engage and negotiate further reductions of deployed strategic nuclear weapons by up to one-third below the level set by the new START.

While there has been suspicion of Russian cheating on START and threatening gestures about the use of nuclear weapons in the Ukraine, President Obama is raising the specter of further dramatic retrenchment. Senator John McCain, chairman of the Armed Services Committee, said, "Further strategic nuclear reductions with Russia would be a dangerously naïve non-starter with the U.S. Senate." In fact, nuclear weapons have grown increasingly prominent in Russian military doctrine, as the growth of its arsenal of tactical nuclear weapons would suggest.

At the Nonproliferation Treaty Review Conference, the five announced nuclear weapon states recognized by the treaty—U.S., Russia, Britain, France and China—will discuss current approaches to nuclear arms control. It is instructive that North Korea, Pakistan, Israel, India and arguably Iran—all nuclear powers, possible nuclear powers or about to be nuclear powers—are omitted from the discussion.

In President Obama's Nobel Prize speech, he reiterated his long-standing belief in a world free of nuclear weapons. But despite these heartfelt sentiments the world is moving ever closer to proliferation, even among those nations that signed the non-proliferation treaty. While the president asserts a "broad international consensus on the need to secure nuclear materials," it is obvious that within the framework on Iran's nuclear materials there isn't any requirement that this state sponsor of terrorism accept international protocols.

Visionaries relying on their own illusions assume that cooperation is possible. But reality intrudes. For Russia, its bristling nuclear arsenal affords comfort in any escalation scenario in Eastern Europe. Should NATO forces confront Russia, the threat of tactical nuclear weapons looms.

Rather than begin the upcoming nuclear security summit by stating our position, Secretary Kerry would be wise to put an emphasis on reinforcing the national deterrent. No sensible person wants nuclear exchanges. Unfortunately not everyone is sensible. A world without nuclear weapons is and should be a goal, but suppose you disarm and your enemies do not? Russia, for example, has already said it will not participate in the preparatory process for the 2016 security summit.

An agreement of the willing is meaningless if the unwilling do not participate. In the nuclear age it is far better to be safe—behind the wall of defensive weapons—than sorry after a failed effort at a freeze. The utopian vision, in this case, can easily emerge as a dystopian saga. President Obama leaves the impression that he is still a naïve Columbia student captivated by illusions. However, there isn't anyone like him in Russia, China or Iran.

Obama's No First Use Proposal (2016)
Originally published on Family Security Matters

When President Obama received his Nobel Prize, he argued that he would regard nuclear proliferation as his primary challenge.

This is hardly surprising since even as a Columbia College student he advocated a nuclear-free world—a position consistent with the idealism of a student who knew very little about the ambitions of U.S. adversaries. Yet now, after eight years in office, the president retains this same arms control illusion.

Since he assumed the oath of office in 2009 the president has pressed for the shrinking and weakening of the U.S. nuclear arsenal, armed with evidence of this signing of the new START with Russia and avoiding modernization of the aging nuclear platforms.

Japan and Taiwan, among others, reliant on the U.S. nuclear umbrella for security, are increasingly uncomfortable with the direction in American policy and are dubious about the reliability of our pledge for nuclear assistance.

To make matters even more confusing for U.S. allies, it appears as if the president is prepared to declare a new policy of "no first use"—a doctrine that contends America would never use nuclear weapons unless an adversary does so first. This seemingly benign gesture undermines decades of intentional ambiguity and the basis of deterrence.

In fact, State Department officials questioned about the matter argue the president's position is wrongheaded. The fatal weakness in his contention is that it signals to our enemies that they need not fear nuclear retaliation from the U.S. even if they attack us with conventional, chemical or biological weapons. In any war-gaming escalation scenario, our battlefield initiatives end where nuclear weapons might be entertained. "No first use" suggests to foes that they should act as aggressively as possible short of nuclear war.

Deterrence, which has kept the lid on nuclear weapons since 1945, is undergoing a monumental shift. The Obama administration's 2010 Nuclear Posture Review contended Russia was no longer an adversary, a contention that recent history in Crimea and Syria would challenge. Moreover, it is likely the president will overlook Constitutional restraints on this matter by submitting a proposal to the United Nations Security Council, thereby usurping Senate treaty power, as he did with the Iranian nuclear deal.

Should this ban gain traction, it would mean in reality that the U.S. would place constraints on itself while dishonest parties like Iran, Russia, China and North Korea would be free to exploit U.S. nuclear concessions. By any stretch of the imagination, the Obama proposal is the nadir of American nuclear deterrence.

Heretofore, deterrence was a rational proposition based on a belief that certain actions would lead to a certain catastrophic result. Fear is the underlying psychological basis for deterrence, since the presumption is neither side in an adversarial situation would be willing to sacrifice its population. However, in an environment when one side is willing to sacrifice its population for theological reasons or concessions are made about when weapons might be used, the essence of deterrence is interrupted.

History has no examples from the nuclear age because deterrence has worked, notwithstanding fears, brinksmanship and mistakes. A system of protocols has maintained international equilibrium because even with a tocsin in the air, controls on nuclear weapons have been effective.

However, these protocols can be overlooked. If the Obama agenda is embraced, there is little doubt the fragility of deterrence will be made obvious, even though President Obama believes this is a major step toward a nuclear-free world. Britain, France and Japan believe he is wrong, but this is one of those issues where you don't want the proposition tested. Even if theoretical, "no first use" takes the U.S. in a highly questionable direction.

Moral Equivocation

President Obama exhibited a generous capacity to overlook the morally perverse actions of dictators and despots if it meant the opportunity to engage in diplomacy. From Iran to Cuba, it was clear that President Obama's legacy as the great negotiator was worth ignoring the atrocities committed by those allowed to sit with him at the negotiation table. The problem with despots, however, is they have no practice in keeping promises.

Restating the Obvious About Dictatorship (2009)
Originally published on PJ Media

At a time when the current administration considers it appropriate to cozy up to enemies, it seems appropriate to understand why we have enemies. Moreover, rather than assume these enemies are victims of American colonial ambitions or historical misdeeds, these regimes should be evaluated on one simple criterion: how they treat their own people.

When we remove the blinders of ideological myopia, what is revealed does not square with President Obama's apologies or the belief that all the wrongs, or most of the wrongs, in the world can be attributed to the United States.

Yoani Sánchez is a dissident blogger in Cuba who has pointed out the dictatorial control of the Castro brothers and the police-state environment they have fostered in this island nation. On October 6 she was walking down a Havana street with three friends when Cuban agents in civilian clothes forced her into an unmarked car and proceeded to beat her relentlessly, screaming at the same time that she had better stop criticizing the government.

Despite the elite American celebrities who travel to Cuba returning to sing the praises of Fidel Castro, this assault highlights how little has changed in the country's record of repression. According to the American Press Association, a watchdog group, there are currently 26 journalists in jail and 102 incidents against Cuban bloggers and writers, including arbitrary arrests, death threats and beatings.

Some contend that the attack against Ms. Sánchez was not personal, but rather a state campaign against the blogger phenomenon that has the potential to undermine the existing government.

Apparently Ms. Sánchez, who provides poignant vignettes of daily aggravations and humiliations, is not easily silenced. Earlier this year, she won a journalism prize from Columbia University, but was barred by the Cuban government from accepting the award. Her courage and drive will assuredly be tested again by a government that cannot tolerate dissent.

On another front, Iran's Revolutionary Guard has formed a new organization to quell internal dissent. Shaken by the scale of street protests that followed the presidential elections in June, the mullahs are intent on repressive measures to thwart the dissidents— suggesting, in effect, that the existing intelligence units cannot be relied on. State media named Hassan Taeb, commander of the Basij paramilitary organization known for its brutal methods, as the new head of the intelligence operations.

In doing so the National Council for Resistance in Iran (NCRI) is being targeted, the same organization that exposed Iran's covert nuclear enrichment activity in 2002 and the Qum facility in 2005, a claim later confirmed by the U.S. and Tehran officials. As Major General Mohammed Ali Jafari, commander of the Revolutionary Guard, noted, "Our enemy has changed face. We face the threat of a soft overthrow instead of military invasion, so the Guard must also transform accordingly."

When unrest surfaced after the June election, the Basij were unleashed to crack down on opposition supporters. And crack down they did. High-profile dissidents were detained inside Tehran's Evin prison, known as "2A," where torture, beating and rape are customary. So secret is this facility operated by the Revolutionary Guard that the ward is even off-limits to prison guards, the judiciary and even the intelligence ministry. Journalists were told that if they were arrested for sympathizing with the protestors, their contacts in the government wouldn't be able to locate them or assist with their release.

That these incidents occur and could be duplicated in dozens of places across the globe should not come as a surprise. The Obama administration has been unable to legislate against evil, and its accommodative stance to dictators hasn't yet yielded reciprocal liberalization. As I see it, Americans need a reminder that the world hasn't changed in the Obama era even if we deny the war we are in, rationalize terrorist activity or assume we can persuade totalitarians to act gently with their own people.

To survive we must remain vigilant. That means being able to tell the truth and avoid illusions and wishful thinking. We may hope for the best in Cuba and Iran, to cite the examples I employed, but realism tells us these regimes deny basic human rights and use abusive and exploitive tactics to maintain power. Any other conclusion, even if advocated by the president, is clearly delusional.

Grand Strategy and Grand Illusion (2016)

Is it possible to detoxify the United States' relations with Russia, China and the Muslim world? Is there a grand strategy that could maintain the honor of America and at the same time introduce stability in areas of the globe fraught with tension?

With a new administration taking hold in DC, new ideas abound. Among them is the offering of a grand strategy—i.e., an ideology that transcends and yet ameliorates competitive states. An example often cited is the Congress of Vienna (1814 to 1815), chaired by Klemens Wenzel von Metternich, which provided a long-term plan for the resolution of conflict resulting from the French Revolution and the Napoleonic Wars. Despite conflicting claims and regional wars, the congress accord did maintain relative tranquility for Europe till World War I, through an elaborate balance-of-power arrangement.

This model has reemerged with Alexander Dugin's Fourth Political Theory and the work of several U.S. political theorists from the Kissinger school of thought. While different in content, all rely on the supposition that "realists" can determine the fate of global affairs based on a system of "recognition and acceptance." Mr. Dugin, for example, contends that if the U.S. were to accept Russian interests in Crimea and Syria, harmony between the U.S. and Russia might emerge.

More significant is what Mr. Dugin describes as "regional globalization," what is usually referred to as spheres of influence. Presumably that would include an Anglo-American sphere, a European sphere and a Eurasian sphere including Russia, Eastern

Europe, the Baltics and Iran. Mr. Dugin is not alone, in my judgment, albeit the carving out of spheres may vary from one philosopher to the next.

It is also presumed that this reconfiguration would occur peacefully through democratic means, on the order of a 21st-century Congress of Vienna. This, of course, would be a metaphysical shift in world affairs were it to be anything more than a utopian fantasy.

But a fantasy it is. Clearly this idea would legitimate President Putin's imperial vision violating the sovereignty of several states. Second, it is hard to believe Eastern Europe and the Baltic states would willingly accede to antebellum Russian domination. Third, the Chinese are already engaged in the subtle but discernible effort to convert the Pacific Ocean into a Chinese basin. Alarm bells throughout Asia have already gone off. Yet these arguments stand in stark contrast to America's core belief in a liberal international order guided by an Enlightenment faith in individual liberty, the rule of law and the free market. Should the U.S. concede on this front in order to acquire global equilibrium, the tenets of international liberalism will be interred.

There are pragmatists in the U.S. and elsewhere who are willing to sacrifice liberty for a secure world order. In an age of weapons of mass destruction, this notion has its appeal. Moreover, it can be argued that the West has lost its commitment to liberal ideals. A change in demography, a fatigue with the burden of freedom, an ignorance about the history of the West conspire to undermine faith in our founding tenets.

Now come the grand design scholars seeking a strategy for order who regard liberal ideals as an impediment to peace or perhaps a peaceful design. Arguably the major backlash can be found in those who embrace a Judeo-Christian mindset in which individual rights are still considered the essence of Western societies. Can this mindset prevail? The answer to this question lies in the education of the young, of those who may be like Ray Bradbury's characters in *Fahrenheit 451*, memorizing the works of great Western books that have fallen into desuetude. This is a slim reed on which to save us from contemporary pragmatists, but it is the only one that offers hope for the future.

A Track Record of Failure

Isolationism, American disarmament, substantial cuts to the U.S. military and talk over action—how did these play out for the Obama administration over the course of his presidency? Our analysis begins with a response to an article of glowing praise by Zbigniew Brzeznski written a year into President Obama's term.

Brzezinski Misses Mark on Obama Policies (2010)
Originally published on Newsmax

In the January/February issue of *Foreign Affairs*, Zbigniew Brzezinski outlines the ambitious efforts of the Obama administration to redefine the foreign policy of the United States and, as he puts it, "reconnect the United States with the emerging historical context of the twenty-first century." According to Mr. Brzezinski, President Obama has done this remarkably well, reconceptualizing foreign policy in several areas, which he outlines:

- Islam is not an enemy, and the "global war on terror" does not define the United States' current role in the world;
- The United States will be a fair-minded and assertive mediator when it comes to attaining lasting peace between Israel and Palestine;
- The United States ought to pursue serious negotiations with Iran over its nuclear program, as well as other issues;
- The counterinsurgency campaign in the Taliban-controlled parts of Afghanistan should be part of a larger political undertaking, rather than a predominantly military one;
- The United States should respect Latin America's cultural and historical sensitivities and expand its contacts with Cuba;

- The United States ought to energize its commitment to significantly reducing its nuclear arsenal and embrace the eventual goal of a world free of nuclear weapons;
- In coping with global problems, China should be treated not only as an economic partner but also as a geopolitical one;
- Improving U.S.-Russia relations is in the obvious interest of both sides, although this must be done in a manner that accepts, rather than seeks to undo, post-Cold War geopolitical realities;
- A truly collegial transatlantic partnership should be given deeper meaning, particularly in order to heal the rifts caused by the destructive controversies of the past few years.

For all of this, Mr. Brzezinski adds, President Obama did deserve the Nobel Peace Prize. Of course, the erstwhile national security advisor does not point out that he heaps praise on a policy he helped to shape. That observation might well detract from his presumptive objectivity. But in almost all respects the reconceptualization attributed to President Obama is either wrong, misguided or based on a set of false assumptions.

Let me cite the ways. The global war on terror is a war against a radical strain of Islam that has imperial goals and a jihadist tactical temperament. The U.S. may avert its gaze or ignore the magnitude of the threat, but the threat remains and weakness as a response only makes it more threatening.

Second, the U.S. was a fair-minded mediator in the Israel-Palestinian issue, as the evolution of the two-state solution suggests. By "fair-minded," Mr. Brzezinski means tilting in favor of the Palestinians whatever objections the Israelis may have.

Third, serious negotiations have been ongoing with the Iranians through back channels and the Europeans for years. Yet despite blandishments and mild threats, they have not had the slightest influence in defusing the Iranian pursuit of nuclear weapons. From the Iranian perspective, nothing the U.S. offers can compare to the regional influence nuclear weapons can confer.

Fourth, counterinsurgency, according to the General McChrystal plan, was conceptualized long before the Obama presidency, and relies on securing strongholds in Afghanistan's urban areas. It is both a confidence building strategy and a military plan.

Fifth, respect for President Chávez and Fidel Castro has not yielded reciprocal reactions from these leaders. On the contrary, they are intent on spreading their brand of socialist revolution throughout Latin America and have done their utmost to undermine President Uribe, a true democratic leader, of Colombia.

Sixth, by agreeing to equalize its delivery capacity with Russia, the U.S. has accorded President Putin and company a unique advantage. Since the U.S. nuclear umbrella protects Japan, Taiwan, etc., we require delivery expansiveness, and secondly, much of the Russian decrease in capacity is composed of planes and subs that were scheduled for mothballing in any case.

Seventh, China is not an ally and not yet a foe. However, with a blue-water navy and patrols in the Sea of Japan, it is engaged in saber rattling that bears careful observation. It is hard to think of China as a partner when it provided the advanced technology for the Pakistani nuclear arsenal.

Eighth, surely acceptance of post-Cold War geopolitical realities should be recognized by the Russians, but President Putin's strategic vision is predicated on the reacquisition of the near-abroad, as recent actions and doctrine indicate.

Ninth, a transatlantic partnership should be recognized and encouraged. But it should be noted that the U.S. has assumed a disproportionate share of NATO expenses, and the Europeans, who have grown to love freedom and prosperity, do not yet know how to defend these cherished concepts.

Alas, what Mr. Brzezinski provides is a cliché-driven set of propositions that have little if anything to do with real-world conditions. In the aggregate these positions make the U.S. look weak and ineffectual in my opinion.

In the end, however, it is not what drives this reconceptualization of policy, but whether or not it is successful. So far, this effort has been a failure, but President Obama has several years to recover from missteps. Perhaps one way to begin is by not taking Mr. Brzezinski's proposals too seriously.

A Pattern of Foreign Policy Failures (2015)
Originally published on Newsmax

Despite administration claims to the contrary, 2014 was a year of failure on the foreign policy front. In every area of the globe, chaos or instability reigns.

The Middle East is a cauldron of warring factions and theological imperatives. Libya is falling under the sway of radical groups, each trying to gain control of Tripoli. In essence, government has ceased to exist. French forces may be the only hope for the restoration of order, but that is not a sustainable solution.

Iraq is struggling to maintain a state that resembles the recent past. With the Islamic State carving out a segment for itself and the Kurds banging the drums for autonomy, the future is indefinite. A modus vivendi between Shia and Sunni leaders is also unlikely. On Iraq's border, Syria is in a similar state of dismemberment. Bashar al-Assad holds on to power precariously with overt Russian support and tacit U.S. acceptance, but his base is restricted to an area around Damascus as rebels of various stripes carve up the rest of the country.

The largely ignored war in the Sinai continues unabated, with Egyptian forces taking significant casualties. Sinai has become a sanctuary for terrorists who threaten Egyptian stability and Israel's southern border.

Iran, a perpetual source of terrorist activity since 1979, has emerged, with U.S. approval, as a stabilizing regional force opposing ISIL ambitions. Yet its own imperial goals remain undiminished. Iranian National Guard members launched a coup against the Yemini government and prevailed. As a consequence, Iran controls the critical sea lanes of the Red Sea and the Strait of Hormuz.

Negotiations in Geneva and Vienna indicate that Iran will possess sufficient fissile material to build nuclear weapons, a decision that will have profound implications for the future of the region. In addition to altering military strategy, nuclear weapons or even sufficient fissile material to build weapons will roil the political waters for the foreseeable future.

Across the globe, on the Pacific front, the Chinese have made it clear they want to assert themselves as the hegemon in the region. Assertion doesn't always mean war, but it does represent a challenge, one that the Obama administration neither understands nor is prepared to openly resist. As a consequence, Japan, South Korea, India, the Philippines and Indonesia are searching for leadership, a helmsman who can lead nations with disparate interests but the same potential enemy.

In South America, U.S. overtures to Cuba seem to suggest that there may be more to gain from opposition to American policies than embracing them. Venezuela, as a proxy for Cuba on the continent, has harbored terrorists and sympathizers of Iran without penalty. The *caudillo* principle hasn't died in South America, but the U.S. as a model of democratic government is fading.

On balance 2014 represents the unfolding of the Obama foreign policy failures. It is one thing to renounce the position of global policeman, but another thing to remove oneself from the adjudication of international disputes. As much as President Obama wants the U.S. to be a state like other states, we are different in kind, size and stature. Notwithstanding denials to the contrary, America is still the light of opportunity that shines across the globe, albeit a somewhat less bright light under President Obama's leadership. Restoring that leadership role represents the task ahead. Needless to say, it will not be easy reversing positions and establishing confidence with skeptics, but that is the challenge that lies before us.

The End of Liberal Internationalism (2016)
Originally published in the Washington Times

At the end of World War II, the United States established a liberal international order that included an institutional commitment to free trade and freedom of the seas. It also included unprecedented assistance to weak nations incapable of fending for themselves, through the Marshall Plan, NATO and other alliances. However one describes the U.S. rule, it did provide a period of equilibrium, notwithstanding challenges from the Soviet Union.

While the U.S. is not likely to be completely displaced from its dominant position in the 21st century, this order will undoubtedly be threatened by a diffusion of power and the complexity of world politics. The openness that enabled the U.S. to build networks and maintain institutions and alliances is under siege. Internally, the populist reaction to globalization and trade agreements illustrates antipathy to the post-war arrangements. Externally, a rising Chinese military presence in the South China Sea and Russian assertiveness in Syria and Crimea challenge assumptions of the past.

In Asia, Beijing seeks to draw American allies such as the Philippines and Thailand into its political orbit. In the Middle East, the U.S. has been unable to guide the region toward a more liberal and peaceful future in the wake of the Arab Spring and has proved to be powerless to halt the killing fields in Aleppo. Russia's geopolitical influence has reached heights unseen since the Cold War, as Russian president Vladimir Putin attempts to roll back liberal advances on his geographic periphery.

For 50 years or more, the European Union seemed to represent the advance guard of a new liberalism in which nations "pool" sovereignty for continental cooperation. But today the EU is fractured. The departure of jobs to Asia and the arrival of migrants from Africa and the Middle East have resuscitated nationalistic impulses. Brexit was merely one manifestation of this trend. After that June vote, the only question that remains is which country will be next to leave the EU and how much more contraction the union can tolerate.

Even though Norbert Hofer of Austria's Freedom party lost the election to a pro-EU party, his strong showing set off alarm bells throughout the EU. Earlier this year, Mr. Hofer said that Islam "has no place in Austria" without explaining what that means for Austria's Muslims.

The Italian referendum also suggested a troubling trend line for the EU. Matteo Renzi's proposal to extend his powers and ease further reforms was seen as a plebiscite on his premiership. It was soundly rejected and Prime Minister Renzi was obliged to resign. The "winner" of the referendum is Beppe Grillo's Five Star Movement, a movement skeptical of the EU and global liberalism.

Over this past decade, buffeted by financial crises, populist insurgencies and the resurgence of authoritarian powers, the liberal international order has stumbled. In part this process of dissolution is related to the belief that the U.S., as the superpower maintaining global equilibrium, is no longer a fully engaged partner. Where the U.S. has lapsed, Russia has intervened—its own economic weakness notwithstanding.

What the world is experiencing is material reduction brought about through the demand for social services and equity without the ability to generate adequate revenue. Debt is the burden that overwhelms Europe. A *cri de coeur* heard throughout the continent is a plea for the delivery of returns to society superior to alternative financial arrangements. In the backdrop of unsustainable financing is a Russian system of centralized and opaque political leadership incompatible with Europe's market- and rules-based system, and a Chinese initiative for global trade managed by a Communist party apparatus that will not tolerate opposition.

Russia and China represent a kind of Nietzschean "will to power" applied to a liberal international order weaker than it has been in three generations. Hence, autocratic governments will attempt to establish an alternative political order managed by might rather than rules. The best that can be hoped for, short of conflicts, is an awkward coexistence between liberal and illiberal nations. But even in this compromise, should it be accepted, the belief that the liberal internationalism that kept the world intact for 80 years is over is tacit.

The Treatment of Allies

Syria

From the very beginning of the unfolding civil war in Syria, President Obama displayed his administration's reluctance to lead. In 2013, Syrian president Bashar al-Assad used chemical weapons on a highly populated rebel-controlled city that resulted in massive casualties, including by some estimates over 400 children. President Obama drew a "red line" and demanded al-Assad change his tactics. Shortly after drawing the line, President Obama backed down. So went his Syrian debacle. The international community watched the Syrian stage with great interest, looking to America for leadership. Russia capitalized on the void and inserted itself into the conflict. Allies in the Middle East anxiously live alongside a bloody civil war. Though America covertly supported rebel activity, the Obama administration showed little desire to take a visible moral stand against President al-Assad's cruelty.

U.S. Betrays Syria's Opposition (2011)
Originally published on Human Events

Reuters headlines indicate that dozens have died and thousands have fled a Syrian tank assault in Hama. At least 45 civilians were killed the first week in August, a sharp escalation in President Bashar al-Assad's campaign to crush the political opposition that has already claimed at least 2,000 people.

So violent have been President al-Assad's assaults that even the U.N. Security Council condemned the use of force—its first substantive response to five months of unrest. But as a diplomat in Syria noted, "The Security apparatus thinks it can wrap this uprising up by relying on the security option and killing as many Syrians as it thinks it will take." President al-Assad has given his security forces a virtual blank check, the same President al-Assad whom Secretary of State Hillary Clinton called "a reformer." After the bloodshed made international headlines, the White House finally responded by noting, "Syria would be a better place without President Assad."

In an effort to understand and placate Syrian opposition groups, Secretary Clinton invited them to a meeting in Washington. However, most of those invited have links to the Muslim Brotherhood. Missing from the invitations are Kurdish leaders, Sunni liberals, Assyrians and Christian spokespeople. According to various reports, the State Department made a deal with Turkey and Muslim Brotherhood representatives to either share power with al-Assad in order to stabilize the government or replace him if this effort fails.

One organization, the Syrian Democracy Council (SDC), an opposition group composed of diverse ethnic and religious organizations, including Alawis, Aramaic Christians, Druze and Assyrians, was conspicuously omitted from the invitation list. This isn't coincidental.

From the standpoint of Foggy Bottom it is far better to promote stability, even if this means engendering the goals of presumptive enemies. However, this is a dangerous game that not only puts U.S. interests hostage to the Muslim Brotherhood, but suggests that the withdrawal of American forces from the region affords the U.S. with very few policy options.

As I see it, it is far more desirable to support the democratic influences despite their relative weakness at the moment. These are the political organizations that require cultivation and support. In the long term—a somewhat ambiguous phrase—these groups of religious and secular groups represent the real hope for the future and the counterweight to the influence of the Muslim Brotherhood.

At the very least Secretary Clinton should hear the SDC argument. Leaving this body out of the Syrian conversation is absurd. Al-Assad should know that his opponents aren't merely those complicit in stabilizing a murderous regime, but those with genuine democratic impulses who represent a significant portion of the Syrian people.

The killing in Syria will not end because of these State Department–sponsored talks. However, a message should be delivered that the U.S. stands behind the one organization that represents democracy in a regime that invariably opposes this political view.

It is instructive that the Obama administration stated unequivocally that President Mubarak of Egypt, ostensibly an ally of the United States, had to vacate his position. Yet no such comment has been made about President al-Assad, a person whose interests are diametrically opposed to those of the United States.

Why isn't what is good for the goose good for the gander? Only President Obama can answer that question.

Syrian Rebels Forgotten by Obama, UN (2016)
Originally published on Newsmax

In its emphasis on defeating the Islamic State, the U.S. delegation in Geneva has sold out the rebels fighting against Syria's Bashar al-Assad. A new chapter in the Middle East has unfolded as America's perceived interests have tilted in the direction of Iran and Russia. Instead of a transitional government that would ease the Syrian dictator out of power, Secretary of State John Kerry said there should be a national unity government for the foreseeable future—a euphemism for "al-Assad stays." In fact, that is the essence of the recently signed cease-fire accord.

Last year, by contrast, when the rebels advanced across Syria, seriously weakening President Bashar al-Assad, the U.S. supported them. In fact, rebel success on the battlefield triggered Moscow's intervention. With Russian airpower deployed on his behalf, President al-Assad can call on Shiite troops, including Iranian Qud forces, to achieve a victory unavailable to him since the civil war began in 2011.

Despite Russian claims to the contrary, the majority of its strikes have hit non-Islamic fighters, mowing down the mainstream rebellion in western Syria. Clearly Russia has achieved its short-term objective: forcing the U.S. to choose President al-Assad or the Islamic State. With the virtual collapse of rebel forces in the Aleppo region, thousands of dejected fighters could abandon their arms and gravitate to the Islamic State.

The encirclement of Aleppo is emerging as a humanitarian disaster of extraordinary magnitude, but the UN and world opinion are silent in the face of this tragedy. More significantly, the Obama administration, in its effort to seal ties to its "ally" in the region, has been conspicuously silent on the matter. Neither Secretary Kerry nor UN envoy Staffan de Mistura is willing to pressure Russia and President al-Assad for fear of jeopardizing the Geneva talks. For our State Department, negotiation is the answer for any crisis.

Moscow understands that without President al-Assad, there isn't any justification for its Middle East intervention. There may be reservations Russian president Vladimir Putin shares about President al-Assad, but he needs him as the devil needs devoted dupes. When the Russian onslaught began, U.S. officials hailed Russian intervention as the best way to check the Islamic State, but thus far the Russian campaign has strengthened the jihadist group in central Asia. This is seemingly the price Washington is willing to pay in order to keep the Geneva process afloat.

Moreover, the concessions to Russia have been accompanied by a weakening of the supply network to rebel groups. The result is that the rebels sense betrayal. The Saudis believe the U.S. is unreliable, and the regional leaders increasingly turn to President Putin as the answer to Middle East instability. Surely there is some justification for a political process, but exposing the rebels to the President al-Assad–Russian–Iranian onslaught without contingency planning is outrageous. President Obama is intent on walking away from the Middle East, but the Middle East cannot walk away from its pathologies. It is haunted by an American position of capitulation.

Over the horizon is an American president in 2017, a condition that guarantees a year of brinkmanship and misery as the actors in Syria and Iraq try to solidify their positions. Whoever the next president may be, he or she will have to recognize Vladimir Putin as the real force in Syria. He will have ousted the West from a NATO neighboring country—which is pivotal for control of the Mediterranean. As the czar of Mare Nostrum, President Putin can determine the strategic consequences for the United States. In 1973 the U.S. employed its influence to oust the Soviet Union from the Middle East; in 2016 we can observe a situation in which President Putin—with the acquiescence of President Obama—will oust the U.S. from the Middle East.

In this year of upheaval, the predication of Alexandr Dugin that the Russian empire would be re-created has some merit. If that assessment seems dubious, just ask the rebels who have been betrayed by their American "protectors."

Iran's Nervous Neighbors

The Gulf Cooperation Council (GCC) is an intergovernmental organization composed of the Persian Gulf states of Qatar, Bahrain, Kuwait, Saudi Arabia, Oman, and the United Arab Emirates. All of these member states are Sunni Islamic states. The GCC was formed in the mutual interests of these Sunni states to counter the regional influence of the Shiite Islamic caliphate of Iran and its proxies (including Hezbollah and the Houthis of Yemen). When the Obama

administration began to make clear its intentions to negotiate a
nuclear deal with Iran, tensions rose among America's Sunni allies.

Mideast Allies Wary About Iran Deal (2015)
Originally published on Newsmax

After a lot of arm-twisting, the Gulf Arab states publicly backed
the Obama administration's nuclear agreement with Iran. On the
surface, this appears to be a diplomatic victory for the president as
he seeks to build support for his signature foreign policy initiative.
But is this true?

The positive response from the Gulf Cooperation Council
(GCC), composed of Saudi Arabia, Qatar, the United Arab
Emirates, Kuwait, Oman and Bahrain, emerged after months of
intense lobbying by the White House. What the administration
gave up to achieve its goal is a matter of some speculation.

There isn't any doubt that the U.S. will offer advanced military
material, intelligence-sharing and training. However, from the
outset Saudi Arabian officials have said that whatever capability
Iran obtains from the deal should be offered to their country as well.

Secretary of State John Kerry held a summit explaining the
terms of nuclear agreement to the GCC, but what is undisclosed is
whether he was willing to agree to Saudi terms. In other words, if
there is a pathway for Iran to obtain nuclear weapons, will the same
pathway exist for Saudi Arabia? Kerry refers to the deal with Iran
as "the best option." What that means for Saudi Arabia remains
unclear.

It is clear, of course, that this GCC backing undermines pro-Israel
groups, who oppose the Iran deal because it threatens America's
Middle East allies, albeit Egypt is conspicuously omitted from
the acceptance group. Republicans continue to insist, despite the
GCC proclamation, that the Iran accord will jeopardize Israel and
American interests in the region. They note, as well, that Tehran
will use new oil money and revenues to fund its militant proxies in
Yemen, Lebanon, Iraq and Syria.

Notwithstanding GCC acceptance of the deal, several notable officials from the gulf voiced concern that Washington may weaken its alliance in the area as it pursues rapproachement with Iran. It is therefore encumbent on Washington to assure these nations that they will not be abandoned. From the Sunni Arab perspective, sophisticated weapons, radars, missile defense systems and enhanced intelligence operations may be insufficient as reassurances.

Even Kerry said of Iran he "hopes that indeed perhaps there could be a turning of the page, but we have to prepare for the possibility and eventuality that it won't." Preparing for the possibility it won't probably means the GCC nations require a deterrent—i.e., nuclear weapons of their own. Is this what Kerry really means when he argues the U.S. will do whatever is necessary to provide security for our allies, or does he mean these nations will come under the U.S. nuclear umbrella? In any unfolding scenario America offers either nuclear guarantees, nuclear weapons or a green light to secure these weapons.

As many analysts have understood from the outset, this Iran negotiation leads inexorably to proliferation, the very condition President Obama said he was trying to avoid. Just as "verification" for President Obama doesn't really mean verification, but rather selective inspection, "endorsement" by the GCC doesn't really mean endorsement, but rather tentative acceptance based on a laundry list of incentives.

Arab states have learned the fine art of negotiation. They also understand *taqiyya*—deception to advance the interests of Islam. What seems to be the case is never quite the case. While Secretary Kerry warns of the worst-case scenario, he acts as if a rosy future awaits the region. Wiser minds see it differently, and I side with the wiser minds.

At Camp David, the Unraveling of Obama's Foreign Policy (2015)
Originally published on The Hill

The unraveling of President Obama's foreign policy has been obvious for some time, but at no moment was it more obvious than Saudi Arabia's declining to send King Salman to the Gulf Cooperation Council (GCC) taking place at Camp David. If there were ever a signal the Saudis are not onboard with the president's negotiation with Iran, this is it. The Camp David meeting is being organized with one goal in mind: Try to convince Sunni allies that the agreement with Iran is in their best interest. This is an uphill struggle, perhaps an impossible one. As one Saudi scholar noted referring to the U.S.: "Our allies aren't listening to us, and this is what is making us extremely nervous."

Sunni Gulf states are convinced the impending P5+1 agreement will boost Iran's support for regional proxies like the Houthi in Yemen, while providing a pathway for nuclear weapons. Of course, the fear is justified. Not only did President Obama indicate there would be no way to stop Iranian acquisition of the bomb in 10 years, but he believes Iran can be a stabilizing force in the region. As one would guess, the Sunni gulf states see it differently.

They are convinced this deal will embolden Tehran to act aggressively. In fact, Iran is regarded as *the* destabilizing force in the region. With the likelihood sanctions will be lifted, Iran will have additional resources to pursue its imperial agenda. This explains, in part, why Saudi Arabia's former head of intelligence Turki al-Faisal noted, "I've always said that whatever comes out of these [nuclear] talks, we will want the same." Alas, the door to proliferation is open and all the assurances President Obama will provide about the U.S. nuclear umbrella won't fly. Saudi distrust can be magnified throughout the region.

President Obama is at the brink. If he backs out of the agreement, he repudiates the most significant initiative in his foreign policy. If he goes forward, he risks proliferation and the gamble a nuclear weapon will be employed. At this point, he hasn't any leverage with Iranian leaders who realize the agreement is the president's legacy. And he has lost the confidence of most Sunni leaders, who do not believe he is acting in their interest.

In the backdrop, the Russians are smiling. President Obama's hand is not only constrained, it has given President Putin an opportunity to assert his interests in the Middle East. The Chinese are perplexed. Every Chinese official asked about the region thinks President Obama has some sort of "secret plan"; they cannot accept incompetence or ideology as explanations for his bungling behavior.

Whether there is a plan or an ideology driving decisions, the president's moves are having a profound effect on the future of the region. Moreover, it is hard to see how anything positive will emerge from the deliberations.

Some contend the president's successor can simply abrogate the deal, assuming it is finally introduced. That may be a facile assumption. Even an *anticipated* arrangement is precipitating changes, including nations scrambling to obtain nuclear weapons. Second, since the P5+1 represent the primary nations in the UN Security Council, the argument will be made that the moral weight of this body gives the agreement legitimacy. Third, the loss of confidence amid Middle East leaders is so great that no matter what a successor president says, it will be treated with trepidation.

President Obama said during the course of his campaigns that he would "change" America. Alas, he has. In fact, he has changed the globe, and in the process all residents of planet Earth were put in far more peril than they were before his presidency.

The Camp David discussions boil down to a sales pitch by the president to quondam allies. But, in fact, it will be a defense of the indefensible. As George Orwell said, "Political language has to consist largely of euphemism, question-begging and sheer cloudy vagueness...the great enemy of clear language is insincerity."

Saudi Arabia

President Obama's actions in the Middle East were at times perplexing to the Saudis, especially since he gave more attention to the nuclear needs of the Iranians than to the existential threat to American Sunni allies as posed by a rapidly expanding Islamic State. The Obama administration's reluctance to decisively engage with the Syrian conflict or the threat of the Islamic State bred distrust with the U.S. and strengthened ties among Sunni states to the exclusion of American interests.

Nonintervention Breeds Saudi-Egyptian Ties (2015)
Originally published on Newsmax

If ever there was a need for U.S. diplomatic intervention in the Middle East, this is the moment. Instead of sitting on the sidelines as a disinterested observer, Secretary of State John Kerry and company should be on a plane to Cairo to discuss an emerging schism in Saudi-Egyptian relations. In February, the Saudi kingdom announced that it was prepared to send ground troops to Syria to fight alongside the international coalition. Cairo objected.

Egyptian foreign minister Sameh Shoukry said the Saudi decision to send ground troops into Syria does not fall within the scope of the Islamic Military Alliance to Fight Terrorism, the 34-member coalition Saudi Arabia launched in December. Shoukry confirmed Egypt's endorsement of a political, not a military, solution in Syria.

As one might expect, spokesmen in both nations said the disagreement would not affect the strong ties between them. But the facts present a different version of the story.

Saudi Arabia under King Salman bin Abdulaziz is extremely sensitive to any political position that challenges the Saudi vision of regional issues. This sensitivity was made manifest when the kingdom rejected $4 billion in aid to the Lebanese army because Lebanon disagreed with Saudi Arabia's stance on Hezbollah.

In addition to its military alliance with Saudi Arabia, Egypt is reliant on Saudi financial assistance, including petroleum needs for five years and $8 billion in capital projects. Obviously Egypt has a stake in the maintenance of good relations. But in politics it is axiomatic to contend there aren't permanent or perpetual friends or enemies.

There is, of course, more that unites Egypt and Saudi Arabia than separates them. The coordination in reviving a Sunni coalition to serve as a counterweight to Iranian ambitions is the primary concern linking the nations. Nonetheless, questions remain about the extent to which Saudi Arabia will use the aid card against Egypt in return for Cairo's adoption of a position consonant with King Salman's agenda during his upcoming visit to Cairo. The visit will include a discussion of military operations in Yemen and Syria, and most significantly, Iranian interference in regional affairs. Salman will undoubtedly be seeking a malleable Egyptian response.

If the U.S. were not regarded with suspicion by both nations, it would be natural for State Department officials to broker a deal. In fact, if President Obama truly appreciated the need for a regional balance of power, he would attempt to solidify a Sunni front as a way to control visions of an Iranian empire.

What the administration has overlooked is that the consequence of non-intervention, in some ways, is as bad as the consequences of intervention in Iraq. President Obama has remained true to his principle that non-engagement, even diplomatic engagement, will have salutary effects for foreign policy. However, the reality, such as the *contretemps* between Egypt and Saudi Arabia, presents a very different view of the world. President Obama's belief in "the arc of history" in which global affairs become less violent, more tolerant and empathetic appears as wishful thinking. Perhaps in time (centuries?) this will happen, but at the moment many nations arc looking for U.S. leadership.

Moreover, the Middle East is an area of persistent tribalism, even if the president sees that as the atavistic stress of globalization. Cultures are in collision. Our allies need healing and our foes require defeat. Instead the U.S. observes Islamic extremism, sectarian conflict and a network of terrorism without a strategy for dealing with them. Even in an area of modest disagreement where the U.S. might play a diplomatic role, Saudi Arabia and Egypt will design their own accord with the U.S. nowhere to be found.

Saudi Arabia Is Both Friend and Foe (2016)
Originally published on The Hill

In the case of China it is not clear if they are foe or friend, with an argument to be made on both sides of the issue. In the case of Saudi Arabia there is little doubt it is foe and friend, a matter that has led to extraordinary confusion.

Recently Saudi officials told the Obama administration that "it will sell hundreds of billions of dollars' worth of American assets if Congress passes a bill that would allow the Saudi government to be held responsible" in U.S. courts for any role in the 9/11 terrorist attacks.

This is an unmitigated threat. Interest rates in the U.S. are relatively low—in large part because foreign governments, like Saudi Arabia, buy large parcels of our bonds. If a substantial buyer sells, the U.S. would want someone else to buy its debt; however, with global deflation that would be hard to do.

Whether any lawsuits against the Saudi government are warranted or even legal is in some sense beside the point. The Obama administration made it clear it will not pursue the matter, raising the specter of capitulation. Nonetheless, an Associated Press dispatch reported that Saudi officials decided not to send a high-level delegation to greet President Obama on his recent visit to Riyadh. This gesture was obviously intended to send a clear message the Saudi government doesn't have much faith in him.

Based on this slight, the president could reveal what is in the redacted 28 pages of the 9/11 commission report, however insignificant the evidence might be. Second, the president could incentivize fracking through subsidies, despite the low price of oil, in an effort to push the price down further, and in the process adversely affect Saudi oil revenue. We might need the cooperation of Saudi Arabia in the bond market, but they need our assistance in the oil market.

For years Saudi Arabia exported its brand of Wahhabism to madrassas across the globe. Places formerly pacific imbibed militancy that emerged from this form of extremist ideology. We averted our gaze until recently, when it became apparent that these teachings can result in violence. Even the Saudi leadership is starting to understand the bitterness their policies have engendered.

While complete repudiation has not occurred, there are hopeful signs, such as the banning of the Muslim Brotherhood. Most notably the Saudi king realizes that the only counterweight to Shia imperial goals in the region is a Saudi-led military alliance that includes Egypt, Jordan and the gulf states. Here is a role that enhances presumptive balance of power objectives and could eventually create regional stability.

Of course there is suspicion on both sides of this equation. The Saudis view President Obama's capitulation to their demands as another example of U.S. weakness in an area where it once was the hegemonic power. It is also the case the U.S. influence in Saudi Arabia is waning. The Saudis may acquire F-16s, but they can no longer easily acquire loyalty. United States dependence on Saudi oil, which was the basis for bilateral understandings, has been modified by dramatic shale oil discoveries and technological innovation making the U.S. somewhat fossil fuel-independent. Put simply: Saudi Arabia is not a front-burner issue in the State Department's agenda.

Managing this relationship won't be easy. Neither bullying nor capitulation will work. History will find a solution but at present we are justifiably angry at what the Saudis have done to radicalize Islam. At the same time we may need the Saudis to stem the tide of Iranian imperialism, a point President Obama does not appreciate. As has been noted before, "There isn't a prize for rain, only for arks." We must build diplomatic arks with a people we would often like to punish. This isn't easy, but it is essential.

Egypt

If Saudi Arabia was perplexed by U.S. foreign policy under President Obama, the Egyptians were staggered. President Obama's actions in Libya removed Muammar Qaddafi only to leave the region in chaos. And, as stated, the U.S. did little to address the growing threat of the radical Islamic State. Closer to home for the Egyptians, President Obama's State Department played an active role in propping up a Muslim Brotherhood takeover of the Egyptian government, only for the group to be deposed by the Egyptian people two years later. After Egypt shed itself of the Muslim Brotherhood, the U.S. withheld previously committed military assistance, only to reverse its decision in 2015.

Obama Sending Mixed Messages on Egypt (2011)
Originally published on Newsmax

A million people are standing in Tahrir Square in Cairo protesting against the government and arguing Hosni Mubarak must go. The military representing the most stabilizing influence in Egypt has immersed itself into the protest, at least to some indeterminate degree. The nation's most notorious prisons have been emptied of criminals, and Islamic extremists and roving bands have destroyed art treasures and looted private property.

While words of freedom and liberty are in the air, there is the distinct danger these protests could result in less freedom for Egyptians than what they have known, especially if those who harbor Islamist goals (read: the Muslim Brotherhood) gain a foothold in government.

Despite the confusion surrounding these protests, Foggy Bottom was completely blindsided. On one occasion Secretary Hillary Clinton said, "Mubarak is a friend"; on another occasion Vice President Joe Biden denied Hosni Mubarak is a dictator. But as the protests persisted, Washington's tone changed. Now the State Department refers to an "orderly transition" to "a democratic, participatory government."

But there is still not an unequivocal call for liberty consistent with the president's Cairo speech. In fact, President Obama has put a greater emphasis on engagement than freedom, as his tactics with the Iranian government suggest. Admittedly a democratic election in Egypt could result in one vote, one time with the Muslim Brotherhood gaining control and, like their Hamas cousins, instituting religious dominance of the nation.

Of course, not everyone views the Muslim Brotherhood as a threat. Bruce Riedel at the Brookings Institution argues the Brotherhood might be troublesome but is not a cause for anxiety. This position overlooks the Brotherhood's basic attitude of subjugating women and the threat to the 30-year peace with Israel.

As I see it, Brotherhood power in Egypt, even if exercised behind the political curtain, would be calamitous for U.S. interests in the region. For the Brotherhood, violence is justified when it is consistent with the cause, and that cause is jihad. History is written in blood, not Western law. In 2007, so-called reform-minded leaders argued that all government decisions must be vetted to ensure they are consistent with Islamic law.

However, it is not clear how much influence the Muslim Brotherhood has among the protestors or the military forces or even among the peasantry. Therefore, keeping your powder dry seems a reasonable position, until the movement of historical forces carries it away on the tide of change. The problem, at the moment, is it is not clear what the Obama administration has in mind. On the one hand, it is calling for stability, which could be interpreted as endorsing President Mubarak; on the other hand, it is continually making reference to "transition," which suggests President Mubarak must be ousted.

Clearly the U.S. wants or should want a stable, civil society in Egypt that is aligned with U.S. regional interests. If that is not possible, the U.S. should curtail its economic and military assistance in excess of $1 billion and bolster the only enduring democracy in the Middle East neighborhood, Israel.

Should Egypt become dominated by extremist forces, the likelihood of war will increase and the resultant chaos will work to the advantage of Iran. Even though it's a Persian nation distrusted by Arabs and a Shia state distrusted by Sunnis, Iran is the strong horse in the region that garners support through its messianic belief in violence.

If the evolving Egyptian story reveals anything, it is how destabilizing a weak and ineffectual U.S. can be. At another time in the distant past, the U.S. would have recognized its interests and known exactly what it must do to secure stability. This, however, is not that time and the U.S. no longer recognizes its strategic interests or how to protect them.

American Foreign Policy Through the Eyes of the Egyptians (2014)
Originally published on Family Security Matters

For intellectuals and government officials in Egypt, American foreign policy is an enigma. From Syria to Afghanistan questions are posed about the stance of the Obama administration. To cite one example, an official asked, how do you explain the president's argument for bombing Syria only to end up not bombing Syria?

Most significantly, Egyptian analysts ask why the U.S. spends its resources and sacrifices its blood to fight al Qaeda, but continues to assert the Muslim Brotherhood is a moderate force. For Egyptians, there is sufficient evidence to maintain the Muslim Brotherhood and al Qaeda are united for purposes of logistics and funding, despite cleverly designed arguments to conceal the relationship. Even the trade of five terrorists for one American captive has alarmed Egyptian foreign policy councils.

Egyptians ask as well why Muammar Qaddafi was displaced and Libya bombed only to see the al Qaeda flag flying over every major Libyan city. Colonel Qaddafi may not have been a reliable ally, but he did provide a degree of national stability. In fact, 3 million Egyptians once found employment in Libya. Now the Libyan landscape is littered with dead bodies and chaos reigns.

Egyptian analysts continually peppered me with questions about Iraq, noting that the precipitous withdrawal of American forces from that nation ushered in a civil war and, perhaps most notably, the influence of Iranian forces.

This query was invariably followed by a statement that the U.S. encouraged al Qaeda through its support of the mujahideen in Afghanistan and then wondered why the Taliban emerged as a national force. With the anticipated withdrawal of American troops from this nation, future stability is clearly in question.

And then there is the major issue: how can the U.S. engage in rapprochement with Iran over the nuclear weapons issue when Iran cannot be trusted and an Iran with enough fissile material for a bomb will invite nuclear proliferation throughout the region?

Whether one accepts the questions is irrelevant. Even if simplistic in formulation, they represent a majority of elite opinion. President Obama is regarded as "a rank amateur" and, in the minds of the many I met, incapable of dealing with regional issues.

The Egyptians were perplexed about the president's reluctance to release the spare parts for the Apache helicopters promised to them. On April 23, 2014, the Obama administration reversed itself and decided to send the helicopters that were urgently requested by Cairo, even though the arms embargo imposed by the Obama team last year, after the ouster of Muslim Brotherhood president Mohammed Morsi, will not be lifted.

As a consequence of U.S. vacillation, the Egyptians are increasingly cynical. For them, the Obama administration and Republicans like John McCain and Lindsay Graham, who defend and rationalize the role of the Muslim Brotherhood, are in *Alice in Wonderland*. The security concerns of Egyptians should be the same security concerns as of the United States. The terror that afflicted and still hangs over the Egyptian nation is the terror Americans were forced to confront on 9/11. Yet, as Egyptians remark, "The Obama team doesn't get it."

Whether the U.S. hasn't explained its position sufficiently or the explanation is inexplicable, Egyptians are generally perplexed. That remains a problem since Egypt, as the most populous Arab state, is often considered the first among equals in the Sunni world. Its policies have been the linchpin on which regional positions depend. If Egypt turns away from the United States, its position will influence others. Healing the apparent rift between Egypt and the U.S. should be at the top of the Obama foreign policy agenda. I don't know if that is the case, but it is certainly worthy of someone's attention.

The Unfolding of the Iran Deal and Its Aftermath

From 2013 to 2015, the world watched as the P5+1 powers (the United States, France, England, China, Russia and Germany) negotiated a deal with Iran over its nuclear enrichment program. The Obama administration enthusiastically led a domestic and international campaign to support a deal. Talks occurred in Vienna and Switzerland, and a deal was finalized in 2015. The Obama White House heralded the deal as "an historic deal that will prevent Iran from acquiring a nuclear weapon." However, many in the U.S., in Israel and across the world saw the deal-making as President Obama's desire to cement a legacy as the great negotiator. If he could reach a deal with Iran, the world's most stalwart actor (and largest state sponsor of terror), then surely his administration would stand out in history. The deal eventually came at the cost of sound terms. Worse yet, the entire deal was predicated on Iran's honesty in reporting the size of its nuclear cache and allowing the international community to inspect its arsenal.

The Iran Deal: An Introduction

Obama's Legacy: Dismal Iran Deal (2015)
Originally published on Newsmax

Since 2009, well before official P5+1 formal negotiations, President Barack Obama was willfully engaged in a plan to achieve an accord with Iran on nuclear questions. It became a matter of pride for the president to contend that he was able to negotiate an accord that his predecessors could not. Yet the president has created a paradoxical box for himself in which the Iranian agreement—leaving aside its merits or lack thereof—forces him to be complicit in assisting Iranian foreign policy.

Hence, Washington's disapproval of the Iranian desire for a "Shia Crescent" runs headlong into those measures needed to forestall this adventurism. Resistance to Iran's foreign policy goals requires sanctions at the very least. But sanctions would undermine the nuclear accord.

It is clear to anyone who observes events in Syria that President Bashar al-Assad is responsible for the death of 400,000 of his own people, the use of poison gas, the migration of millions to Europe and the destruction of the Sunni opposition. His removal was stated American policy when the civil war in Syria began (2011). However, with the Iranian Revolutionary Guard fighting to retain al-Assad's dominance, American Special Forces and aircraft would be obliged to kill Iranians with whom an accord has been signed. It is hardly coincidental that the Obama administration has learned to live with President al-Assad. Military action by the U.S. is certainly not in the cards, and "snap back," or the application of sanctions, is almost as distasteful.

As a consequence, President Obama's "box" is America's dilemma. Neither Hillary Clinton nor Donald Trump is likely to alter facts on the ground, because it doesn't appear as if they have much leverage. Clearly the deal with Iran could be rejected by the next president, and perhaps should be, but the question arises as to what is next. Direct intervention is not possible unless the U.S. is willing to put a troop force of 50,000 on the ground. Considering rhetoric used during the campaign season, this is unlikely and unpopular.

So for the time being, Iran is an ally of a dubious kind and a foe. Iran is assisting in the war against the Islamic State, or so it says, and at the same time is fighting to retain President al-Assad's power in Damascus. Iran describes the U.S. as the "Great Satan," and in the next breath demands further liberalization of sanctions.

To repair the obvious contradictions in policy, the Obama team engaged in a fantasy. With Deputy National Security Advisor Ben Rhodes at the ready with his pen and a vivid imagination, two levels of Iranian leadership were invented. There are, according to his narrative, the "bad guys" who lead the chant "Death to America" and the "good guys" who are working to achieve moderation in policy, a modus vivendi. Of course, the good and the bad are really all bad, but if the Democratic congressional leadership was truly informed, the deal with Iran would not have survived.

The reality of the nuclear deal with Iran is that it rests on a fiction. Ben Rhodes admitted as much and even flaunted the deception, but, more importantly, the legacy President Obama has worked so hard to create has the solidity of pie crust. It is a policy direction out of George Orwell's *1984*. We are in a box of President Obama's making, and it is hard to breathe and very difficult to escape.

In 1946 Mr. Orwell in *Politics and the English Language* wrote: "Political language…is designed to make lies sound truthful and murder respectable, and to give an appearance of solidity to pure wind." I can only imagine what Mr. Orwell would say about the Obama "box."

Strategic Stability in the Second Nuclear Age (2014)
Originally published on Family Security Matters

The negotiations in Vienna to restrict or prevent Iran from enriching sufficient fissile material to build nuclear weapons raises the specter of yet a new round in what some have described as "the second nuclear age." For the uninitiated, the first nuclear age was the period in the Cold War when the U.S. and allies confronted the Soviet Union's nuclear arsenal. The second nuclear age is defined by the multiplicity of nuclear powers linked by varying levels of cooperation and conflict.

Although the Soviet Union and the United States had tense and hostile moments, they did reach some accord for maintaining strategic stability. However, in the second nuclear age, deterrence involving threats from two or more potential adversaries is complicated. Actions of self-defense by nation one against nation two may be threatening to nation three. Furthermore, non-nuclear technologies such as missile defense, cyber attacks and precision weapons could challenge strategic balance.

Hence, there is a need to carve out a unique and unalterable restraint mechanism among nuclear powers to avoid endangering stability—what I have described as a "safe zone" to reduce the risk of deliberate, accidental or unauthorized use of nuclear weapons.

At the moment five nuclear powers, the U.S., China, Russia, France and England, maintain an uneasy but recognized regimen under the 1968 Non-Proliferation Treaty, with India and Pakistan included in the forum. Clearly North Korea is an outlier and Israel is an ambiguous supporter. But despite tensions on the foreign policy front among the Big Seven, equilibrium, however shaky at times, has held. Surely this fragile system needs buttressing with transparency and confidence-boosting measures.

The fear is that by adding Iran to the mix, as the leading state sponsor of terror, not only is the status quo unsettled, but a nation outside the command, control and communication network that forestalls breakout and possible deployment will now be in a position to alter the fragile deterrence mechanisms on the world stage. Moreover, recognizing the stated motives of Iranian leaders, a P5+1 deal that gives Iran a green light for further uranium enrichment and the likelihood of nuclear weapons could trigger a cascading desire for nuclear weapons in Saudi Arabia, Egypt and elsewhere.

Fierce low-intensity conflicts such as the Indian Pakistani dispute over Kashmir could escalate into the strategic realm, but thus far deterrence has worked. Whether it will continue to work is dependent to some degree on restraining Iranian nuclear ambitions. Can an Iran with nuclear weapons or simply fissile material be counted on to maintain nuclear stability?

Multilateral participation in the maintenance of stability is essential. But an unreliable nuclear power assuming its own rules and motivated by theological or imperial goals could set in motion a nuclear exchange with catastrophic consequences for mankind. It is in everyone's interest to maintain a vigilant balance; yet a nation inspired by terror has a distinct advantage if it strikes first and can withstand retaliation. This is the Iran dilemma. Can the U.S. and other nuclear nations bring Iran into a community in which strategic balance trumps regional hostilities? Will Iran foster confidence by avoiding "breakout"?

Answers to these questions are mystifying, but without answers the world will be entering a long, dark and dangerous tunnel of uncertainty.

Why Obama Made the Deal

Expect Obama to Compromise with Iran (2014)
Originally published on Newsmax

It is something of an old saw to contend that if a woman says "no," she means "maybe." If she says "maybe," she means "yes," and if she says "yes," she is not a "lady." Similarly if a man says "yes," he means "maybe," if he says "maybe," he means "no," and if he says "no," he could not possibly be a negotiator in Vienna for the Obama administration.

So keen is President Obama on a deal with Iran, he cannot say no. The fact that zero tolerance for an Iran with nuclear weapons is no longer a negotiating point is telling. The fact that Iran's missile force site is not on the agenda suggests yet another concession. The fact that the U.S. has already conceded the existence of at least 1,500 centrifuges enriching uranium indicates U.S. "flexibility." And the fact that the plutonium facility is not a discussable item suggests preemptive acceptance of the Iranian position.

After one failure on the foreign policy front after another, President Obama needs a victory or, more accurately, the appearance of victory. He is likely to get one and only one concession from the Iranian negotiating team: it will pledge not to weaponize its missiles. The translation is that Iran will have the fissile capability to build nuclear weapons and a delivery force with the Shahab-3 and the Kavoshgar-3 rocket used as a space launch. But it will say the two are not to be united. Of course, no one but President Obama will take this claim seriously.

Nevertheless President Obama amid some media fanfare will argue that through the negotiating skill of his team, he has achieved an understanding with Iran that will avert hostility with this once-adversarial nation.

Iranian president Hassan Rouhani will merely shake hands with Secretary Kerry for a photo op and go on his merry way, knowing that he duped the feckless Obama representatives into a deal that will give Iran enormous leverage in pursuing its dominant long-term regional goal.

Recognizing the flaws in the agreement, senators on both sides of the aisle will object to being left out of the negotiations. Some will even cite a Constitutional provision that maintains the Senate must ratify treaties, but President Obama will argue deceitfully that this deal isn't a treaty but merely an understanding or accord.

The Israeli president and representatives will balk, contending that this agreement sets the stage for a second Holocaust. Not only has Iran pledged to wipe Israel off the map; it will have the means to do so. Secretary Kerry will be dispatched to Tel Aviv to assure Israeli leaders deterrence will work. No one is likely to believe him, but that too doesn't make any difference.

With the completion of the deal, the Middle East will be forever changed. All escalation scenarios in regional conflict will have to account for the prospect of an Iranian bomb. To deter acts of aggression enhanced by this prospect, Egypt and Saudi Arabia will acquire nuclear weapons from Pakistan. The region will now be hostage to a possible nuclear war. President Obama may get his political victory but at a price that puts the international community in a precarious state into the distant future. Thinking the unthinkable becomes thinkable again.

John Dryden wrote, "Fool'd with hope, men favor the deceit." One might contend that the naïve person hopes for the best and believes it will be achieved, but the sly enemy thinks hope is his ally in the effort to pursue negotiating advantage. Let the forces of innocence betray themselves on the altar of acceptance. The Ides of March are before us, and we must entertain very bleak and uncomfortable scenarios.

Obama's Obsession

As early as the first year of Obama's presidency, his ambitions for a deal with Iran were apparent. After Iranian president Mahmoud Ahmadinejad's contested (and suspicious) reelection in 2009 left the country sharply divided, President Obama saw an opening for his administration into Iranian politics. With the nuclear deal, Iran was afforded a level of trust that many would argue it doesn't deserve.

The Iranian Election in Historic Terms (2009)
Originally published on Pundicity

The 2009 election in Iran has exposed the problematic dimensions of President Obama's "soft power" approach. By any standard this election of President Ahmadinejad appears to be a sham. Millions of votes were counted in just two hours after the polls closed. Internet sites were shut down. Protestors were beaten and arrested. And in the village where Mir Hossein Mousavi, the chief rival to President

Ahmadinejad, resides, anecdotal evidence indicates widespread tampering.

Yet, even though Vice President Biden said there is "some real doubt" about the election result, the United States government is committed to continued efforts at negotiation in order to halt Iran's nuclear weapons program. "Talks with Iran," it was noted, "are not a reward for good behavior, they are only the consequence" of President Obama's decision that talks with Iranian leaders are in our national security interest.

But is that really the case?

A thunderstorm of protest across Iran clearly demonstrates that many Iranians, perhaps most Iranians, feel cheated. It appears as if the so-called green revolution has traction with a passion for change evident with youthful demonstrators on the streets of every major Iranian city. Despite efforts at suppression by government authorities, outlets such as Facebook, YouTube and Twitter, among others, offer a communications network for the disenchanted.

As I watched YouTube clips from the comforts of my home, I heard crowds shouting, "Death to the dictator."

Mr. Mousavi has formally asked the Guardian Council to annul the election result he described as a fraud. But there is little doubt his plea will not be heeded. How this discontent will unfold remains to be seen, but a network of young, middle-class dissenters could emerge as a force putting pressure on President Ahmadinejad and Iran's theocracy to take a less confrontational posture toward the West.

This, of course, is precisely the dilemma President Obama now faces. On the one hand, he has staked out a position as a negotiator with the Guardian Council—the 12-member clerical body associated with Supreme Leader Ayatollah Ali Khamenei. On the other hand, he must recognize that overtures toward the existing regime run headlong into the emerging grassroots spirit for change. If through negotiation he legitimizes the mullahs, he will lose the youthful demonstrators who have put their lives on the line for liberalization.

The question the president must address is, which side of history will he be on? Will he consider the passion for change inexorable or will he, like President Ahmadinejad, consider the demonstrations like the unrest after a soccer match?

The backdrop for President Obama's stance is the Iranian enrichment of uranium and probable development of nuclear weapons. Should the president embrace the view of demonstrators, his negotiation position will be compromised. Should he negotiate with the mullahs lending legitimacy to the present regime, he will be seen as the opponent of democratic reform. What if the negotiations do not result in the cessation of Iran's nuclear program? Will this investment of political capital be viewed as a foolish gesture that only alienated those who might bring about a regime change?

Clearly history has a way of intruding on grand designs. The demonstrations on the ground could be the beginning of a major shift in the fortunes of Iran. A stable Iran, without imperial goals, could set in motion reforms that might cascade through the region. Is this the beginning of the end for the Iranian theocratic state, or is this merely a momentary pause in the move for ever-tighter controls on the Iranian people?

President Obama had better be prepared to answer these questions, since the pace of change could be unpredictable. On one matter there cannot be any doubt: the confidence in "soft power" espoused by the president has been called into question. He sits on the horns of a dilemma, and historical movements will decide questions he has only started to consider.

Obama Mistakenly Sees Iran Deal as Escape from Mideast (2015)
Originally published on Newsmax

With even Obama supporters now questioning the deal with Iran, with the revelation that Iranian leaders made a side deal with the IAEA, with the recognition that al Qaeda has a sanctuary in Iran, with the U.S. excluded from the inspection team, with leaders in Iran shouting, "Death to America" and with the supreme leader indicating that Israel must be "annihilated," why does President Obama insist on this arrangement?

From a perspective that is coming into focus, President Obama and his colleagues see themselves as the Sykes-Picot of the Middle East. That is to say, like members of the British and French foreign offices in 1916 who drew lines in the sand creating states out of the dismembered Ottoman Empire, President Obama regards the nuclear deal with Iran as a way to redraft Middle East geography and, simultaneously, have the U.S. withdraw from the region.

If Iran is in possession of nuclear weapons—a pathway created through the "deal"—it becomes the regional "strong horse," a condition that justifies U.S. withdrawal. While there is the recognition Sunni nations will object to this hegemonic status for Iran, the Obama team contends that Iran will be a more reliable (President Obama used the word "responsible") partner in stabilizing the Middle East than Egypt, Saudi Arabia, Kuwait and Jordan. That is a strategic calculation that many regard as misguided. Why would you put Iran, the major state sponsor of terrorism, in a position to stabilize a region it has helped to destabilize? This is the question that many, including Democratic officials, are asking.

The answer lies in a belief that Persian Shia are better prepared and more stable than their Sunni counterparts, a hypothesis that requires further explication.

Since Egypt has recently had two revolutions in three years, even the presence of popular President al-Sisi isn't reassuring. After all, he has a bull's eye on his back with the Muslim Brotherhood taking aim.

The House of Saud is in disarray. King Salman is aging and ailing. Succession could be a problem. Moreover, a growing secular influence in the country could profoundly disturb the seeming equilibrium. One would be unwise to wager on a Saudi Arabian government in five years that resembles the present one. Change is on the near horizon and probably dramatic change at that.

Jordan is a nation populated by a majority of Palestinians who are restless with King Abdullah. The Hashemite family, which claims to be descended from the Prophet Mohammed, has ruled Jordan since 1946. With the Islamic State on its border and terrorism internally, Jordan is also in a fragile political position that could lead to violent revolution.

That there is instability in the three leading Sunni nations does not detract from the problems Iran faces as well. Twenty percent of the population over age 15 are drug addicts. Fertility levels have collapsed. Chlamydia infection rates, as David Goldman points out, are three times the worldwide average. By any objective measure Iran is a civilization in decline; one might even say one that is dying.

Yet it is being bolstered by an Obama administration that believes this is the only government in the region that has a chance of stability. While this calculation is probably wrong, it nonetheless offers President Obama his dream of extricating the United States from the Middle East. In his judgment—if I read minds accurately— Israel is a distraction that interferes with the plan, since ties to Israel force the U.S. to remain in the region. Better to leave the fate of this ally to the United Nations so that our involvement is limited.

With this as a plan, the Iran deal from President Obama's perspective makes sense even if it is entirely one-sided. The U.S. has justification for withdrawal; the president can concentrate on his plan to extend government influence at home and the U.S. can channel foreign policy through the United Nations. Yes, this is a different America and a very different world.

What We Will Do for a Deal (2015)

Supreme Leader of Iran Ali Khamenei publicly rejected a key component of the nuclear deal when he said: "We don't accept a 10-year restriction" on the development of nuclear weapons.

Moreover, he noted, "all economic, financial, and banking sanctions implemented either by the United Nations Security Council, the United States Congress or the administration, must be lifted immediately when the deal is signed." Both of these unequivocal statements clearly challenge understandings in the framework.

In addition, the Iranian parliament approved legislation that bans international inspectors' access to military sites and scientists in any final deal. Secretary of State John Kerry indicated the United States was not concerned with Iran's past nuclear work. Based on statements of this kind, it would appear as if the U.S. is bending over backward to consummate some arrangement, but don't call it a treaty.

However, it is not only that concessionary statements have been made. According to a report on Bloomberg View, the U.S. military is sharing a base in Iraq with Iranian-backed Shiite militias, militias that have killed American soldiers in the past. American and Iranian cooperation in the war against the Islamic State has been reported on several occasions, but the sharing of a base means U.S. operations could be compromised by militia spies.

The militias are led by Abu Mahdi al Muhandis, a Hezbollah official closely associated with Quds force head Qassem Suleimani, who is believed to have planned the bombings of the U.S. and French embassies in Kuwait in the 1980s. To make matters even more contradictory, the Iranian-backed militias have been fighting to support President al-Assad in Syria, even though the Obama administration has formally stated President al-Assad has lost legitimacy and must step down to make way for a political transition.

Is it any wonder that former Sunni allies are perplexed about U.S. policy perspectives? The effort to accommodate Iran suggests a direction that has altered confidence among many Sunni leaders in the Middle East. From their perspective, the U.S. appears to be breathlessly at work to create a deal, any deal, as a legacy for President Obama.

There was a recent report that the U.S. is willing to build nuclear facilities in Iran, assuming, of course, they are not built to manufacture weapons. But how would we know? Secretary Kerry made reference to "absolute intelligence" about Iranian practices, a point vehemently denied by those with access to intelligence files.

What is not in question—in fact has never been in question since negotiations began—is the flexibility of the U.S. negotiating team. At this point, the U.S. is prepared to add "incentives" to the deal in the form of technology transfer. The U.S. has used its resources to assist Iranian troops in Iraq and Syria. Secretary Kerry has continued to assert Iranian compliance with the framework despite clear denials from the supreme leader. The secretary has maintained a desire to lift sanctions, assuming he can obtain some concession from the Iranian side.

President Obama has locked himself into an unenviable position. If this arrangement fails, Iran will pursue weapons development unless we deploy military means to stop it. If this deal succeeds, we will sanction an Iran with nuclear weapons, buying some inestimable time for breakout at a price of $100 billion and a loss of influence in the region. Since the goal at the outset was a deal, it is hardly fortuitous that the president is in this Procrustean bed. How he gets out may be a question for the ages.

A Deal at All Costs: Catastrophic Consequences for Iran's Neighbors and America's Allies

Don't Trust, Just Verify (2009)
Originally published on Human Events

The buzz at Foggy Bottom is that Secretary of State Hillary Clinton is in serious negotiation with her Russian counterparts to squash the deployment of an anti-missile system in Eastern Europe.

In return for this non-deployment—which the Putin-led government regards as an incitement even though this system is aimed at thwarting a possible Iranian attack—the United States wants Russian diplomats to urge Iranian cessation of its nuclear weapons ambition.

On every level this negotiation is foolhardy. It should be clear to everyone by now that the benefit of nuclear weapons for Iran far exceeds the pain the West can inflict for their development. Nuclear weapons immediately give Iran hegemony in the Muslim Middle East and inspire its imperial aspirations. President Ahmadinejad has already noted that the program "has no brake and no reverse gear."

Moreover, even the so-called moderates in Iran (a term I use loosely), Mohammad Khatami and Akbar Hashemi Rafsanjani, have promoted the nuclear weapons program. Despite all of the blandishments European and American diplomats have offered, the Iranian regime adamantly pursues its uranium enrichment program, and at this point, probably has enough fissile material to produce a nuclear bomb.

It should also be noted that even if the Russians agree to this arrangement, there isn't any way to verify the results, since the IAEA has been powerless to monitor the dispersed nuclear sites in Iran. Should negotiations take place between Russia and Iran, the diplomatic conversation could serve as appropriate cover for Iran to build and test a nuclear device.

Russian complaints about a missile system in Eastern Europe belie a Putin-led belief that Russia has a sphere of influence over those nations that border it, notwithstanding the breakup of the Soviet Empire. In accepting Russian demands to cease construction on missile defense, the United States would be conceding Russian ambitions to control the "near abroad."

And if that isn't bad enough, this deal also suggests that the United States must make its Eastern European allies in Hungary, the Czech Republic, Poland and other states vulnerable to a potential Iranian threat. How can the United States sacrifice the bonds of its alliances for such a slim reed of hope?

The question that arises from this deal is, why would the State Department pursue an arrangement in which we give up so much in return for so little? The answer, of course, is that no one knows what to do about Iran, and since the Russians have been enablers in the Iranian nuclear program, perhaps they can be coaxed into being disenablers. One might describe this as the "frustration policy."

Secretary Clinton has said, "we are under no illusions about Iran, and our eyes are wide open." The policy being pursued, however, is entirely illusory, and State Department eyes may be wide open, but so are their minds. Seeking a solution to this Iranian problem baffled the Bush administration, even though the erstwhile president continually said an Iran with nuclear weapons is unacceptable.

Now a new diplomatic gambit is being pursued in large part because the government is unwilling to concede that only a military option—as horrible as the prospect is—offers any hope that this matter can be resolved. As a consequence, we will engage in mind-bending acrobatics to convince ourselves this latest negotiation will work, and in the process we will give the Russians tacit control over the near abroad and sacrifice our allies to potential nuclear blackmail.

Why the Iranians Are Smiling (2014)
Originally published on The Algemeiner

November 24, 2014, loomed as a strategic date in the history of the globe. Since the P5+1 decided a deal with Iran could not be reached, history was moved ahead seven months. President Netanyahu of Israel among others has said, "No deal is better than a bad deal," but it appears as if the Obama team and P5+1 are seeking any deal rather than no deal.

There is no surprise at the rising confidence of the Iranian government. Without the slightest fanfare or notice by the international press, Shia rebels supported by Iran captured the capital city of Sana'a in Yemen. This extraordinary geostrategic move gives Iran entrance to the Red Sea. Along with its command of the Strait of Hormuz in the Persian Gulf, Iran will be in a position to control the sea lanes surrounding the Arab world.

With Beirut, Bagdad, Damascus and Sana'a under Iranian control and influence, the dream of a Shia Crescent appears as a reality. Moreover, with Yemen on the doorstep of Saudi Arabia, Iran has an ideal staging area for attacks against its main Sunni rival.

Moreover, through virtual silence, the United States government is complicit in these actions. Since President Obama will not deploy U.S. forces in the war against the Islamic State, the Iranian Revolutionary Force is considered a surrogate army, even though no one in the State Department will admit to the concession. Iran's role as a putative "stabilizer" in the roiling Middle East offers it enormous latitude at the Vienna negotiating table, where a decision will be made about Iran's nuclear capability. Despite a bipartisan congressional declaration opposing any deal that permits Iran to have nuclear weapons or develop nuclear weapons, it appears as if the negotiating team representing the U.S. and most of the Europeans is willing "to split the difference." In other words, there is a growing consensus that if Iran agrees not to weaponize its missiles in Parchin, it would be allowed to retain enough enriched uranium to build a bomb at a later date, what I have described as the "Japanese solution—i.e., Article 9 in the Japanese Constitution prohibits the development of nuclear weapons, but it does not prohibit the storage of fissile material that could be used for nuclear weapons.

I doubt Israel or France will be enthused by this agreement, but the Obama team seems intent on muscling this through, even ignoring Senate approval. All through the talks the world "treaty" has been replaced by "agreement" or "accord." Presumably this would be the Obama legacy. He will contend that through skillful negotiation rather than saber-rattling or direct confrontation, he has reached an accord with our primary enemy in the Middle East. Many will appropriately call this agreement a Chamberlain-like arrangement that brings the Middle East closer to the boiling point. One thing is for sure: this will bring Iran one step closer to its goal of Middle East domination.

Surely the Sunni states won't sit by idly. Already Egypt, Saudi Arabia, the UAE, Kuwait and Jordan have announced joint military operations to oppose Shia imperial goals. And it would not be a surprise if Israel, operating under the radar, agrees to be an active, albeit unregistered, member of this emerging defense condominium.

Although the U.S. government will contend its intention is to mitigate Middle East tensions, those tensions will rise as a hesitant and willful policy tilting to the Shia is put in place by the Obama administration and European governments eager for "resolution," any resolution.

Unfortunately the clock is ticking and the options are limited. A sanctions regimen offers some leverage, but probably less than has been advertised, since sanctions already in place have not deterred the Iranian government from proceeding with its enrichment program. It is also obvious that even if the U.S. goes through another round of sanctions, assuming a deal isn't consummated, the Chinese, Russians and Turks are not likely to comply.

So we are spiraling down a dangerous hole that makes military action more likely, rather than less, in the future, an option that no one wants to embrace. Unfortunately, the forces of history proceed without an ethical compass.

Iran's Plan to Wreak Havoc on Israel with Missiles (2015)
Originally published on The Algemeiner

The Iranian desire to acquire nuclear weapons involves several political and military scenarios, including the oft-repeated desire to "annihilate" the state of Israel. However, Supreme Leader Khamenei has made it clear that even without nuclear weapons, he intends to surround Israel from the north (Hezbollah), the south (Gaza and Hamas) and the east (the West Bank) with an unbroken ring of rocket and missile arsenals.

Since the end of the war between Hamas and Israel, Iran has openly supplied advanced missiles to its surrogates in the region without a word of condemnation from the West. The Iranian military doctrine is clear: encircle Israel using missiles smuggled into the hands of Hamas in Gaza and the West Bank and Hezbollah in Lebanon.

As Iranian leaders note: "We have passed through the barrier of denominational discord. We helped Hezbollah (Shia)…in the same way that we helped Sunni groups, Hamas and Islamic Jihad." Of course few things unite disparate Muslims more than hatred of Israel.

Ahmad Bakhshayesh, a member of the Iranian National Security and Foreign Policy Committee, emphasized the belief that in arming the areas contiguous to Israel, a blow has been struck against Israeli security, and through encirclement Iran has forestalled any Israeli effort to attack Iranian nuclear facilities. Supreme Leader Khamenei has noted that in bolstering the missile arsenal of Hamas and Hezbollah with missiles that have pinpoint accuracy, Israel security will be challenged and "the liberation of Jerusalem—which is the duty of every Muslim" will be achievable.

It has also been noted that the Fateh-110 missile developed in Iran has sufficient range to strike at every target in Israel from the north to the south. While Iran has been engaging in nuclear negotiations in Geneva and Vienna, its arms industry has been working overtime to develop advanced offensive rocket capability and has made it part of military planning to place these upgraded weapons in the hands of Hamas and Hezbollah.

With the withdrawal of U.S. forces from the region, the rapprochement toward Iran by the Obama administration and the strengthening of Iran's influence in Syria, Lebanon, Iraq and the Palestinian organizations, Israeli security—to some degree—has been compromised. Under these circumstances, one can count on an escalation in Iranian declarations and continued assistance for the "resistance front." As Iran sees it, the stage is set for a propaganda, ideological and military confrontation against Israel and the West.

Surely Israeli military planners understand the new challenges that have emerged. Terrorist mobilization in the Golan has increased dramatically in the last year. At the moment, Israel is quiescent, but this is likely to be a temporary reprieve from battle.

Each day that passes introduces new complications for Israeli security. Israel won the war against Hamas, and from a tactical point of view Operation Protective Edge provided information about Hamas leadership, planning and infiltration methods. But it is also true the enemy learned a good deal about the capacity of Iron Dome, the deployment of Israeli forces and Israel's intelligence apparatus.

Iran's transparent encirclement strategy is not entirely new, but it is being reinforced based on accumulated knowledge. Encirclement is also a variable that must be entertained in any preemptive strike against Iranian nuclear facilities.

Iran's obsessive desire to destroy Israel must be met by an equally obsessive desire to defend the Jewish nation. If encirclement compromises Israeli defenses, a strategy must be developed to break through missile intimidation with a clear and unequivocal response. That is a response that will undoubtedly be left to the Israel Defense Forces.

Iranian Influence in Iraq (2015)
Originally published on the St. Croix Review

In an ironic twist of fate, the future of Iraq may be dependent on the goodwill of Iran. A Shiite-led government commission in Iraq is currently examining which Sunni politicians are eligible to participate in upcoming elections. This is disconcerting because the last time Sunnis were restricted, using a de-Baathification policy to do so, the Sunnis launched an insurgency drive for political influence. A potential Shia-Sunni split represents an opportunity for Iran to assist its Shiite brothers with political, intelligence and military assets, including, of course, the prospect of nuclear weapons.

For Iran, history appears to be moving in its direction. The desire to influence, indeed to dominate, Iraqi politics has long been a strategic goal going back to the Iran-Iraq War several decades ago. One might even contend that the nuclear weapons program is linked to its ambitions in Iraq.

In the days leading to Iraqi elections, Iran's influence in this neighboring nation is palpable. The Iranian seizure of the al Fakkah oil well in southern Iraq was a poignant example of encroaching dominance, an event that received almost no attention in the United States and one in which Iraqi prime minister Nouri al-Maliki averted his gaze. In fact, to demonstrate that Iraq's government and Iran were dancing to the same tune, a government spokesman said any U.S. attempts to save a place at the government table for the Sunnis would "not achieve anything." Our State Department may not read the signals, and the Obama administration seems mired in domestic program concerns, but the message being delivered loud and clear is that Tehran, not Washington, has the upper hand in Iraq.

Based on its influence in Iraq, Iran is using this development as a bargaining chip with the U.S. in nuclear negotiations. Since the Obama administration has made it clear it wants to disengage from Iraq, Iran holds the key to regional stability and must be considered a negotiating partner in any future arrangement. A potential Sunni insurgency could upset U.S. withdrawal plans. Hence Iran has the ability to assist or thwart U.S. goals, a position that complicates negotiations over Iran's nuclear program and puts the U.S. in the position of seeking assistance on the one hand and chastisement on the other.

This leverage gives Iran an enormous negotiating edge. If the U.S. wants to avoid an eruption in Iraq that is tantamount to a civil war, then according to Iranian leaders, Washington will have to meet Tehran's terms on the nuclear weapons issue and forestall any military option by the U.S. or Israel. As Iran sees it at the moment, it is holding all the cards. Arguably the ace in the deck is the apparent cooperation between Prime Minister Nouri al-Maliki and the Iranian mullahs. Since Prime Minister al-Maliki understands he cannot rely on U.S. forces to maintain stability—with withdrawal the overarching goal—he has thrown in his lot with the Iranians.

It is apparent the Obama administration has not considered the law of unintended consequences. The announced plan for withdrawal has set in motion actions American military commitments were designed to prevent. It is ironic that the United States is dependent on Iran to bail it out of a dicey situation at the same time it claims to oppose Iranian nuclear ambitions.

As I see it, the die has been cast. The United States government will allow Iran to develop nuclear weapons, notwithstanding rhetoric to the contrary. Furthermore, it will seek to obtain Iranian influence as a regional stabilizer even if it means the mullahs will insinuate themselves into Iraqi politics.

Clearly the spin doctors in Washington will attempt to put the best possible gloss on this situation, but as I see it, this is a loss-loss for American diplomacy and a significant blow to U.S. policy in the Middle East.

Obama's Delusions

Obama Constructs Iran Deal Fantasy (2015)
Originally published on Newsmax

After weeks of wrangling, a framework for a nuclear agreement with Iran was reached, albeit the details still must be worked on. As expected, President Obama "guaranteed" that this "historic" deal—please don't call it a treaty—"would cut off every path to Iran developing the bomb." While one could surely appreciate the president's enthusiasm since this is regarded as his legacy, it would seem that the president did not read the fine print.

In most respects, the agreement is capitulation to Iranian dictates. It is a paean to utopia that ignores reality. The framework leaves Iran with extensive nuclear capability. It can continue to enrich uranium. It can continue to deploy 6,500 centrifuges. It will not be obliged to shut down one nuclear facility, particularly its underground center in Fordow. It will not face the threat of sanctions.

President Obama, in what can only be described as hyperbole, maintains that this arrangement is an alternative to war. But the real alternative to a bad deal is not war, but another deal, one that forecloses on Iran's ability to produce nuclear weapons. According to the framework, breakout is permitted in 10 years. Remarkably the P5 + 1 negotiation underscores a deal that *approves* Iran's nuclear option, notwithstanding the initial goal of prevention.

Most significantly, not a word was struck on Iranian aggression. This center of state terrorism was not restrained in any manner on its worldwide terrorist activity and its threat to destroy Israel. Apparently it is okay for Iran to provide sanctuary for al Qaeda leaders, supply Hezbollah with rockets that target Israel and realize its dream of a Persian empire throughout the Middle East. Here again, President Obama dipped into the wishing well to contend that in time—with U.S. compliance—Iran will enter the community of nations and act responsibly. Of course, there is not a shred of evidence to support this claim.

This is not the first time President Obama has confused what he wants to be true with what is actually true. When the president discussed the withdrawal of American forces in Iraq, he said the war in that nation is over. Well, it may have been over for President Obama, but it was not over for the Islamic State.

The American people desperately want solutions and peace. They want the anodyne of a future without war, a world where U.S. intervention is not necessary. And as this nuclear framework suggests, President Obama is giving it to them—at least rhetorically. What he is really giving is a world far more dangerous than the one he inherited. Knowing that Iran can possess nukes in 10 years— sooner if it cheats on the accord—every nation in the Middle East will be scrambling to get nukes of their own as a deterrent.

What should Israel do? An Iran that has vowed to annihilate Israel will be in possession of nuclear weapons that can re-create the Holocaust. Should Prime Minister Netanyahu sit on his hands and wait? Assuming a compliant Iran—a dubious assumption— does that mean Israel has a 10-year window before attack occurs?

Prime Minister Netanyahu has several options: he can campaign against the deal with members of Congress in the hope the P5+1 arrangement will be rejected or modified; he can attack Iran unilaterally, setting back the Iranian nuclear program several years but not indefinitely; he can attempt to coalesce with Sunni neighbors in a multilateral attack on Iran; he can attempt a naval blockade, since Iran depends on imported refined petroleum. These are certainly not the only options. But he cannot simply sit back and assume deterrence will work.

The questions abound. President Obama may have found his legacy. But history has a strange way of converting smiles into tears. Now that we know the framework, it is scary to entertain the upcoming details in June. There is a reason why Persia invented chess and we invented Disney World. They love checkmate; we love Mickey, Donald and fantasy land.

Perception Is Strong, Sight Is Weak (2015)
Originally published on Accuracy in Media

For the cognoscenti, seeing is believing; what eyes see must be true. But recent events suggest vision is often flawed. In many cases believing is seeing; the mind casts a vision of what it wants to see. Reality becomes what one's ideology shapes. Clearly events in Ferguson and the University of Virginia reinforce this assessment.

Yet nowhere is it more in evidence than the Obama White House. The president insists his deal with Iran over nuclear weapons restrains that nation from the pursuit of the nuclear goal. He insists negotiation is working, even though details still have to be ironed out. Moreover, he insists on this position despite evidence to the contrary.

Speaking in the Farsi equivalent of the subjunctive, the supreme leader of Iran, Ali Khamenei, uses the word "might," while President Obama employs the verb "will." Supreme Leader Khamenei notes as well in his assessment of the preliminary accord or framework, "What has been done so far does not guarantee an agreement, not its contents, not even that the negotiations will continue to the end." What is there about this declarative sentence that President Obama does not understand?

It is obvious President Obama will persuade himself of any illusion in order to get a deal, any deal. That, in itself, explains Supreme Leader Khamenei's objections. From his perspective, the more he objects, the more concessions he may secure. For example, the framework suggests that sanctions removal will be calibrated to meeting certain milestones. However, Supreme Leader Khamenei said recently, "The day a final agreement is reached, all sanctions should be lifted." In this case the subjunctive case was not used.

To defy reality by contending conditions will conform to your beliefs sometime in the future is to assume Panglossian scenarios for the arrival of entropy. President Obama asserts that at some point Iran will be a member of the community of nations, a responsible member at that. Yet there isn't a shred of evidence to support this assertion. In fact, Iran has been the leading sponsor of global terrorism for more than three decades. It is a host to al Qaeda, an imperialist in the Middle East, an organizer of assassinations and an underwriter of both Hezbollah and Hamas. To which community does Iran belong?

In 1976 Professor Robert Jarvis, at Columbia University, wrote: "It is striking that people often preserve their images in the face of what seems in retrospect to have been clear evidence to the contrary. We ignore information that does not fit, twist it so that it confirms, or at least does not contradict, our beliefs, and deny its validity."

Of course Professor Jarvis was not alone in making this observation, nor is President Obama the only person guilty of delusional thinking. The stakes are the problem in the present case. A belief that you are preventing a pathway for Iran to obtain nuclear weapons is dangerously different from setting the stage for an Iran in possession of these weapons. When the president says, "Not on my watch," does he really mean on someone else's watch?

It would appear that the belief system in the Obama administration trumps present reality. Yes, if the evidence doesn't square with what you want, twist it, shape it, deny it, but never recognize it.

Miyamoto Musashi, a 17th-century Japanese swordsman, said, "Perception is strong and sight is weak. In strategy it is important to see distant things as if they were close and to take a distanced view of close things." In my judgment these are astute observations, but I doubt Secretary of State Kerry or President Obama refers to 17th-century Japanese literature for guidance. Perhaps they should.

It's Only a Paper Moon (2015)
Originally published on Newsmax

Iranian defense minister Hossein Dehghan recently reaffirmed Iran's position that issues involving Iran's missile program are not matters for discussion. Presumably Iran is determined to keep developing its missile force. As for attempts to clarify Iran's past activity regarding the "military dimensions" of its nuclear program, Dehghan noted that Iran will definitely not grant anyone access to its security and military "secrets."

Concerning statements made by President Obama and Secretary Kerry after the deal was signed, Minister Dehghan said, "The U.S. officials make boastful remarks and imagine that they can impose anything on the Iranian nation because they lack a proper knowledge of the Iranian nation…the time has come now for the Americans to realize that they are not the world's superpower and no one recognizes them as such any longer."

In fact, in a clear reference to President Obama's "red lines" that seemed to exist only as disappearing ink, Iranian Revolutionary Guard Corps commander Mohammad Ali Jafari said that several provisions of the resolution constitute "the crossing of red lines" that Iran set, particularly on the issue of military capabilities. As far as Iran is concerned, military matters, including access to ballistic missiles, aren't on any agenda, will not be a bargaining chip and remain none of the business of the P5+1.

So despite all the claims about peace and stability, the agreement is basically a statement of intention. Verification, to which President Obama refers, is a chimera. Iran will permit inspections when it chooses to do so, notwithstanding Secretary Kerry's assurances to the contrary.

In 1933 Billy Rose and Yip Harburg wrote "It's Only a Paper Moon" with the lyrics, "It's a Barnum and Bailey world/Just as phony as it can be/But it wouldn't be make-believe/If you believed in me."

As I see it, the Iran resolution is a "make-believe" document filled with intentions that rely on Iranian goodwill. The one person who contends the "make-believe" becomes real is the president, if you believe in him. As a consequence this arrangement, however you cut it, is a presidential initiative to refashion the Middle East by "offshoring" responsibility for regional stability to the leading state sponsor of terrorism. In this case a belief in the president must exist without any doubts.

Alas, as Alfred Lord Tennyson noted, "The old order changeth." But it is a question of whether the new order enhances stability. From the Obama perspective, U.S. foreign policy is being woven into the fabric of multilateral decision-making, a step closer to world government. President Obama is not a naif, as some conservatives contend; he has a plan for a new world order.

The deal with Iran is merely one stage in a multistage process to reduce the American footprint on the world stage. In President Obama's mind, this agreement will release the U.S. from Middle East obligations and hasten the day when regional powers will fill the vacuum. President Obama's choice for the role of surrogate policeman is Iran. Hence an Iran that can and will acquire nuclear weapons becomes a military and political force with which to be reckoned.

The problem, of course, is that Iran has its own imperial agenda that goes beyond President Obama's romantic perception. Iran envisions a Persian empire that includes the oil fields of Saudi

Arabia and swaths of territory from Yemen through Iraq and Syria and Lebanon. President Obama is the romantic dealing with his dream of a new world order; Iranian leaders see a metaphorical chessboard that allows them to move directly to an assault on the queen.

The question that emerges is, who is right? Thus far, there isn't any reason to place confidence in the president's plan, since the Iranian leadership is in open defiance. Iranian leaders encourage "death to America" chants, then suggest the treaty will be upheld. In discussing romantic yearnings in foreign policy, Isaiah Berlin once said, "Passionate effort at self-assertion both individual and collective, leads a search after means of excusing an unappeasable yearning for unattainable goals." This seems to be an accurate depiction of the present administration's position. Despite warnings about the danger of an accord in which the U.S. makes the major concessions, President Obama appears to be driven by an "unappeasable yearning," a yearning that cannot be realized when the goal of a cooperative Iran is unattainable.

Why It's a Bad Deal

The Stark Choice with Iran (2014)
Originally published on Town Hall

It is high time to face reality. The extension of talks in Vienna suggests that despite flexibility in negotiations on the part of P5+1, Iran believes it can get a more conciliatory deal by holding out another seven months.

By all known accounts, Washington is reported to be seeking assurance that Iran will remain at least one year away from testing a nuclear weapon. This is the *best* of the terms we can get from the Iranian side. In fact, all negotiations at this point deal with the number and scale of centrifuges. The idea that Iran has violated every nuclear agreement it has ever signed and should not have the enriched uranium to produce a bomb is not on the negotiating agenda. Iran will have that fissile material and could produce a weaponized missile at a time it chooses to do so, all comments and assurances to the contrary notwithstanding.

Legislators here and abroad continue to assert a sanctions regimen offers leverage that modifies the Iranian stance. Like a mantra, Obama administrators contend sanctions brought Iran to the negotiating table. Perhaps this is true, albeit the point isn't provable, but sanctions have not halted the path to nuclear enrichment. In fact, negotiations have led to a modification in the sanctions regime and have provided a "legitimate" pathway to further enrichment and plutonium development.

At the same time these negotiations are underway, the putative leader of Iran, Ayatollah Ali Khamani, called for Israel's elimination, writing that Israel "has no cure but to be annihilated." This statement was issued against a backdrop of Iran's continuing the military dimensions of its nuclear program in defiance of the Framework of Cooperation signed in November 2013 with the International Atomic Energy Agency and the P5+1 Joint Plan of Action.

In addition to violating agreements it has signed, Iran continues to foment terrorism throughout the region, with proxies in Hezbollah and rebel groups in Yemen. Most significantly, it has promoted incitement among Palestinians and supported the rabid comments of President Mahmoud Abbas.

As I see it, the Vienna negotiators on our side of the table have bent over backward to make a deal, including a willingness to offer Iran enough fissile material to produce a bomb in a year, in clear defiance of the Nuclear Proliferation Treaty, to which Iran is a signatory.

Despite what many politicians assume, sanctions cannot inflict enough pain to moderate opinion among Iranian leaders. Moreover, as long as talks go on, sanction rules will be violated by Turkey, Russia and China.

In treating Iran as a legitimate state instead of a rogue state, the promotion of terrorism is ignored, as are the existential threats against Israel. Iran is regarded as merely one of the states in the community of nations. Its aspiration for a Shia Crescent is a matter for another time.

Hence the choice is stark: an Iran with nuclear weapons or an attack. Clearly no one wants war, and there is no doubt this war would not be easily contained. The Sunni nations would most likely avert their gaze to an attack on Iran, secretly breathing a sigh of relief. But there would be consequences in widespread terrorism throughout the Middle East and beyond.

On the other hand, an Iran with nuclear weapons or the capacity to build them is the worst of choices, since rational deterrence is not likely to work with a regime driven by theological assumptions. Nuclear proliferation would be the logical outcome, with Saudi Arabia first in the queue to purchase these weapons from Pakistan. A nuclear exchange of any kind would set back mankind centuries, and a doomsday scenario would become increasingly plausible.

So the best of bad choices is a bad choice, but almost an inevitable one. The Iranians know we don't want to fight, and they know as well they are at the table with a "full house." All our side has is a "pair of deuces." So whether the bad news comes in seven months or seven days is irrelevant. The news is bad and the choices remain stark.

U.S.-Iran Deal on Nuclear Weapons (2013)
Originally published on Family Security Matters

A presumptive deal between the United States and Iran to curb the Iranian nuclear program in exchange for an easing of sanctions is regarded in the White House as a breakthrough, cutting the Gordian knot between intractability and persistence. Yet before the acclamation begins, a cautionary note is warranted.

Israeli prime minister Benjamin Netanyahu recently said, "I believe that adopting them [the deal proposals] is a mistake of historic proportions." There is much to suggest that he is right.

For one thing, perhaps most notably, Iran retains the capability of making nuclear weapons. The deal—described as unfolding—merely freezes the most advanced aspects of its nuclear program, including the production of near-weapons-grade fuel. With uranium enriched at the 20 percent level, as is presently the case, Iran can probably produce six Hiroshima-like atom bombs today. Moreover, it possesses the missiles to deliver them over a 1,000-kilometer distance.

Second, Iranian leaders have been known to lie. The assurances offered in the past have disappeared like soap bubbles. After all, negotiations of one kind or another have been going on for decades. Prime Minister Hassan Rouhani, in his previous role, was the chief Iranian negotiator at a diplomatic table with American and European representatives. Despite his pleasant smile and moderate demeanor, he is a jihadist who is eager to promote Iran's imperial agenda, and that political position is enhanced by the possession of nuclear weapons.

Third, although this deal is the first phase in what is presumed to be a step-by-step process, verification procedures are obscure. It has been established from intelligence sources that Iran has several projects deeply hidden underground on heavy-water nuclear production and centrifuges. Even if one or two are "frozen" to satisfy IAEA inspectors, how can one be sure other facilities aren't operating at full tilt?

Fourth, the acceptance of an Iran with nuclear capability will lead inexorably to nuclear proliferation in the region. Saudi Arabia has recently completed an arrangement to buy nuclear weapons from Pakistan that are congruent with its present delivery capacity and in defiance of U.S. admonitions. This arrangement was precipitated by the American "rapprochement" with Iran.

Fifth, the acceptance of the U.S.-Iran deal means that Iran will be perceived as the "strong horse" in the Middle East. It is, in effect, precisely the perception Iran has been trying to cultivate with its neighbors.

Sixth, this deal is actually little more than a public relations bonanza for the president, even though it weakens U.S. ties to allies in Saudi Arabia and Israel. President Obama will hail this diplomatic "achievement" as a Neville Chamberlain-like "peace in our time" deal. In fact, as was the case with Prime Minister Chamberlain's concessions to Hitler, this deal probably brings us closer to the brink of war than was formerly the case.

At the risk of hyperbole, this "exchange" with Iran is part Munich and part Yalta. The concession designed to promote better relations with Iran is probably an illusion, a case of believing before seeing. Moreover, the concession catapults Iran into a Shia leadership position that threatens surrounding nations.

The Saudis believe that in the last phase, when sanctions are finally eliminated, Iran will still have nuclear capability. It will resemble the "Japanese solution," a point at which there is sufficient fissile material to build several bombs, but the missiles are simply not yet weaponized. This may be an arrangement the U.S. is prepared to live with, but it is not one the Saudis can embrace.

Since this is the era of illusions, it is easy to predict what is likely to occur. President Obama, with great fanfare, will announce to the American people that this tension over nuclear weapons in Iran has been resolved. There will be a national sigh of relief. However, behind the curtain of illusion, the dogs of war will be plotting. What they will see is a U.S. devoid of military commitment and struggling to maintain a peace at any price.

Money and the Iran Deal (2015)
Originally published on The Hill

Lead performers in Cabaret sing, "Money makes the world go round." Little did these performers know about the Middle East, where money not only makes the world go round but props up dictators like Syria's Bashar al-Assad. Iran is presently spending billions to keep him in power and prosecute a war in which more than 230,000 people have been killed and poison gas has been employed.

Moreover, should the "treaty" with Iran be consummated, this sponsor of global terrorism will receive at least $100 billion in sanctions relief. Not only will this money be used for President al-Assad, but it will bankroll Hezbollah and Hamas with a new generation of rockets and weapons.

For Tehran, money buys weapons, and weapons buy power and influence. President Obama is counting on an accommodative Iran that receives foreign assistance. But is there any reason to embrace this hypothesis? And even if someone does, at what point can the IAEA, or any other relevant body, determine the turnabout in Iran's nuclear program? How do we know when a genuine peace has arrived?

Iranian leaders have made it clear that dreams of a Persian kingdom dance like sugarplums in their imagination. For that to happen, the money pump cannot run dry. There is a need to support their Houthi surrogates in Yemen; resupply Hamas rockets that were destroyed in the last war with Israel; continue to add to the Hezbollah war machine, which is poised to attack Israel; and keep President al-Assad afloat—that is the mechanism by which control of Lebanon will be retained.

It is hardly surprising that Iranian leaders insist that sanctions be dropped now that the deal with P5+1 has been signed, while U.S. negotiators contend sanctions will be reduced based on certain milestones being met. What is not said may be most significant: the bonus received from any deal should not be used for terrorist activity or the promotion of imperial goals. Since money is fungible, this provision is difficult to enforce. Nonetheless, it represents a statement of intention that the U.S. should not gloss over.

One way to defeat militant Islam is to dry up its resource base. Oil pays the bills at the moment, but it may not in 10 years. Hence, trade and FDIs (foreign direct investments) are what the Iranian leadership seeks. One scenario, however, is for Iran to unite with the Shia population in eastern Saudi Arabia, where the major oil fields are located. Saudi oil, along with Iraqi and local oil production, would give Iran clear dominance in oil production (about 70 percent of global supply), thereby generating enough capital to sustain the Shia empire and offer enough of a hedge to secure Iranian leadership decades ahead.

Iranian leaders not only think strategically, they think as carpet peddlers. There is always a profit to be made, an advantage to be generated. The West, most significantly the U.S., thinks money will alter behavior; indeed, puts the Iranians in the position of thinking as we do. But there isn't any evidence to support this conclusion. It is a policy stance based on hope.

Money can obviously be used for many purposes. We would be wise to withhold our generosity until there are signs of behavioral change. I doubt that we will see any; yet cynicism shouldn't dictate policy, nor of course should naïveté.

Since 1979 Iran has behaved as a rogue state, fomenting death and destruction and taking at least 1,500 American lives. It has a vast terror network in Argentina, Cuba, Venezuela and even parts of Asia, all outside narrowly defined regional interests. Will Iran scale back these investments because of Western assistance, or will it promote its worldwide goals? Surely, we should obtain answers before one dime changes hands. Are you listening, President Obama?

Iran Cheats, Iran Wins

Iran Cheats Again (2015)
Originally published on Family Security Matters

Despite the murder of at least 1,200 Americans, including service personnel at Khobar Towers; despite lying about its nuclear weapons program; despite the largest terrorist attack in the western hemisphere before 9/11, which killed 85 Argentinians; despite support for Hamas and Hezbollah attacks against Israel; despite trumped-up charges against Americans who have been imprisoned or murdered; despite being a refuge for al Qaeda leadership; despite the apparent murder of Alberto Nisman, who was investigating the terror attack in Buenos Aires; despite the cries of "death to America"; despite repeated cyber attacks against the U.S.; despite the export of weapons to Syria and Yemen in violation of the arms embargo; despite the egregious violation of the nuclear accord with the UN Security Council with the testing of nuclear-capable ICBMs; despite all of this and so much more that hasn't been mentioned, the United States continues to assert that with the nuclear deal now completed—albeit still not signed by Iranian leaders—Iran will enter the ranks of a responsible nation.

For many, and I am among them, this is comparable to asking a leopard to change its spots. Since the signing of the nuclear deal in July 2015, Iran has twice tested Ghadr-110 missiles in direct violation of the accord. UN Security Council Resolution 2231 states that Iran cannot undertake any activity related to ballistic missiles that can deliver nuclear weapons for eight years. But President Hassan Rouhani said that "Iran will not ask for permission or abide by any resolution" regarding the development of weapons. U.S. Ambassador to the United Nations Samantha Power called the first October test a violation about which she is "deeply concerned." But despite appeals to the UNSC Iran Sanctions Committee, no action has been taken. Nor is it likely any action will be taken.

Notwithstanding the recent release of the International Atomic Energy Agency (IAEA) report indicating Iran lied about its nuclear program and was working on a nuclear weapon as late as 2009, the IAEA argued its study was complete; thus closing the file on Iran's past nuclear program and offering a green light for lifting nuclear-related sanctions. Lying, cheating, stonewalling will be rewarded, making it virtually impossible to engage in any serious verification of Iranian compliance with the accord.

As the agreement presently stands, the JCPOA, or Joint Comprehensive Plan of Action, allows Iran to bar international inspectors from entering suspicious sites for 24 days or more—ample time to remove evidence of malfeasance. Since Iran has violated the agreement twice—that we know of—since the signing and has blatantly lied about its past activity on enrichment, why should it not be emboldened to ignore any inspectors or any agency that seeks to enforce the nuclear deal?

A precedent has been created—not unlike public commentary from the Obama administration. Words mean whatever we want them to mean. Logic and reason have been subjected to the cauldron of post-rational analysis. And as Jonathan Swift once noted, how can you hope to reason someone out of a position, if he hasn't been reasoned into it?

President Abraham Lincoln once asked, "How many legs would a dog have if you call the tail a leg? Four. Calling a tail a leg doesn't make it a leg." Similarly, calling Iran a nation that will evolve into a responsible regional partner in the Middle East doesn't make it so. What we want is so often what we do not have. In this case, what we have is not what anyone would want, including those who negotiated the deal.

Yet we slide down the rabbit hole persuading ourselves or being persuaded that this deal is good for America. When someone says, "Wait, there is a problem," he is shunted off center stage. I can hear Scarlett O'Hara in *Gone With the Wind* facing impending problems, saying "I'll think about it tomorrow." Welcome to Tara or Obamaland. Yes, Iran lies and cheats, but the deal is the best we could get and we'll think about it all tomorrow.

The Iran Deal Is a Turning Point (2015)
Originally published on the St. Croix Review

Among scholars World War I was a turning point in modern history. The war elicited a Communist party ruling a nation; the war was the seedbed for the rise of Nazism, and the war led to the dismemberment of the Ottoman Empire and the Austro-Hungarian Empire. Clearly the post-war global map was altered. History was bisected into pre– and post–World War I.

Alas, we are in another turning point in this new century. Roughly a hundred years from World War I, the P5+1 deal has bisected 21st-century history into pre- and post-Iran negotiation. The world, as we have known it, has been interred, replaced by a series of monumental changes.

Pre–Iran deal will seem halcyonic compared to what awaits us. Just as pre–World War I was considered an age of innocence, pre–Iran deal will be thought of as the era of denial. The globe will not be same again as the tectonic changes come into focus.

First, Iran will be regarded as a "strong horse" in the Middle East. Not only does Iran have sufficient capability for a bomb at a time of its choosing, but the lifting of sanctions will energize its economy and expand its regional aspirations.

Second, the state system that Sykes and Picot helped to create a century ago no longer exists, creating a Middle East map that is unrecognizable. A power vacuum emerging from the U.S. regional withdrawal has opened a Pandora's box as Islamic extremists, subjugated ethic groups and warlords compete for the contested space in Libya, Syria and Iraq.

Third, new alliances have emerged, with Egypt, Jordan, Saudi Arabia and possibly Turkey joining Israel in opposition to Shia expansion through Iranian military activity. The U.S. rapprochement with Iran has alarmed the Sunni states and Israel, leading to a belief that American military strength to counteract hostile regional forces is no longer an option—in fact, cannot even be summoned.

Fourth, Russia under President Putin's leadership has inserted its military into a dominant role in the eastern Mediterranean with U.S. retreat. Taking the lead in the war against the Islamic State, Russia has developed a "coordination cell" in Iraq that includes the Iraqi army and the Iranian Quds. Hence Russia is the presumptive "stabilizing" influence in the region with motives that are not benign.

For President Putin any form of chaos that results in high oil prices is desirable. Therefore it is plausible that the real prize is not the Russian footprint in Syria, but an influence over the Saudi Arabian oil fields. Moreover, the Russian military presence in Syria influences Israeli ability to retaliate when Hezbollah and Hamas engage in missile attacks. Israel understands its hostile neighbors, but it does not want to go to war with Russia—if that can be avoided.

If Iran is the emerging strong horse in the Middle East, Russia is its jockey. The cooperation between the two states does not bode well for Sunni states. President Netanyahu recently met with Putin, pointing out—one can only assume—that Israel is obliged to defend itself but in so doing it does not want to encounter Russian forces on the other side of the military divide.

As President Putin sees it, the "humiliation" the Soviet Union faced in 1989 with the dismemberment of its empire must be restored. His chessboard moves in Crimea and the eastern Ukraine, his challenges to NATO, his humiliation of the U.S. and his intrusion with military force into Syria are efforts to restore the "near abroad," the empire he saw dismembered. Moreover, he can accomplish his goals with the U.S. enfeebled by a president who can only engage in wishful thinking and doesn't possess a scintilla of strategic awareness. This is the Russian moment, a point both President Putin and Middle East leaders recognize.

President Putin presents himself to the U.N. as the man who can save the Middle East from entropy. Perhaps he can, but at a price that may be unacceptable. The face he is wearing at the moment belies real intentions.

I am reminded of a quote from Nathaniel Hawthorne's *The Scarlet Letter*: "No man, for any considerable period, can wear one face to himself and another to the multitude, without finally getting bewildered as to which may be true." So far President Putin has pulled it off. The question, of course, is when will the mask of President Obama be removed?

Advantage Iran in the Nuclear Negotiations (2014)
Originally published on Real Clear Politics

Six world powers and Iran are at the last stage in pursuing a final settlement on Tehran's disputed nuclear program, despite caveats from both sides that a breakthrough deal may prove impossible. This is clearly understandable.

Notwithstanding the obvious, the American delegation in Geneva, led by Secretary of State John Kerry, is seemingly upbeat in its negotiations with Iranian leaders. But the Panglossian smiles that emerge from the meetings are deceptive.

How can one assume that any substantive roll-back of Iran's nuclear program can occur when the Iranian leadership states unequivocally that a red line has been drawn on the plutonium production reactor, further uranium enrichment and ballistic missile development? What can possibly emerge from those talks when the essential talking points are off limits? It strains the limits of credulity to believe the Obama administration team thinks there is a "carrot" that will encourage Iranian flexibility.

At the outset of these negotiations—in order to bring Iran to the negotiating table in the first place—the U.S. and its Security Council partners lifted the sanctions regimen, thereby improving Iran's weak economy. In fact, in January, due to a round of oil deals with China and others, oil production leaped upward by 1.3 million barrels a day, which translates into $4 billion a month and $48 billion a year. Ironically this improving economic picture is likely to harden the Iranian negotiating stance.

While the U.S. is obsessed with these Iranian negotiations, the Russians have inserted themselves into Middle East affairs in a nefarious way. The brokered settlement with President al-Assad for the destruction of his poison gas arsenal has put Putin in a position of protecting the al-Assad regime and insinuating Russian interests into Syria. But that is only part of President Putin's agenda.

Since the U.S. has frozen the sale of Apaches to the al Sissi regime in Egypt, the Putin charm campaign could lead to another Russian beachhead in the Middle East. It has weapons on sale that the Egyptian government believes it needs to counter internal terrorist organizations, such as the Muslim Brotherhood and al Qadea's affiliates in the Sinai. After forcing the Soviet Union and

Russia out of the Middle East for over four decades, a bungling U.S. foreign policy has given Putin the opportunity to reestablish Russia in Middle East affairs.

Notwithstanding President Obama's contention that regional tension has been reduced, Iran has supplied Hezbollah and Hamas with about 100,000 rockets capable of reaching every Israeli population center. Israel's anti-missile systems including the Iron Dome and David's Sling would be stretched to the limit with a saturation bombing of these missiles.

Complicating matters further, the Iranian government boasted that it is sending two warships to patrol the East Coast of the United States. The latest reports indicate these ships are near the southern tip of Africa, soon to be rounding the Cape of Good Hope. This isn't the first time Iran has shadowed the U.S. shoreline, but the timing of this foray is revealing.

This flotilla does not pose the slightest threat to the U.S., but suppose it was nuclear capable? Clearly Iran wants to flex some muscle to counter the presence of the U.S. fleet in the Persian Gulf, give the U.S. "a taste of its own medicine." However, this sideshow seems to foreshadow Iran's global intentions. It explains why restraining Iranian nuclear ambitions is critical. It also explains why Iran's intention is transparent; nuclear weapons give Iran enormous political influence in the region—an influence no amount of U.S. assurance can negate.

Here is the stalemate: A United States position based on goodwill and fear of nuclear proliferation versus an Iran hell-bent on pursing its imperial agenda with nuclear weapons as the instrument for doing so. One side is flexible and the other uncompromising. It isn't hard to see which side has the advantage.

The Aftermath

The nuclear deal lifted many economic sanctions on Iran, which resulted in a cash windfall. Iran now has the ability to generate nuclear materials, so long as it is done under the guidelines of the nuclear agreement—an assurance that is mostly satisfied by Iran's *word. But has the world benefitted from the diplomatic relationship that the Obama administration promised as a result of the deal? In 2016, a year after the deal, Iran seized two American navy vessels and 10 American soldiers in the Persian Gulf. The soldiers were held captive and later released, but the release coincided noticeably with a $1.7 billion cash payment to the Iranian government from the United States of America. The administration claimed it was money ($400 million plus interest) that the U.S. owed Iran from the Iranian Revolution of 1979. Many in the international community saw it as ransom pay. Either way, the event didn't seem to support the narrative of "close diplomatic relations" between the U.S. and Iran that the president was acclaiming.*

Questions Persist on Iran Ransom Controversy (2016)
Originally published on Newsmax

President Obama emerged from his White House utopia to tell Americans his $400 million cash payment to Iran was not a ransom payment for the return of 10 Americans held hostage. Even if true—a highly dubious truth—there are questions that emerge from the incident that the president has not and will not address.

If this payment is an overdue judgment that goes back to 1979, why now? If this wasn't a ransom payment, why did the Iranians contend the prisoners would not be released till the plane landed? If this was a legitimate payment, why pallets of cash in foreign currencies? Money could be wired to Iran via a third party rather than sending an unmarked aircraft in the middle of the night. And if this wasn't a ransom payment, because as President Obama noted, "We do not pay ransom for hostages…because if we did we'd start encouraging Americans to be targeted," how does he explain the three Americans taken hostage since the January payment?

Whether one accepts the improbable legalistic argument President Obama offers, what matters for future U.S.-Iranian dealings is what the mullahs believe. It is obvious they believe that arresting and holding Americans pays off. In a country on the brink of bankruptcy, the U.S. has bailed it out.

The larger question remains: Why would President Obama do that? Behind the monetary exchange lies the naïve belief that the assistance the president gives Iran will be reciprocated with the claim President Obama prevented yet another war in the Middle East. That is to be his legacy.

Iranian imperial ambitions have made a mockery of this claim with the testing of a new generation of long-range missiles and an upgrade in the weapons employed in Lebanon, Yemen and Syria. President Hassan Rouhani has called his negotiations with the U.S. "the greatest diplomatic victory in the history of Islam." He is probably right.

The reported transfer of $1.7 billion would mark a new chapter in Iran's economic history. It will also allow this notorious state sponsor of terrorism to buy more weapons from the Russians and to enhance Iran's posture in the region. Despite these obvious developments, the current American administration believes the canard that "moderates" in Iran can be persuaded to move that country in a desirable (read: peaceful) direction.

This can only be described as a grand illusion. President Obama cannot free himself from the firm belief that he, by dint of his ingenious negotiating skill and appeasement tactics, can fundamentally shift Iran's Khomeinist ideas to placid Sufi-like considerations. Evidence to the contrary is rejected, as Secretary John Kerry continues to tell the president about the smiles and congenial behavior of Iranian diplomats on the other side of the negotiating table. As Secretary Kerry noted recently, Mohammad Jarad Zarif is one of us. The translation is that he can be trusted.

President Obama still has the opinion that Iran can be a stabilizing influence in the Middle East and a "constructive partner" going forward. For him the money exchange is a down payment on a liberalized Iran, one that rejects the 1979 revolution.

This grand illusion is not only naïve, it is dangerous. The apparent U.S. tilt in the direction of Iran has alarmed Iran's neighbors. Sunni nations are scrambling for a strategy that serves as a counterweight to Iranian ambitions. Most notably, the U.S. is not in this calculus. The loss of confidence in President Obama and his team is palpable.

From Cairo to Riyadh, official conversations deal with "what happened to America?" Can another administration reestablish ties to the key Sunni states? That remains to be seen, but it won't be easy.

Iran Wins, We Lose (2015)
Originally published on Newsmax

In discussing the Cold War, President Ronald Reagan said his strategy was simple: "We [U.S.] win and they [Russia] lose." On the basis of the current comprehensive plan with Iran, that statement seems like ancient history. Iranian president Rohani in addressing the agreement said that all of the goals they aspired to in these negotiations were achieved. In effect he is suggesting, "We win and you lose."

Iran had four goals and each, in turn, has been achieved.

As President Rohani noted, "The first was to continue nuclear capabilities, the nuclear technology and even nuclear activity." In the beginning of negotiation, the P5+1 said Iran could have 100 centrifuges; after many deliberations, they arrived at a mutually agreed level of over 6,000 centrifuges, over 5,000 of which will be in Natanz and over 1,000 in Fordo. All centrifuges at Natanz will continue to enrich uranium.

Moreover, the period of restrictions on nuclear development—i.e., the bomb—was to be 20 years, a point the P5+1 said was firm. But in the final days of negotiation, there was agreement on eight years. On the issue of research and development, there was initial insistence on low-level-capable centrifuges, but here too concessions were made so that Iran can inject gas into the advanced IR-8 centrifuge, thereby accelerating the enrichment process. On the heavy-water reactor at Arak, President Rohani contends, "This reactor will be completed with the same heavy-water nature and with the characteristics noted in the agreement." At Fordo there is one cascade of 164 centrifuges, but over 1,000 centrifuges will be installed at this facility for the purpose of "R&D on stable isotopes."

The second Iranian aim was "to remove the mistaken, oppressive and inhuman sanctions." On the day of the agreement all sanctions— even the embargo on weapons, missiles and proliferation—will be lifted. All financial and banking sanctions and those related to insurance, transportation, petrochemicals, precious metals and other economic sanctions will be completely eliminated, "not frozen."

The third goal was to have the Security Council revoke the anti-Iran resolutions. Under the agreement approved by the Security Council, all previous resolutions against Iran for violations and non-compliance with the IAEA will be revoked. In other words, despite overwhelming evidence that Iran violated the non-proliferation treaty and rejected its own promises, the historic record has been wiped clean.

Last, in conjunction with the third goal, the nuclear dossier on Iran and its misdeeds will be completely removed from the Security Council after 10 years of implementation of the agreement, "and regardless of the IAEA." Here too the IAEA's prior investigations and even future ones are subject to deracination.

What this agreement has done from President Rohani's point of view is legitimate Iran as a nuclear power, ignoring its role as the leading state sponsor of terror and a nation responsible for the death of at least 1,000 Americans. No wonder Iran celebrates. This agreement is a victory the Shia have sought for 1,400 years since the split with the Sunni majority.

Now the pathway for Iran's political ambitions is set. From the Iranian point of view, President Rohani has performed a small miracle; he has brought the United States and the UN to recognize Iranian ambitions.

Needless to say, President Obama will not accept President Rohani's rhetoric. He will maintain a victory for "peace," but in objective terms, the Iranian statement may be closer to the truth than President Obama's claims about the accord.

In a sense, Leo Tolstoy anticipated this administration's position on Iran when he wrote: "I know that most men, including those at ease with problems of the greatest complexity, can seldom accept even the simplest and most obvious truth if it be such as would oblige them to admit the falsity of conclusions which they have proudly taught to others, and which they have woven, thread by thread, into the fabric of their lives." Here, then, is the Obama stance.

Russia

Perhaps the best analogy of the Obama administration's relationship with Russia is in the symbolic gift that Hillary Clinton gave her counterpart at the Russian Ministry of Foreign Affairs at the beginning of Obama's presidency. It was a plastic red button that was supposed to have the word "reset" written on it in Russian. Instead, Hillary's button said "overcharged." President Obama's soft power approach to world diplomacy moved America aside as Russia became a major player in Syria and the Middle East, annexed Crimea and danced around its obligations under the new START nuclear nonproliferation agreement. Arguably, the harshest tone President Obama took with Russia came in 2016, when he found in Russia a workable scapegoat for his party's catastrophic losses in the American election.

Russia Courts American Allies with Signs of Strength

Cairo and Moscow: So Happy Together (2014)
Originally published in The American Spectator

While America's attention was focused on Robin Williams' suicide, the Ebola virus and events in Gaza, Iraq, Ukraine and Ferguson, Missouri, a single 130-word *Wall Street Journal* dispatch on Tuesday described events in Sochi, Russia, that might portend a dangerous shift in the allegiance of one of America's most important allies.

While it missed the attention of most news editors, newly elected Egyptian president Abdel Fattah al-Sisi arrived in Sochi Monday for two days with Russian president Vladimir Putin on the Black Sea coast.

The duo toured the Olympic cross-country ski center, but not until President al-Sisi got to view an elaborate and tempting display of Russian military hardware that President Putin had kindly set out before him, right there at the Sochi airport.

President Al-Sisi was barely out of his plane when he got to gaze upon a massive array of armored vehicles, missile systems and other weapons goodies—all of them available for sale.

Welcome to the new era of Russian diplomacy: as relations with the United States sour, longtime allies like Egypt are being courted by a Russian president eager to expand his influence through economic assistance and military cooperation.

While our president navigated his golf cart around the fairways of the Vineyard Golf Club, President Putin was sitting down with the president of the most populous Arab state for two days of discussions about Israel, Gaza, Iraq, Libya and Syria.

"The views of Russians and Egyptians about Middle East issues coincide to a large degree," said a Kremlin statement that was issued in advance of President al-Sisi's arrival—words that should stir fear deep in the souls of everyone concerned with safety and security in the Middle East.

The matchmaker behind this burgeoning friendship is, unfortunately, the man riding the golf cart on Martha's Vineyard.

Our president badly misjudged events in Egypt, suspending military aid in response to what the Obama foreign policy apparatus considered a coup d'état—but that was, to any studied observer of Egyptian politics—a national upheaval to end the Muslim

Brotherhood's drive for Islamization of Egypt through the person of Mohamed Morsi.

It took a series of bloody assaults in and around Cairo (and for al Qaeda leader Ayman al Zawahiri to openly call upon jihadists to attack Egyptian security forces) before President Obama finally backed down and approved the sale of 10 Apache helicopters so Egypt could defend itself against a full-blown insurrection in the Sinai. However, the delivery of these helicopters is being held up by Democrats in Congress, and the aircraft remain in storage at Fort Hood.

Vladimir Putin has no such tender sensibilities: the smorgasbord of military equipment was laid out on the tarmac, and all President al-Sisi had to do was make his choices.

In Washington, President al-Sisi is viewed with suspicion as a usurper of some failed but grand democratic experiment.

In Sochi, however, he is viewed, accurately, as an Egyptian national hero—a military giant in a country where military life is a staple of state affairs, and the one man who may be capable of unifying his country and the various disparate forces that could tear it apart.

In my two hours of meetings with President al-Sisi earlier this year, I found him highly intelligent, articulate and capable of thoughtful analysis of American foreign policy.

Clearly, he is also smart enough to seek out new friends when old ones abandon him—and that should be a cause for concern here in the United States.

"Soft Power" Is Not Enough to Keep Russia to Its Promises

Start-Up May Be a Start-Down (2015)
Originally published on the St. Croix Review

Aquarius the show is in revival on Broadway and in revival in the Obama administration. The utopian idea of "the zero option," of eliminating nuclear weapons, of an Apollonian globe where lions and lambs live in harmony, is alive and well and evident in the new START.

Of course it would be wonderful if we had a world without nuclear weapons, but the genie is out of the bottle and weapons of mass destruction offer influence, prestige and power even for nations that cannot adequately feed their people.

While START reduces delivery capacity of Russian and U.S. missiles, planes and submarines using arcane accounting methods, the real issue, as I see it, is that Russia reserves the right to withdraw from the treaty if it deems missile defense deployment in Eastern Europe threatening.

The obvious question is, why should the United States Senate ratify a "conditional" arrangement? If the treaty is ratified (a likely prospect), the United States is committing itself to unilateral compliance. In other words, Russia determines on its own whether the treaty remains in effect.

This is a truly unprecedented matter, one that may indeed violate national security interests.

Moreover, in an effort to convince other nuclear powers that they should embrace our disarming impulse, the president has circumscribed "no first use policy" to only those adversaries employing nuclear weapons and has announced that the U.S. will not develop a new generation of nuclear weapons. I'm sure that this heartfelt gesture has resonated appropriately with Kim Jung Il and Mahmoud Ahmadinejad. It would take a leap of illogical proportions to assume that if the U.S. does not modernize, China, Iran, North Korea and Pakistan will follow suit.

This treaty also means in effect that President Obama will not upgrade U.S. missile defenses. If he were to do so, the Russians would pull out of the treaty. The one major bargaining chip former President Reagan had in his negotiations with the Soviet Union was Star Wars or missile defense. Now the Obama team is willing to give it away and receive nothing in return. The only way to describe this negotiating strategy is political ambition wrapped in the cellophane of naiveté.

One gets the impression that the president operates from a view of what he would like the world to be, not what the world is. Unfortunately the globe is an unwieldy place where national interests invariably trump international equilibrium. There is no way to eliminate nuclear weapons so long as rogue nations cheat, the non-proliferation treaty is ignored without penalty and nuclear weapons offer nations political clout. Who would care about a backward nation like North Korea if it did not possess nuclear weapons?

The fear for those of us who believe in "peace through strength" is this START agreement is merely the beginning of a unilateral disarmament campaign following President Obama's lifelong adolescent vision for a world without military tocsin in the air. It is already rumored that the president will attempt to join the Comprehensive Test Ban Treaty and limit defense deployment in space. What can allies like Taiwan, Japan and Canada, to cite a few examples, be thinking when the U.S. nuclear umbrella that affords deterrence is now laden with holes?

The voluntary abandonment of U.S. superiority in space technology and nuclear weapons could haunt our people and our allies. It is as if the U.S. is suffering from leadership fatigue and wants to halt the course of history. However, historical forces march to their own drumbeat. What we may want—whatever utopia we may envision—is often undermined by the constraints of reality. As I see it, President Obama hasn't learned that lesson. I can only hope our enemies aren't looking and listening too closely.

There is a Russian tale that takes place in a zoo where a lion and a lamb reside together in the same cage. Onlookers are astonished to see this unlikely union. At one point, a sightseer asks the zookeeper how this happens. "Oh," he notes, "it isn't difficult. We put a new lamb in the cage each morning." If only President Obama knew this Russian tale.

Russia in the Middle East

Russian Aims in the Middle East (2015)
Originally published in The Washington Times

So what are the Russians doing in the Middle East? The downing of a Russian jet by Turkish F-16s raises questions about Russian ambitions and goals in the region, with President Obama and President Hollande of France outlining changes Russia should make to its military strategy in Syria and to its position vis-à-vis the Islamic State. Perhaps the first and obvious point is that Russian military power is being exercised to keep President Bashar al-Assad in his present position as president of Syria, a post that has secured Russia naval presence in the eastern Mediterranean and an air base in Latakia.

But this is merely one aspect of a strategic plan. Without much fanfare Egypt and Russia signed a nuclear agreement, which, along with a $2 billion arms deal, seals the return of Russia to Egypt for the first time in four decades. It also represents the eclipse of American preeminence.

In the wake of the 1973 Yom Kippur War, Russia was forced out of the Middle East, but as a consequence of the P5+1 agreement and a precipitous U.S. retreat, it is the emerging strong horse in the region. In fact, the cost of the Egyptian Dabaa nuclear station will be borne by a Russian loan over 35 years, giving Russia a foothold in Egypt for the foreseeable future. Deals signed with President al-Assad for the construction of two nuclear plants are also long-term arrangements.

Russian engagement is not driven only by military concerns, albeit the proximity of these Muslim nations to the southern tier of Russia where many Muslims reside should not be underestimated. As I see it, hard currency in Russia is derived from one primary source: natural gas. President Putin is aware of the natural gas veins discovered in the Mediterranean off the coast of Syria. He knows as well that a Turkish pipeline to be completed in 2017 will challenge the virtual monopoly Russia maintains in providing natural gas to Europe. Hence the tension with Turkey. It is not merely the question of toppling President al-Assad, as the Turks would like, or keeping him in authority, but rather whether the natural gas monopoly can be sustained.

There is another dimension to this complicated picture. President Putin has said in several interviews that the dissembling of the Soviet Union was "humiliating." He has noted that empire and the glory of national destiny can be reacquired. This goal can be achieved in one way: undermining the dominant role of the U.S. on the global stage. In President Obama, he has a willing and acquiescent partner.

President Obama contends retreat is an appropriate stance since U.S. engagement either exacerbates an already difficult situation or forces a long-term commitment the nation is unwilling to endure. As a consequence, the U.S. involvement in the Middle East, which served as a balance wheel—however precarious—has been dislodged, leaving a vacuum in its place, a vacuum President Putin has been pleased to fill. From President Putin's perspective, this is a major gift. A nation suffering from the effects of a stagnant economy, longevity rates declining, alcoholism on the rise and, despite claims to the contrary, a second-rate military, has been accorded the gift of empire and international standing. Russia has risen from despair to the height of Middle East power broker. From President al-Sisi to Prime Minister Netanyahu, from Supreme Leader Khomeini to King Salman, leaders meet with President Putin to determine the fate of their respective nations.

While the U.S. has deployed 3,500 Special Forces units in the fight against the Islamic State, Russia has vowed to send 150,000 troops into the Middle East, albeit the mission of these troops isn't clear. Most likely these troops will be deployed to assist President al-Assad in the Syrian civil war, but based on international opinion after the Paris atrocities, Russia might build its global standing further by attacking ISIS strongholds.

On one matter there cannot be any error: Russia is in the ascendency throughout the region and the U.S. is in decline. When

President Obama said that "climate change is the great threat to the world" at a G-20 meeting, late-show talk personalities in Egypt described his comment as "laughable." In fact, the president's name is a laugh line throughout the Middle East. If one of President Putin's goals was to humiliate the United States, that has been accomplished. President Obama contends that his legacy will be the withdrawal of the U.S. from the region. What he won't say, in fact doesn't have to say, is that he has opened the door to a Russian-dominated area that has dangerous implications for the long term.

Russia and the U.S. were arguably engaged in a proxy war in Syria from 2013 to 2016. Russia consistently sided with Syrian president (and the current government of) Bashar al-Assad. The U.S., unwilling to put boots on the ground, armed various rebel groups looking to overthrow the al-Assad regime. Add to that mix the influence of militant Islamic groups of varying degrees of capability, and the Syrian civil conflict was born. Through Syria, President Putin flexed against President Obama's unwillingness to act and inability to draw and keep a firm red line.

Kerry-Putin Talk Resolves Nothing (2015)
Originally published on Newsmax

Secretary of State John Kerry and Russian President Vladimir Putin met recently in what they euphemistically described as a kumbaya moment. Presumably there was a pledge to work together to resolve crises in Syria and the Ukraine. Secretary Kerry said neither side was seeking a "major breakthrough," but instead they seek to keep "communications open"—this is "diplospeak" for "resolution isn't in the cards."

Before meeting with Secretary Kerry, President Putin called for a continued buildup of Russian forces. He also contends that Russia should "retool its military industry to replace foreign suppliers." If there was concession on President Putin's part, it is in "continued talks." Of course, there was consensus on one issue: Tehran's nuclear program.

Secretary Kerry was expected to express opposition to the advanced S-300 air defense system the Russians sold to Iran, but didn't. Since the sale had been completed, any objection would have been meaningless at that point, albeit this gesture might have assuaged the Israeli government. What Kerry did discuss was the role of the Soviet Union in defeating Nazi Germany 70 years after the war's end.

Yet this make-nice meeting is disconcerting. The U.S. negotiates from a positon of weakness. It is obvious that the administration is reluctant to arm the Ukrainians or buttress NATO capabilities. President Putin knows there isn't any real opposition to his aggressiveness. Most European states are in an appeasement paralysis. They want Russian natural gas and investment and are quite willing to avert their gaze over Russian troops in eastern Ukraine and Crimea.

Syria is yet another case in which the U.S. voluntarily surrendered its leverage. Despite a claim by President Obama that President al-Assad crossed the "red line" when incontrovertible evidence was released that he used poison gas, the administration asked Putin to manage the problem. Manage it, he has. The Russians converted Syria into a vassal state, supplying arms to President al-Assad and supporting his position in the Security Council. Moreover, without the slightest objection from the United States, the Syrian government continues to use sarin gas against its enemies.

If there is a U.S. position vis-à-vis Russia, it is acquiescence. There is the hope President Putin will act responsibly. The idea that President Putin is like Russian leaders over the last 300 years, with imperial ambitions and a sense of Russian empire, hasn't entered the mindset of the Obama foreign policy team.

As a consequence, the U.S. is a proverbial weather vane blowing in the winds of history. It is now a casualty of foreign forces, whether they are Iranian, Chinese or Russian. As Winston Churchill noted, "Jaw-jaw is better than war-war," but there is a time to recognize the futility of empty talk. When U.S. interests are in jeopardy, when allies can no longer trust the word of our leaders, when the world convulses over the prospect of nuclear proliferation, the talk is not only silly but dangerous.

Secretary Kerry is a puppet for President Putin's ventriloquism. It is President Putin who pulls the strings. And from this relationship only chaos can emerge. On December 1, 1862, Abraham Lincoln addressing Congress said, "Fellow citizens, we cannot escape history. We of this Congress and this administration will be remembered in spite of ourselves. No personal significance or insignificance can spare one or another of us. The fiery trial through which we pass, will light us down, in honor or dishonor to the latest generation." I ask, as Lincoln did, will this administration be recalled in honor or dishonor? Will the stage of history be enlightened by our action or will it darken as Act Three comes to a close?

Russian Attacks on U.S.-Backed Rebels (2015)
Originally published on Newsmax

For several successive days Russian planes have targeted Syrian rebel troops backed by the Central Intelligence Agency. Even the recalcitrant Obama administration had to admit this is an intentional campaign to degrade U.S. efforts at deposing President al-Assad. According to official reports the Obama administration is "angry."

Clearly President Obama doesn't want to get sucked into a proxy war in Syria, but at the same time he cannot (should not?) abandon CIA-backed rebels who have put their lives on the line to oppose President al-Assad's army.

There is little doubt in any quarter that Russian attacks on U.S. allies are a direct challenge to President Obama's policy of *partial* intervention.

Russian officials contend the air campaign in Syria is designed to fight the Islamic State and other terrorists. However, targeting tells a different story. There is also a report that a Russian aircraft destroyed a U.S. surveillance drone.

Rebel spokesmen in Syria argue that Russian planes struck Ezzeh Gathering in Hama province, catching fighters off guard. Seventeen more strikes followed over a three-day campaign, injuring 25 rebel fighters. Obama administration officials considered asking Russian forces to avoid certain areas in Syria, but came to the conclusion that the Russians could use this information to even more directly target U.S. allies. Clearly the U.S. is not only on the defensive, it does not have a strategy to protect its allies.

When several rebel forces gained a foothold in northern Syria, President al-Assad lost confidence in his ability to protect coastal areas, including Latakia province. That condition was most likely the catalyst for Russian advancement in the area and the desire to build a major military facility there.

Weakening moderate rebel forces is central to Russian ambitions. President Putin is attempting to put President Obama in the position of having to accept President al-Assad, despite all the claims about deposition. Should that happen, the U.S. will have lost face with its former Middle East allies; Russia will have demonstrated its hegemony in the region; President al-Assad will have been "rewarded" for killing 250,000 of his own people and using poison gas; and American alliances will be called into question around the globe.

Rebel forces are understandably disheartened. They were trained by the CIA and offered American support. Now they have been left to dangle. When asked about future support, several officers said, "There is nothing specific."

Here too is another graphic sign of American weakness. Without deploying a force of our own in the region—which President Obama justifiably wants to avoid—there could be a demand for "safe areas" and "no-fly zones" that U.S. aircraft could defend. It is morally unconscionable to train rebel troops we place in the battlefield, only to see them open to Russian air strikes.

Russia's goal is clear: protect President al-Assad. Assertions about the war on terror are a pretense. According to reports, there has been one bombing mission directed at the Islamic State and al Nusra, the Syrian al Qaeda operation; all of the others are directed at rebel troops.

The stakes in this conflict go well beyond Syria. They involve the geography in the Middle East, Russian influence in the Ukraine and even the waves of immigrants floating to European shores. A "what, me worry?" president either doesn't fathom the consequences of inaction or it is part of his scheme for withdrawal and retreat. Either way, the U.S. is backed into a corner from which recovery will not be easy.

Putin's Syria Withdrawal Could Strengthen Iran (2016)
Originally published on Newsmax

There was a Hollywood film of yesteryear with the title *The Russians Are Coming*. If one were making that film today it might be called, "The Russians Are Going." In a move that has surprised many in our State Department, Russian president Vladimir Putin ordered the withdrawal of the "main part" of the Russian military contingent from Syria. He noted that the principal tasks "for the armed forces were accomplished"—i.e., stabilizing the regime of Syrian president Bashar al-Assad.

There is no doubt Russian airpower pushed back rebel forces in key areas and reinforced the Shiite hold as al-Assad's military force around the northern city of Aleppo. With settlement talks underway in Geneva, President Putin believes a ceasefire can be brokered with President al-Assad affixed to the future of Syria and a U.S. team, left without any alternative, accepting President al-Assad. Keep in mind, President Obama on several occasions argued that "al-Assad must go." That refrain is a distant memory.

Some analysts have speculated that President al-Assad was resisting Russian demands for a near-term power sharing arrangement and long-term constitutional reform. But, as I see it, this speculation enters the realm of wishful thinking. President al-Assad is in the driver's seat, firmly ensconced by the combination of Russian air power, Iranian military force and U.S. equivocation. Moreover, the Russian draw-down should not be considered a regional withdrawal. Russia will continue to maintain a presence in Syria with an air base in Hmeimim and a naval base in Tartus.

Some contend the price tag associated with this military engagement was not worth the investment. Here too I would take exception. The relatively modest investment has given Russia a foothold in the Middle East and a key seat at the table during ceasefire deliberations. Moreover, the Russian initiative diminished the role and stature of the United States. President Putin can assert, "We stand by our allies." It would be hard for President Obama to make the same claim to the Syrian rebels he once supported.

Others attempting to explain Russian motives contend that President Putin wished to extricate himself from a Middle East quagmire. While there are pathologies in the region that won't soon be resolved or even fully understood, it is precisely this confusion and the power vacuum created by U.S. withdrawal that allowed for the ease of Russian intervention. President Putin has consolidated his alliance with Iran, and by creating the illusion of "responsible" behavior through the draw-down of forces, he undoubtedly hopes to gain concessions from the U.S. and Europe on relief from sanctions that had been imposed over the Russian invasion of Crimea.

Looking at this partial withdrawal of Russian forces dispassionately, it appears as if President Putin has grabbed the mantle of moderation and is regarded as the stabilizing influence in Syria. This has been accomplished with a modest outlay of resources and without the loss of Russian lives.

The downside—if there is a downside—is that President Putin's strategy reinforced the Iranian goal of a Persian Crescent throughout the region. That condition could come back to haunt the Russians through Iranian influence in Turkmenistan, Uzbekistan and Kazakhstan on Russia's southern flank. An Iran with nuclear weapons and a missile delivery system is not only a threat to Israel and the Sunni nations, but to Russia as well. At the moment the

Russian-Iranian alliance is intact because those states each benefit from the relationship. However, if history is any guide, Russians are nervous about Shia ambitions, and Iranian religious views aren't exactly compatible with the Russian Orthodox Church.

So the globe spins and the Middle East spins even faster than the rest of the world. Where it lands and when it lands is anyone's guess, but these questions will surely confound for a lifetime, if not longer.

In February of 2014, Russia made covert military moves on the peninsula of Crimea, installing a pro-Russian government. Russia contends that the choice to become independent and install a new government was a move for independence on behalf of Crimea. As Putin amassed Russian military assets on the Ukrainian border, President Obama responded by expressing "concern."

Russian Policy and American Timidity (2014)
Originally published on Townhall

As Russian troops secured the Crimean peninsula, its currency hit a record low and the stock market figures plummeted. American and European officials maintain there is more pain to inflict in the form of sanctions and the freezing of assets. This is a costly proposition for Russia. One might well ask: why did President Putin choose to invade? The answer is not dissimilar to Adolph Hitler's response when asked why he invaded the Rhineland: "Because I can."

No matter how much economic bite there is to countermeasures, they do not add up to the benefits President Putin derives from the invasion. After all, his goal is the restoration of "the near abroad"— those nations unleashed from the Soviet orbit at the end of the Cold War. Ukraine is the key, the linchpin in the plan for reconquest.

At Munich Hitler argued for the consolidation of the German people in Austria, Czechoslovakia and the Sudetenland. President Putin employs the same argument today, contending the Russians in eastern Ukraine and Crimea should be united with Mother Russia. Of course, the same contention could apply to the Baltic States, where there are sizable Russian minorities.

The upshot of all the speculation about motive and aims is the startlingly obvious point that President Putin can invade because there isn't a United States with the political fortitude to stop him. Aggressors in world affairs count on timidity. A combined French and British force could have stopped Hitler's troops in the Rhineland, but they could not bring themselves to act.

The Obama foreign policy is predicated on soft power—the use of diplomacy to convince and persuade. But soft power works when hard power is behind it. Al Capone once noted that he talked to his rivals, but they tended to listen when he carried a gun. The so-called reset with Russia, which President Obama has promoted, is reset on only one side. We give, they take. The notion that U.S. flexibility will result in similar Russian flexibility is now fully exposed for what it has always been—a fantasy.

Russia has as its one foreign policy goal the promotion of national interest. At the moment that interest is defined by Vladimir Putin, who is quoted as saying, "The dismemberment of the Soviet Union was the great tragedy of the 20th century." Redressing this tragedy is his aim.

In most respects, Russia is a backward nation. Average life span is in decline; alcoholism is on the rise; the birth rate is below replacement level. The economy is reliant on primary industry-mining, oil and natural gas. Despite outstanding mathematicians and technologists, high-tech development is virtually non-existent. In real terms, economic conditions for the average person have not improved in decades. What gives Russia clout is nuclear weapons, sophisticated missiles and a large standing land and sea force. That said, the Russian military machine could not stand up to U.S. forces in any confrontation, notwithstanding retrenchment in the American defense budget.

This calculation, however, is predicated on the will to act when action is necessary. By any measure, Putin has President

Obama's number. He senses indecision and weakness. He realizes consequences do not follow provocative actions.

That, of course, is the rub. President Obama has given his enemies a signal that bluster is not policy. His rhetoric was appropriate after Syrian president al-Assad used chemical weapons. But in the end, his policy reinforced the influence of the al-Assad regime. He promised the Russians he would not deploy radars in Poland and the Czech Republic in return for Russian cooperation in the war against terrorism. They got what they wanted; we did not. At the Cairo speech, President Obama reached out to the Muslim Brotherhood as a group with whom we can negotiate. In return, the Muslim Brotherhood spearheaded its ties to al Qaeda and President Obama has been left waving at the wind.

The result is a Russian invasion that embarrasses the president, illustrates in graphic terms the fecklessness of President Obama's policies and undermines the prestige of the nation. This is a dark hour in our history, one that I pray can be reversed.

China

Power Plays in the South China Sea

Just south of mainland China, the South China Sea is considered international waters, with competing territorial interests shared among China, the Philippines, Brunei, Vietnam and Malaysia. A number of islands and natural gas deposits in the sea are points of dispute among China and her neighbors. To the northeast, China and Japan are engaged in similar disputes. Both the Philippines and Japan have a reciprocal agreement with the United States that would require U.S. intervention should China take military action against either. U.S. allies have agreed to allow the U.S. to maintain a naval presence in the region.

China frequently takes issue with U.S. naval craft entering the Chinese Exclusive Economic Zone (EEZ), a 200-mile track of water that surrounds the country as recognized by international agreement. The exact boundaries of the EEZ itself are disputed (largely due to China's territorial disputes). It is also disputed as to whether the presence of military vessels from other countries within the EEZ violates international agreement.

In short, the waters surrounding China are primed with delicate situations that could easily devolve into international conflict. Allies in the region look to the U.S. for strength. China knew of President Obama's reluctance to assert influence abroad, and acted with bravado during the eight years of his presidency.

Fading U.S. Influence in Asia (2016)

If one requires any evidence that the United States is a fading power, the recent events in the South China Sea offer ample evidence. Two Chinese fighter jets intercepted U.S. military reconnaissance aircraft and, to add to the humiliation, rebuked the Obama administration for any surveillance near China. The incident took place in international airspace on what has been described as a "routine U.S. patrol." This latest encounter comes on the heels of another interception in which Chinese jets mimicked an all-out attack on a U.S. naval vessel that sailed close to a disputed reef. These are merely two recent war-like actions by the Chinese in a series of interceptions since 2014.

China now claims most of the South China Sea, through which $5 trillion in ship-borne trade passes each year. The Philippines, Vietnam, Japan, Malaysia, Taiwan and Brunei all have claims of one kind or another in the Chinese-created perimeter, and all of these nations depend on the U.S. to enforce those claims. Washington has accused Beijing of militarizing the region, but China responds with a shrug, suggesting that there are diplomatic channels available for the resolution of disputes.

The weakness of U.S. naval forces in the Pacific and the South China Sea is apparent. New naval vessels—desperately needed to relieve the demands on the existing force—are not in production, and with sequestration are not likely to be in production. There are an insufficient number of Aegis-equipped ships to provide an acceptable level of sea-based protection. And now, after several incidents in which there wasn't a military response, Chinese officials believe the U.S. has acquiesced in their regional domination.

Moreover, and quite tellingly, the nations that have claims on islands in the South China Sea have either dropped their protests or softened their language. There is the growing realization the U.S. is not prepared to protect island claims or even protect freedom of the seas.

The president-elect of the Philippines, Rodrigo Duterte, explained, "America would never die for us. If America cared, it would have sent its aircraft carriers and missile frigates the moment China started reclaiming land in contested territory, but no such thing happened....America is afraid to go to war. We're better off making friends with China." This is a sentiment resonating throughout the continent.

Chinese sorties against the U.S. are not a casus belli, even as they have increased regional tension and have exposed the U.S. as an ill-prepared protector of Asian allies. Having eviscerated national naval strength, there isn't much the U.S. can do except express our dismay at the UN and in bilateral talks.

The Chinese installation of the DF-21 "carrier killer" surface-to-ship missile, and its current iteration, has a range of 2,500 miles. Of significant concern is the Russian air defense, the S-500 anti-aircraft and anti-missile systems that are likely to neutralize the effectiveness of the F-35 stealth fighter before it becomes operational, which the Chinese claim to have acquired. These technical breakthroughs give the U.S. Navy pause; while not dispositive, they are factors that militate against activism.

Chinese long-term plans for the 21st-century version of the Silk Road are on the way to fruition. As Chinese leaders see it, a supine U.S. is an unwitting ally on the pathway to commercial domination. Xi Jinping sees China as the "central kingdom," a land of incomparable influence consistent with its historic past. In most respects, notwithstanding neglect of our defenses, the U.S. is still more powerful than China. But the Chinese advantage lies with a discernible plan and a military buildup commensurate with its goals. As General Clausewitz noted, the will to act can be as significant as one's capabilities—particularly when an adversary will do almost anything to avoid confrontation.

Is a restoration of U.S. naval supremacy in the Pacific possible? The answer lies in money and time. The F-35 aircraft has sapped funds from every aspect of military preparation. It also takes years to build another carrier force and other naval vessels for a show of maritime muscle. Most significantly the commander in chief of our military must grow a spine—i.e., the backbone to assert our interests and protect our allies. Ultimately, this matter is more important than all others. If the president is not up to the challenge, American interests in Asia will continue to fade. That may be the real legacy of this president and the one best remembered by our "former" allies.

Chinese Get Aggressive in the South China Sea (2015)
Originally published on Newsmax

Recognizing the unwillingness of the Obama administration to assert itself in foreign affairs, the Chinese government has engaged in a major strategic effort to maintain sovereignty over the vast South China Sea, a body of water larger than the Mediterranean and an area long recognized as a sea lane under international law. Fifty percent of the world's maritime trade in tonnage passes through this body of water. By any stretch, this Chinese gambit is reckless, breathtaking, dangerous and imperial.

Despite claims by the Philippines over the Spratly Islands and the Japanese over the Senkaku Islands, China is asserting its role as the Middle Kingdom. The purported Mischief Reef and other artificial islands built by China are what American admiral Harry Harris calls "a great wall of sand" giving China control of South China Sea waterways.

These man-made islands have runways that can support military flights. And there are reports heavy weapons have been deployed as well. Needless to say, Asian neighbors are concerned.

Japan has reinforced its naval force; Taiwan may secure nuclear weapons; South Korean military units have been put on alert; and Philippine naval assets have gone through maneuvers in the area. U.S naval aircraft have flown over the islands as a way to reject Chinese claims of sovereignty, but they leave when Chinese planes scramble to intercept.

The United Nations convention on the Law of the Sea is unequivocal on what constitutes an island with territorial water (which does include man-made structures), but the Chinese government chooses to ignore the law. By dogged insistence, many nations have been persuaded by the ham-handed Chinese argument, but not those in the region. In fact, China has awakened a sleeping giant in the form of a South Korean, Japanese, Philippine, Indonesian and Australian defense condominium.

The Chinese strategy is clear: secure this crucial waterway for shipping as one part of its effort to build a new "maritime Silk Road." However, this aggressive and impatient stance has mobilized resistance that the Chinese did not anticipate. Can China back down?

The investment in the artificial islands and the assertion of territorial claims have put the Chinese government in an awkward position. Had the Chinese opened serious negotiations on the contested islands, notwithstanding several egregious encounters with Philippine fishing boats, some kind of compromise might well have been achieved. Now the stakes are high for all parties. For the U.S, this face-down may be a prelude to hegemony in the Pacific by Chinese naval forces. The Chinese blue-water navy is nearing parity with the U.S naval presence in the Pacific, and if anticipated growth rates are realized, Chinese forces will outnumber those of the U.S. in a few years.

It is clear the U.S. does not acknowledge Chinese control of the South China Sea. But is there more the U.S. can do or is willing to do? And is this aggressive Chinese position a casus belli?

First, the U.S. can use its logistical support and diplomacy to reinforce the defense arrangements unfolding as a counterweight to Chinese strategy. Second, the U.S. should send a major naval task force to the South China Sea as a symbol of American power and influence in the region, albeit the ships should remain 12 miles from the islands in question. Third, the U.S. should tell our allies we are there to support their efforts, not to direct defense alliance activities.

Since the Chinese cannot easily retreat, the possibility for escalation is high. China may have overplayed its hand, but after all, it is the Chinese hand with power and prestige attached to it. In his book *Roots of War*, Richard Barnet described American foreign policy as "permanent war," a belief that the U.S. must remain "number one in the world." This trope of the left is now challenged by 21st-century reality: American weakness and apparent unwillingness to challenge aggression bring us and the world closer to war. President Obama may have learned a lesson from the left's attitude of yesteryear, but he is now obliged to consider it against the present backdrop of international challenges.

The Art of War (2015)
Originally published on Family Security Matters

In Sun Tzu's *The Art of War*, present Chinese military strategy in the South China Sea comes into focus. Sun Tzu argued that the best war is one not waged, one in which the cleverest leader wins without fighting.

The Chinese declaration over its perimeter zone incorporates a number of islands claimed by other regional nations—e.g., Japan and the Philippines. With the construction of reefs that can accommodate air force assets, the government is sending a message: the so-called contested islands are part of the Chinese Middle Kingdom.

This message reverberates across the Asian fairway to Taiwan. China will not go to war to secure control of this breakaway island, but it will attempt to intimidate it with targeted missiles and seduce it with collaborative commercial ventures.

A similar strategy is employed throughout the region. Recognizing the fact that control of the South China Sea affords China de facto control of the Strait of Malacca, through which 60 percent of commercial tonnage is transported, China can dictate to states dependent on open sea lanes.

Moreover, this strategy carries over to the Pacific basin, where the U.S. once had clear hegemonic authority. Despite the so-called pivot to Asia, the administration has done virtually nothing to counter Chinese initiatives other than fly a B-52 over the air perimeter and send a destroyer within the 12-mile radius of claimed Chinese territory.

Chinese officials do not consider this self-declared zone a casus belli. Should the U.S. project the real power at its disposal, the Chinese would be obliged to back down, with some face-saving gesture. But with the Obama presidency, that isn't necessary. President Obama is at least as wary of war-provoking gestures and has signaled in several ways that the U.S. will no longer serve as the balance wheel in preserving Asian equilibrium.

What this ultimately means is that China—without firing a shot in anger—will gain control of the South China Sea, the Pacific and possibly the Indian Ocean as well. This evolving strategic picture is increasingly apparent, but it is given scant attention in the White House. When asked to comment, State Department officials contend the U.S. Navy is superior and capable of dealing with any threat to our interest.

This, of course, is somewhat valid. Our navy is superior…at the moment. However, that moment is being eclipsed by an uptick in Chinese defense spending, specifically on its blue-water navy and a corresponding reduction in U.S. naval expenditures. A key variable in assessing this profile is the will to act. Chinese leadership is aggressive; ours is passive. Xi Jinping wants to engage his neighbors with threats and incentives. The U.S. is often described by Asian leaders from the Philippines to Japan as missing in action, an unreliable ally that has turned inward.

Sun Tzu was not merely a guide, he was prescient. China could win a war without fighting it—a bloodless victory over the continent. There is a danger that Sun Tzu warned about—miscalculation that emerges from arrogance. If Asian nations perceive China as overtly aggressive and heavy-handed, they might dismiss the commercial overtures and band together as a defense condominium. Although this is an unlikely scenario based on the history of Asian fragmentation, it is a position the U.S. should encourage if only someone at the State Department had a strategic vision.

Sun Tzu offered lessons for all nations, particularly the U.S., which has the ability to project power. The alternatives between conciliation and war are not realistic. There are many positions between the extremes, including active diplomacy, saber-rattling, military maneuvers, alliances and defense assistance. The key to our involvement in the Pacific is not simply the projection of power, albeit that is important, but a strategic vision that considers goals and capabilities, national will and alliance assurances. At the moment there are merely tactical maneuvers like fly-overs; an overarching strategy is missing.

Sun Tzu noted that "strategy without tactics is the slowest route to victory. Tactics without strategy is the noise before defeat." As I see it, the noise is deafening.

The Senkaku Islands and the Chinese ADIZ

The Senkaku are a group of uninhabited islands southwest of Japan and east of China. Japan has claimed the islands as part of its territory since 1895, but the Chinese have contested this claim starting in the 1970s. Dominant theories suggest that the Chinese became aware of oil deposits on the islands. China has since been making power plays to assert its claim over the islands. In 2013, China extended its Air Defense Identification Zone (ADIZ) over them, and placed unusually heavy restrictions on a Japanese and Taiwanese presence in those areas at the behest of its own authority. The move was an overt escalation of the dispute over the island chain.

The U.S.-Japanese-Chinese Triangle (2013)

Prime Minister Shinzo Abe of Japan said recently: "The U.S.-Japan alliance is the central foundation for our regional security." This comment was uttered as a fear and a hope. Since the dispute between China and Japan over the Senkaku Islands, the State Department position has been one of diffidence at best and neutrality at worst. President Obama appears to be missing in action, stirring fear that the U.S. does not have an appetite to play its historic role as a Pacific power capable of maintaining the U.S.-China-Japan entente.

For the first time in close to a century, the U.S. has achieved good relations with Beijing and Tokyo simultaneously. Those good relations are now in jeopardy. It is not so much a dispute over rocky islands in the East China Sea as an increasingly assertive blue-water Chinese navy seeking regional dominance. As the governor of the Tokyo prefecture noted: "I don't want Japan to end up as a second Tibet."

President Obama's wavering has instilled uneasiness in Japan. Prime Minister Abe is not prepared to go to war over the Senkakus, but he cannot live with the impression he will acquiesce in China's maritime push. First the South China Sea, then the Sea of Japan, an ocean where Chinese subs are already active.

Should China sense weakness from the U.S., it could overreact. In doing so, it might awaken a somnolent U.S. giant and it would assuredly strengthen U.S.-Japanese ties. In fact, the worst-case scenario for China is pressing the panic buttons that result in an unleashed Japan with nuclear weapons.

A China on the rise may be tolerable if it doesn't overstep the bounds of Japanese sovereignty and key regional interests. What is essential is the U.S.-Japanese defense pact, the true balance wheel in Asia. What many analysts are asking is whether President Obama is as committed to its retention as his predecessors. Does he have the resolve to defend American interests with conviction? Wishful thinking may not be enough.

What the president should consider is a broad Asia policy that goes beyond China and Japan to include a condominium of Asian states devoted to regional stability, something on the order of SEATO. Presumably a military force that includes India, Australia, South Korea, New Zealand, the Philippines, Japan and the U.S. could serve as a deterrent to Chinese adventurism, simultaneously reducing the U.S. footprint in the region. This condominium does not foreclose on areas of cooperation with China. Commercial ties in the area should grow and can be enhanced through multilateral stability.

The Chinese understand that force as a counterweight and hubris as a weakness must be included in their military calculus. A multilateral force can deter extremist action, and overplaying one's hand, however strong, could unleash forces that harm Chinese regional interests. As long as all parties recognize their interests and as long as the U.S. returns to its longstanding Pacific role, regional stability is likely. Should another scenario emerge, all bets are off.

Chinese Air Defense Zone (2013)
Originally published on Family Security Matters

The negotiations over Iran's potential nuclear weapons arsenal have pushed all other foreign policy issues out of the headlines. But as Washington muses about Iran, one of the boldest attempts to challenge the U.S. as a Pacific power has occurred with very little commentary.

Recently China unilaterally created an "Air Defense Identification Zone" in the East China Sea that has the Senkaku Islands within its perimeter. These islands now claimed by China have been administered by Japan since an accord signed in 1972.

While the Chinese describe this perimeter as "air defense," in actuality it is "air control." In fact, the perimeter as drawn comes within 80 miles of Japanese territory. These Chinese air patrols have already encountered Japanese Coast Guard vessels and air defense planes in what can only be described as a game of who blinks first.

This "zone" has already had a profound influence on regional states. The South Koreans distrust Chinese ambitions, but may distrust Japan even more. Some commercial airlines have already agreed to recognize the Chinese identification zone, albeit Japan's aviation authority ordered national airlines to disregard the Chinese air zone. Most analysts assume China will employ this zone of influence to push aggressively for the "satisfactory" resolution of island disputes with Brunei, the Philippines, Taiwan and Vietnam.

But the most significant development is the challenge to U.S. hegemonic regional influence. Recognizing that the U.S. government is distracted by Iranian negotiations in Geneva, the Chinese acted. The head-to-head confrontation between these Pacific superpowers, which the American government wants to avoid, is now upon us. If the U.S. allows this perimeter to stand unchallenged, the East China Sea will be regarded as a Chinese aerial protectorate in a few months.

In an effort to calm jittery allies in the region, the U.S. government sent a pair of B-52 bombers over the disputed islands and well within the Chinese perimeter. At this point, there hasn't been a Chinese response. But there will be other challenges as long as China and her neighbors are jostling for control of waters with potentially rich hydrocarbon reserves.

China's defense ministry noted that the Chinese military would take "defensive emergency measures" against aircraft that didn't obey the rules of the newly created zone. White House spokesman Josh Ernest said the dispute between China and Japan should be settled diplomatically, but also noted, "The policy announced by the Chinese...is unnecessarily inflammatory."

It was merely a question of time before U.S. supremacy in the Pacific was tested. For years the U.S. and China have been on a collision course, notwithstanding American efforts to placate Chinese ambitions. As China sees it, this is the ideal time for a confrontation.

The U.S. is withdrawing forces in several nations, indicating both war fatigue and budgetary restraints. Negotiation with the Iranians has become a State and Defense Department preoccupation. Despite

President Obama's "pivot" to Asia, our allies on the continent are apprehensive about the American defense commitment. At a recent conference I attended in Tokyo, the most often heard refrain was, "Where is the United States?"

The question, of course, is really, "Where is the U.S. when we need it?" Japan, Taiwan and the Philippines need her now. Clearly the U.S. does not want a confrontation with China, a view probably shared by the Chinese government. But the Chinese believe the United States will back down. B-52s may fly today and possibly tomorrow, but does the U.S. have the will to sustain resistance to the assertion of Chinese power? In the answer to that query lies the future of the Pacific. An unchallenged China will regard itself as dominant over the contested islands in the East China Sea and even regional nations, soon to be viewed as satellites in the reconfigured Middle Kingdom.

Obama Offers "Strategic Patience" While China Bullies (2016)
Originally published on Newsmax

It is fairly obvious based on all accounts that the Chinese government will maintain a formal Air Defense Identification Zone (ADIZ) in the South China Sea. According to a well-placed Chinese source, any formal declaration of the existence of an ADIZ will depend on U.S. military presence in the region and China's relationship with its neighbors.

On one point, the Chinese government need not worry. Although the Obama administration has backpedaled on the use of language, it is unmistakable that the president is committed to "strategic patience." In fact, he has employed similar verbiage about the war against militant Islam.

The question that arises is, what does he suppose will happen during the period of patient waiting? Will the Islamic State roll back on terror? Will the Chinese government engage in peaceful negotiation with nations contesting island control in the South China Sea?

To offer the best face of the Obama stance, it might be said that problems often resolve themselves. Moreover, President Obama believes that nations like China and Iran will ultimately see their interest being served through *stabilization* of global affairs. The president often talks about being on the right side of history.

The problem is no one can predict what "the right side" is and who is on it. There is also the obvious contention that American patience is not seen as a sign of strength, but as a display of weakness. What is on the other side of patience? Will the Chinese control 40 percent of commercial tonnage that seeks passage through the China Sea and the Strait of Malacca? If the U.S. cannot tolerate this effect of waiting in the wings, what strategic options are left?

In the "long war" with militant Islam, the present administration has shown itself to be unable, or perhaps unwilling, to deal with the challenge. A strategic vision hasn't emerged because the government has adopted a wait-and-see attitude. Patience is not a strategy, albeit the tactical dimensions of the position can, at times, have a salutary effect on conditions. However, when a totalitarian force is about to strike with full fury, patience is not a virtue.

The glaring issue with strategic patience is that it lacks any apparent desire to deal with problems. Terrorism is more abstract than imperial aims, but neither can be enjoined by waiting.

Before the 1941 attack on Pearl Harbor, the U.S. government may have assisted our allies through Lend-Lease, but we did not join the fray directly. This was an example of strategic patience until one could be patient no longer.

The fear that many share is that it is increasingly more difficult to cope with an enemy advancing than one in retreat. In a world of weapons of mass destruction, patience could be devastating.

This does not mean patience is wrong; it is a question of when it is applied and what the costs and benefits of waiting will be. Patience in the Cuban Missile Crisis worked. At the moment, it is a mistake. This era calls for activism, whether it is saber-rattling or taking measures to fight an ideational war. Either this administration is awakened from its slumber or history will wake up with a thunderclap.

Taiwan

President Obama's soft power foreign policy has done more than embolden China; it has given our allies cause for concern that the U.S. would not intervene in an existential crisis of Chinese making.

The island of Taiwan is ruled by and claims itself the Republic of China (ROC). The ROC was the mainland Chinese governmental authority until Chinese civil war pushed the ROC to formerly Japan-controlled Taiwan after World War II. The mainland Chinese government is now the People's Republic of China (PRC). The ROC and the PRC both claim to be the official government of China, but the mainland PRC has demanded the world engage only with it, under a strict policy known as "One China."

The U.S. has a purposefully ambiguous relationship with Taiwan, so as to act accordingly with the One China policy, but the expectations are U.S. intervention should the PRC move to invade the island.

Weaker U.S. Leads to Insecurity in Taiwan (2009)
Originally published on PJ Media

Despite "the era of good feeling" that has emerged between Taiwan and China, tensions in the Taiwan Strait have not disappeared. There are 1,500 missiles aimed at Taiwan. It is also the case that Beijing's military posture toward Taiwan has hindered efforts to create a thaw in the relationship. China has not given up the notion of using force against Taiwan.

In the latest edition of its biennial military review, the Taiwanese Ministry of Defense released a metaphorical bombshell. It noted that with China's continuing and unrelenting military buildup, "it can now deter foreign militaries from assisting Taiwan." This, of course, is a euphemism for deterring the United States. Since the U.S. deployed an aircraft carrier in the Strait a decade ago when conditions heated on both sides of the divide, China has vowed to thwart any American military assistance for Taiwan. And if the report is accurate, that moment may have arrived.

Taiwan and China have been ruled as separate nations over the last 60 years, but Beijing claims the island must eventually unify with the mainland. The only question that remains is what is meant by "eventually." Whenever the word "independence" has been used by Taiwanese politicians, China has ratcheted up the threat level.

Since the election of President Ma Ying-jeou, who is noticeably cautious in reference to independence, Taiwan's relations with China have improved. The two nations now have regular commercial flights and are negotiating a possible free-trade deal. What has not received much publicity is the fact that Taiwanese business investments in China have led to the employment of millions of Chinese mainlanders. However, these developments exist against a backdrop of China's insistence that Taiwan is part of "One China."

Holding China at bay is Taiwan's most important international ally, the United States. According to the 1979 Taiwan Relations Act, the U.S. government has noted it will provide defensive weapons and would intercede if China attacked the island. This report by the Taiwan ministry, however, indicates that vows of intercession are meaningless gestures now that China's military strength is sufficient to deter U.S. involvement.

It is also the case that Obama administration impulses to withdraw from foreign commitments make it extremely unlikely the U.S. would respond militarily to Chinese adventurism. For all practical purposes Taiwan is a literal and figurative island at the mercy of Chinese leadership.

This is not to suggest that China is prepared to attack Taiwan. Such an event would poison Chinese ties to the West and its position in the World Trade Organization. What it does mean, however, is that China can apply pressure on a vulnerable Taiwan, thereby accelerating the goal of unification and forcing Taiwanese leaders to make concessions of various kinds.

Presumably Taiwan can seek military alliances in Asia with Japan, South Korea and India in an effort to thwart Chinese ambitions. But, with the exception of India, most nations in Asia recognize putative Chinese regional leadership in the face of America's evanescing Asian presence. The new Japanese government, for example, is already making overtures to Beijing in an effort to forestall Chinese inroads into the Sea of Japan.

It is instructive that a world with a less powerful United States leads to political instability in many parts of the globe. The Taiwanese are a resilient and remarkable people who have taken a once largely barren island and converted it into one of the most vigorous economies on the globe. Yet this development could not have occurred without the protective shield of the United States, and one can only wonder how it can be sustained without active American assistance.

To learn that the Taiwanese now recognize checkmate in the Strait is upsetting for any of us who admire the fierce determination of the island's people. A new day is dawning, and from the perspective of democracy and prosperity, it is a very gray day indeed.

China in the Middle East

Historically, China has never had much of a presence in the affairs of the Middle East. However, like Russia, China has taken notice of the wealth of natural oil and gas deposits in the region. A weak and soft-spoken U.S. under President Obama made conditions prime for China to take a more active interest in Middle Eastern affairs.

A Chinese-Russian Alliance that Complicates the Middle East (2015)
Originally published in The Washington Times

Though on a very small scale, Russian and Chinese navies have engaged in their first joint exercises in the Mediterranean. On the one hand it shows a level of cooperation and the expanding horizons of Chinese maritime interests in the Middle East; on the other hand, Russian and Chinese interests in the region are divergent.

Since the end of the Cold War, Russia has been eager to restore its naval presence in the Mediterranean. Russia retains a foothold in the Syrian port of Tartus, albeit the future of Russian interests is tied to the future of President Bashar al-Assad.

China has, until recently, been uninvolved in the Middle East, delegating responsibility for the maintenance of regional stability to the United States. With the withdrawal of U.S. forces and the continued Chinese reliance on Middle East oil, the military equation has shifted, with the Chinese keen on securing shipping lanes for trade. As a consequence, the Chinese have been caught up in the region's upheavals, picking up several hundred Chinese workers from Yemen and Libya who were in perilous positons.

The joint exercise not only provides a timely opportunity for Moscow to develop its Sino-Russian defense relationship, it is an exhibition of strategic theater as Russia flexes its muscle in the Ukraine and the eastern Mediterranean simultaneously. Clearly this show of force is aimed at the United States and NATO.

While the joint maneuvers suggest cooperation, it is also obvious that the Chinese plan for a "new Silk Road initiative," which would lead to control of the "heartland," is incompatible with Russian interests. Russia envisions area instability, which increases the price of oil and keeps pressure on the United States and its putative allies such as Saudi Arabia. If a crude oil tanker's passage through the Strait of Hormuz is disrupted, China would be the big loser, with Russian interests advanced.

By contrast, the Chinese government has major "futures" contracts with Saudi Arabia and wants regional stability. While not as outspoken as Russia at the P5+1 meetings, it does oppose an Iranian armed nuclear power that can threaten the eastern Shia region of Saudi Arabia where most of the oil fields are located.

At the moment, this likely tension has been submerged. However, it is only a matter of time before it surfaces. It would seem that U.S. interests and Chinese desires are consistent, but here too Chinese dreams of controlling the heartland, as Alfred Thayer Mahan once argued, will force the U.S. into a decidedly ancillary role in international affairs, one that U.S. allies in Japan, Israel, India and other nations would find quite destabilizing.

Moreover, the U.S. tilt to Iran on nuclear weapons threatens Chinese oil transports in both the Red Sea and the Strait of Hormuz. An Iran with nuclear weapons is likely to be far more aggressive in controlling tanker traffic than it is at the moment, thereby threatening Chinese economic interests.

If there is a foreign policy emanating from the Obama administration, it is composed of "less foreign policy." The opt-out position adopted by the president has created a vacuum that Chinese and Russian strategists are salivating over. U.S. withdrawal offers opportunities for enemies and potential enemies in the Middle East and elsewhere.

The mutual defense pact the Chinese and Russians have established challenges U.S. interests directly and indirectly: directly through military assertiveness and indirectly through a loss of confidence among our allies. However, the natural competition between these superpowers will lead inevitably to tension and perhaps conflict. President Obama may believe a U.S. retreat from world affairs makes the globe a safer place than it was previously, but this misguided analysis is harvesting rotten fruit in the Middle East and beyond. History has a way of asserting itself even if you choose to ignore it.

North Korea

North Korea purposefully keeps its military assets and operations a secret from the world. The country has spent the first part of the new millennium engaging in a number of nuclear weapons tests, four of which took place during President Obama's term. China has turned a perplexing blind eye to North Korea's activities, but in the void of President Obama's international leadership, China may be poised to use North Korea as a means to assert itself as an international superpower.

The North Korean Nightmare yet Again (2010)

Originally published on the Daily Caller

As Secretary of Defense Gates noted, any question about North Korea has only one response: "I don't know." There is indeed so little we know about this barbarian kingdom with nuclear weapons. Hence almost anything one does say is speculative.

As I see it, the nuclear facility recently disclosed is designed to be inflammatory. What it means is that North Korea can increase its supply of weapons and use them as negotiating instruments. Since there is nothing of value in North Korea, since the economy is moribund, since the government cannot supply basic necessities for the population, nuclear weapons—at least the threat of deployment—is a negotiating wedge for foodstuff, oil and hard currency. By any measure, this is an extortion ploy.

In a curious way, the Chinese government is complicit. China has the ability to clamp down on this backward kingdom, but it averts its gaze. From a Chinese perspective, North Korea is an effective pressure point on the United States and its allies in Japan, South Korea and Taiwan. What the stalemate with North Korea demonstrates is the relative ineffectiveness of U.S. diplomacy and the obvious fact that the U.S. is an unreliable ally, perhaps even an untrustworthy ally.

What the U.S. cannot deliver—a stable East Asia—emerging Chinese military prowess in the region may. In other words, China uses North Korea as a tool to promote its regional dominance and, in the process, undermine U.S. influence.

This strategy has its advantages for China at the moment, but it could backfire. If Japan uses North Korean saber-rattling and Pyongyang's deadly artillery barrage on a South Korean island as a catalyst to dismantle Article 9 of its Constitution and start producing nuclear weapons, China's military dominance could be challenged. Anti-Chinese sentiment in Japan should not be underestimated.

North Korean gamesmanship and Chinese cleverness are proceeding down a dangerous path in which an escalation scenario is quite plausible. The world waits to see how this situation will unfold with bated breath, and the Iranian regime watches with intense interest. What the U.S. does in North Korea—or doesn't do—is regarded as a portent of the U.S. position on Iranian nuclear weapons as well.

In yet another unfolding chapter in this tale of conflict, the United States and Seoul began joint naval maneuvers, an unmistakable message that sufficient force exists in the neighborhood to counter North Korean aggression. Moreover, even in South Korea, known for its restraint, there is increasing pressure to respond to Kim Jung Il's unprovoked attacks. South Korean president Lee Myung-bak told Chinese emissaries that now isn't the "right time" to resume disarmament discussions. In fact, President Lee bluntly said Beijing should adopt "a more fair and responsible position" on Korean issues. Furthermore, President Lee said North Korea "would pay a price" for further aggression.

U.S. admiral Michael Mullen, chairman of the Joint Chiefs, said, "It is hard to know why China doesn't push harder. They clearly are interested in this—in the region not spinning out of control— so my sense is they try to control this guy, and I'm not sure he is controllable." Of course that is one man's theory. There are others, including a China that benefits from the chaos by diminishing the U.S. role in the region and creating the impression with U.S. allies that only China can stabilize the unruly situation.

This is a scenario with dangerous implications, but strangely the world has seen it unfold before and diplomats seem to believe it will unfold again.

China's Other Means of World Influence: Economic Expansion

A Global Survey and U.S. Decline (2013)
Originally published on Family Security Matters

The road to the future has been set by the Obama administration. According to a recent global survey of more than 38,000 people in 39 countries, more people see China as eventually surpassing or already having surpassed the U.S. as the world's leading superpower, notwithstanding the fact that many more people hold a favorable view of the U.S. While it is difficult to assess why people embrace a point of view, the declinist psychology during the Obama years has clearly been a factor in shaping global opinion.

This Pew survey indicates that the global impact of China's economic expansion over the past three decades and the stumbling economic record of the U.S. have reordered perceptions. The data also suggest deepening mutual suspicion. Only 37 percent in the U.S. view China favorably, similar to the 40 percent in China that have a positive view of the U.S.

China does have a positive image in areas of science and technology, soft power influences on the general profile. But these achievements do not offset China's role as a police state and its violations of human rights. For the U.S., these data represent a dramatic attitudinal shift, one that indicates unquestioning support for the U.S. is on the wane. The U.S. role as the unchallenged global leader since World War II is over; the consequences of this change are perceptible, but not yet entirely discernible.

When nations believe the U.S. cannot be a reliable partner because of an economic downturn, its faith in alliances wavers. The roiling of political forces throughout North Africa and the Middle East is due, at least in part, to the diminished role of the United States. Withdrawal of American troops and a president who continually refers to withdrawal of commitments lead inextricably to a political vacuum, a vacuum that has been and will be filled by other parties, including our enemies.

For something on the order of 70 years, the U.S. maintained global equilibrium. Although wars were fought without victory, the U.S. indicated to those that cared that we were willing to sacrifice blood and fortune for their security. The projection of power was taken for granted by our allies and foes. When China would engage in saber-rattling toward Taiwan, the U.S. would send the Seventh Fleet to the Taiwan Strait as a show of our military commitment to an ally. President Obama may not appreciate "hard power," but at the time of its use, Chinese leaders understood it all too well.

In the world of foreign affairs, perception can easily be reality. What you believe to be true becomes true. The implication in the global survey is that the U.S. is in decline and, as a consequence, no longer a reliable military partner. That perception could lead and has led to very dangerous outcomes.

In fact, the U.S. is paralyzed on the North Korean nuclear question; it has been unable to halt the nuclear weapons program in Iran; it does not have the capability of thwarting Chinese adventurism in the Pacific; and it is increasingly tweaked and chastised by Russia. Clearly the U.S. still possesses military assets and could be a force to contend with, but President Obama's assertion of "leadership from behind" has put the U.S. way behind the international curve.

Most of those who responded to the survey realize the U.S. is a far more agreeable nation than China. Yet they also contend with a reality increasingly evident: the Chinese economic success will translate into political and military power. These respondents may not be inclined to join the bandwagon, but in the end there may not be alternatives.

The Chinese Strategic Vision (2012)
Originally published on Newsmax

It has been widely reported that the Chinese government is providing loans and outright grants to Latin American and African nations for the construction of schools, clinics, power plants and even soccer stadiums. The Chinese have flexed their economic prowess across the globe, generating approval in many quarters and raised eyebrows and concerns in some diplomatic circles.

Spokespeople in Foggy Bottom do not see a security concern, since these involvements aren't in military installations and bases. But the investments are formidable, with a reported $6.3 billion spent in Caribbean governments and more than $10 billion in Africa. Speaking out about this matter, Dennis Shea, the chairman of the U.S.-China Economic and Security Review Commission, said, "I am not particularly worried, but it is something the U.S. should continue to monitor." Sir Ronald Sanders, a former diplomat from Antigua and Barbados, noted, "They [the Chinese] are buying loyalty and taking up the vacuum left by the United States and Canada and other countries, particularly in infrastructure improvements."

What are the Chinese up to? It seems to me the answer can be found in Sun Tzu's *The Art of War.* Sun Tzu contended there are ways to defeat an adversary without going to war. You can create an environment in which defeat is inevitable. For example, if Caribbean states are beholden to China for the infrastructure gifts that have been conferred, the U.S. and its regional influence will be neutralized, exposing the southern flank. One need not anticipate a Soviet-style government in Cuba and the Caribbean to recognize a subtle but real challenge to American interests through Chinese humanitarian and commercial investments.

Similarly, the Chinese vision for the future can be characterized as "food, fuel and minerals." Dominance in these three areas could create a stranglehold on basic resources the world requires. It is not coincidental that the Chinese government overpaid for Potash Inc., one of the world's major fertilizer companies. If the Chinese can control fertilizer, the Chinese can control food supplies.

Chinese government officials have moved aggressively to control commodities wherever possible. Oil futures have been purchased in East and West Africa and, as significantly, mineral deposits such as manganese and titanium have been pursued throughout the continent without regard to the present market rates. The Chinese are notorious for paying handsomely in order to control mining rights.

The long-term strategy—if seen as a strategy—is that control of key commodities offers control of the globe, or at least, global influence without a shot being fired. It is clear that U.S. military requirements are dependent on minerals in control of a potential enemy. Already the signs of prospective compromise are emerging.

It has been said the U.S. plays checkers, while our enemies play chess. But if one were a student of Sun Tzu, it would be evident the Chinese have a strategy, a vision of the future, while the U.S. is pragmatic, ad hoc, without an idea of what is over the horizon.

Middle East Follies

"The world is less violent than it has ever been," President Obama said in 2014. These words came from the president against a backdrop of global terror networks, authoritarian arms proliferation, and a surge in Chinese, Russian and Iranian world influence. Iran sits atop a newfound regional influence, on the winning side of a negotiation to legally produce nuclear material while sanctions have been lifted. The Islamic State has plundered and murdered its way across Iraq, Afghanistan and Syria. U.S. Sunni allies are anxiously preparing for the worst in the void of U.S. leadership. And Israel faces an existential crisis from extremist neighbors that call for its complete annihilation.

A Test of U.S. Mettle (2011)
Originally published on Family Security Matters

Two Iranian warships traveled through the Suez Canal on their way to Syria with weapons material onboard, in defiance of American government restrictions, and there has been barely a word of denunciation from our State Department.

Radical sheikh Yusuf al Qaradawi spoke to a million Egyptians in Cairo's Tahrir Square, urging the new Egyptian government to open the Rafah border into Gaza so that "we can facilitate aid to our brethren" in their effort to defeat their enemy (Israel) and "capture Jerusalem." Sheikh Qaradawi extolled the Muslim Brotherhood, calling for "freedom and democracy" as a vehicle for an "Islamic state based on sharia." Yet remarkably neither the State Department nor most intellectuals condemned Qaradawi's speech.

In Libya Colonel Muammar Qaddafi has used overwhelming force, including air bombings, to resist the national movement of rebellion. Despite the use of military weapons to kill his own citizens, it took five days before the Obama administration responded to the bloodshed, and even then the response was divided, with Secretary of State Hillary Clinton saying the U.S. would consider a "no-fly zone over Libya" and Secretary of Defense Gates arguing that is not a policy option.

In his 1928 book *La Trahison des Clercs* (*The Treason of the Intellectuals*), Julien Benda explained how the abandonment of truth abetted totalitarian ideologies in the 20th century. He noted with prophetic accuracy how a denial of reality led directly to World War II. Clearly one can extrapolate from this analysis 93 years ago to the present, a present in which intellectuals and government leaders deny the reality of radical Islamism, including sharia, jihad and infidel hatred.

With the Arab government roiled by rebellion, the question that emerges is whether this is the moment for the efflorescence of democratic sentiment or a slide back into a past in which violent theological states were created for the essential purpose of creating caliphates. How conditions will unfold remains unclear, but on one matter there isn't any confusion: the United States has a stake in the outcome.

Yet to the regret of many, the U.S. has not asserted any leadership. It is as if we are mere observers of a revolution that has the potential to alter international relations permanently. The level of institutional blindness was evident when intelligence chief James Clapper argued that the Muslim Brotherhood is largely a secular organization. I wonder if Mr. Clapper asked why it is not named the Secular Brotherhood.

This response may not be treasonous, but it assuredly is inept. The lack of coordination, the many voices claiming to speak for the administration and the striking and conspicuous silence of the president have produced an air of uncertainty.

Most significantly, it has produced in the mindset of our enemies in Iran, Hezbollah, Hamas, Syria and even Turkey a U.S. that is weak and ineffectual. Its rhetoric is inconsistent with its action or lack thereof.

In the film *First Knight*, an antagonist of the hero played by the late Heath Ledger says, "You have been weighed and measured and found wanting." The hero's courage and will were being tested. It is not far-fetched to contend that our national will has been weighed and measured, and it appears as if we have not met the challenges of our time.

Instead of playing the role of a key protagonist, we are mere spectators confused by what we see on the global stage and in a state of denial. History is passing us by the way it did for a generation in the 1930s that had the opportunity to forestall war, but couldn't marshal the will to do so. This drama has not yet reached its final act, and it is certainly not too late for decisive action. However, the curtain may close soon enough, revealing a world condition distinctly inhospitable to our interests.

The Coming Crisis in the Middle East (2010)
Originally published on Pundicity

The gathering storm in the Middle East is gaining momentum. War clouds are on the horizon, and like in the conditions prior to World War I, all it takes for explosive action to commence is a trigger.

Turkey's provocative flotilla, often described in Orwellian terms as a humanitarian mission, has set in motion a flurry of diplomatic activity, but if the Iranians send escort vessels for the next round of Turkish ships, it could present a casus belli.

It is also instructive that Syria is playing a dangerous game with both missile deployment and rearming Hezbollah. According to most public accounts Hezbollah is sitting on 40,000 long-, medium- and short-range missiles, and Syrian territory has served as a conduit for military material from Iran since the end of the 2006 Lebanon War.

Should Syria move its own Scuds to Lebanon or deploy its troops as reinforcement for Hezbollah, a wider regional war with Israel could not be contained.

In the backdrop is an Iran with sufficient fissionable material to produce a couple of nuclear weapons. It will take some time to weaponize missiles, but the road to that goal is synchronized in green lights, since neither diplomacy nor diluted sanctions can convince Iran to change course.

Iran is poised to be the hegemon in the Middle East. It is increasingly considered the "strong horse" as American forces incrementally retreat from the region. Even Iraq, ironically, may depend on Iranian ties in order to maintain internal stability. From Qatar to Afghanistan, all political eyes are on Iran.

For Sunni nations like Egypt and Saudi Arabia, regional strategic vision is a combination of deal-making to offset the Iranian Shia advantage and attempting to buy or develop nuclear weapons as a counterweight to Iranian ambition. However, both of these governments are in a precarious state. Should either fall, all bets are off in the Middle East neighborhood. It has long been said that the Sunni "tent" must stand on two legs; if one falls, the tent collapses.

Should that tent collapse and should Iran take advantage of that calamity, it could incite a Sunni-Shia war. Or if Iran feels its oats and is no longer dissuaded by an escalation scenario with nuclear weapons in tow, war against Israel is a distinct possibility. However implausible it may seem at the moment, the possible annihilation of Israel and the prospect of a second Holocaust could lead to a nuclear exchange.

The only wild card that can change this slide into warfare is an active United States policy. Yet curiously, the U.S. is engaged in both an emotional and physical retreat from the region. Despite rhetoric that suggests an Iran with nuclear weapons is intolerable, it has done nothing to forestall that eventual outcome. Despite the investment in blood and treasure to allow a stable government to emerge in Iraq, the anticipated withdrawal of U.S. forces has prompted Prime Minister Nouri al-Maliki to travel to Tehran on a regular basis. And despite historic links to Israel that gave the U.S. leverage in the region and a democratic ally, the Obama administration treats Israel as a national security albatross that must be disposed of as soon as possible.

As a consequence, the U.S. is perceived in the region as the "weak horse," the one that is dangerous to ride. In every Middle East capital the words "unreliable" and "United States" are linked. Those seeking a moderate course of action are now in a distinct minority. A political vacuum is emerging, one that is not sustainable and one the Iranian leadership looks to with imperial exhilaration.

It is no longer a question of whether war will occur, but rather when it will occur and where it will break out. There are many triggers to ignite the explosion, but not many scenarios for containment. Could it be a regional war in which Egypt and Saudi Arabia watch from the sidelines, but secretly wish for Israeli victory? Or would this be a war in which there aren't victors, only devastation? Moreover, should war break out, what will the U.S. do?

This is a description far more dire than any in the last century and, even if some believe my view is overly pessimistic, Arab and Jew, Persian and Egyptian, Muslim and Maronite tend to believe in its veracity. That is a truly bad sign.

Removing U.S. Presence from the Middle East

Since his candidacy, President Obama has been intent on removing the U.S. from the Middle East, no matter what might result from the vacuum of power. Despite initial acquiescence to requests by American military leaders for more troops in 2009, President Obama took every opportunity to advertise the draw-down of U.S. forces from Afghanistan from 2014 onward. To fit President

Obama's worldview, the war on terror had to be over, no matter the divergence from reality required to make such a statement.

The U.S. Withdrawal from Iraq (2011)
Originally published on Family Security Matters

President Obama announced that the United States would pull the remaining troops out of Iraq by year's end. As he noted, "After nearly nine years, America's war in Iraq will be over." This claim has a nice political ring to it, but if parsed, it really means the U.S. participation in Iraq's war is over, but the war goes on. In fact, U.S. withdrawal may exacerbate the violence on the ground. "The tide of war is receding," argues the president, but is that true?

For military commanders, including General Lloyd Austin, U.S. commander in Iraq, the president's hypothesis is questionable. Without a secure, orderly transition, U.S. successes have been put at risk. Politics does not tolerate a vacuum. Iran's ability to meddle in Iraqi politics has soared with the announced U.S. withdrawal.

From the Iranian point of view, the Lebanon model that relies on Hezbollah as a political balance wheel is probably the strategy Iran has in mind for Iraq. There are already signs of Iranian influence in the al-Maliki government. And it doesn't involve high-level strategic thinking to envision a Shiite vassal state with Iran's Quds force operating in the shadows to impose its will on the Iraqi people.

Alas, it is ironic that after spending our treasure and the blood of our soldiers to create the only working Arab democracy in the Middle East, its future is now dependent on the actions of our Iranian enemies. President Obama may indeed believe the tide of war is receding, but the events he put in motion could yield a war far more intense than any we have recently encountered.

Iran, since 1979, has made the point that the United States' forces must vacate the region. Their wish is now realized. It is only a question of time before American troops leave Afghanistan as well. The question that remains is what is in store for this region, with hostile regimes, religious friction and nations possessing nuclear weapons—e.g., Pakistan and most likely Iran?

Every sensible American wants to see our troops at home and war at an end. But it is simplistic to assume that if we walk away from a conflict our enemies will do the same. We are engaged in a long war with radical Islam. It is not likely to disappear because we have lost our appetite for battle. A long peace, perhaps the word "stability" applies, is only possible through the demonstration of our strength, our willingness to stay the course.

The U.S. left thousands of troops in Germany after World War II, and the U.S. still retains close to 30,000 troops in South Korea in order to maintain stability in this hostile peninsula. These troops were and are deployed to maintain the gains achieved on the battlefield. The same could certainly be said for Iraq.

One can only hope that the president's risky decision will not require redeployment of our forces at some time in the future. As I see it, there would be some sense in retaining a force of 15,000 in Iraq in order to bolster the Iraqi army. But that stance has been rejected. So we are left with the strategy of prayer. Perhaps President Obama has a special relationship with the gods. If not, God help us all.

Wishing Doesn't Make It True (2013)
Originally published on Family Security Matters

President Obama recently noted that "this war, like all wars, must end." In other words, the president is outlining revisions in the legal and moral framework that have guided policies since 2001. Presumably this speech is guided by the president's belief that we have "turned a corner" in the war with al Qaeda and other terrorist entities. Moreover, the president argued that the 2001 congressional Authorization for the Use of Military Force adopted after the 9/11 attack should be revised and eventually repealed to recognize the diminished capability of al Qaeda as a terror organization.

The president also insisted that despite his belief in ending the war, unmanned, remotely piloted drones remain a legal, effective and moral tool for fighting terror. One might well ask, if the war is over, why are drones needed at all? But this is begging the question. The fact is that wars do not end by declaration.

Our mission in Afghanistan is concluding because the president made a unilateral decision to withdraw our forces. What is not clear is whether the Taliban got the message. From all that has been reported, their guns have not been converted into plowshares. And that is precisely the problem the nation now confronts. The president may believe that this war must end, but it doesn't seem as if our enemies agree.

All of this talk about "history's guidance" in this speech overlooks last September's al Qaeda attack on the U.S. embassy in Benghazi. It overlooks the role al Qaeda now plays with the rebel forces in Syria. It ignores as well the resurgence of violence in Iraq.

The president obviously is intent on writing the War on Terror out of existence, but the War on Terror has a persistence the president's assertions ignore. If we wish something to be true, is it necessarily true? Here is the juvenile make-a-wish dream converted into foreign policy. The president appears to be converting national security concerns into local policing vigilance. If so, should we be reading Miranda rights to apprehended terrorists? Are the Tsarnaevs merely misguided thugs who have gone astray? Is the knife-wielding Islamist who beheaded a British soldier on the streets of London a criminal with religious impulses?

As I see it, this speech by the president is not only naïve, it sets in motion a host of actions justifying defense retrenchment in the national budget. After all, if the war is about to end, if al Qaeda's ability to do us harm has been thwarted, why do we need so many soldiers, planes, ships, drones, etc.? Sequestration, thy name is "peace in our time."

Rather than the end-of war-speech, this should be the preamble. We should be asking if the president's claims are realistic. We should be going through a defense assessment review, considering what assets are needed should al Qaeda or its offshoots raise their ugly head.

Happy talk belongs in *South Pacific*, not in the Oval Office. A president has an obligation to be thoughtful, not pollyannaish. And most noteworthy, the president should be someone the public can trust. Once President Obama decided he could go to bed early on the day the embassy in Benghazi was attacked, virtually ignoring the death of our ambassador, his assistant and two Navy Seals, he forfeited the trust Americans normally confer on those in the White House.

Now the war is "winding down." If you believe that I assume you believe that the IRS responds dispassionately to all requests. This latest speech gambit by the president shows yet again that appearance in this administration is more significant than substance, that reassuring words are all that is necessary to bring about the absence of conflict. Very soon the president will learn this is not "what history advises…and what our democracy demands."

The Islamic State (IS, also known as ISIS or ISIL)

*The Islamic State (IS) found a home in the void of power created by the American withdrawl from Iraq after Operation Iraqi Freedom. Virtually unchecked by world military powers, IS has large regions of control in Iraq and Syria; holdings in Libya, Egypt, Turkey, other parts of North Africa and Southeast Asia; and billions of dollars on hand in cash and assets. The IS has killed unprecedented numbers of people in its global campaign of jihad, with over 10,000 of those kills performed by execution. It is the most ruthless, violent and well-equipped militant Islamic group that the world has ever seen. In 2014, President Obama referred to the IS as a "J.V. team." He later took back his statement but took no action. Aside from limited airstrikes in Iraq and Syria, President Obama's response to the rise of IS has been to stay out of its way. Allies in the region plead for assistance and Europe falters under the weight of those displaced by the IS. In an interview with **The Atlantic** in 2015, President Obama was asked if he had regrets about his handling of the fight with IS. "I don't think we're losing," he stated.*

A Resolution to Be Irresolute (2015)
Originally published on Family Security Matters

With great fanfare, President Obama asked Congress to consider his proposal—some would call it his strategy—for military operations against the Islamic State.

The powers requested from Congress have initiated a debate among Democrats and Republicans, with Dems arguing for strict limits on presidential war powers and Reps contending more flexibility is needed in the fight against IS than the president has proposed.

In fact, the president has called for a three-year authorization for military force that locks in action for President Obama's successor. The president also proposed repeating the 2002 war authorization act that gave President George W. Bush the authority to invade Iraq. Not only does the president call for a time limit, but he is also "handcuffing" his successor.

The effect of the president's resolution is to win bipartisan support for irresolution. It simply defies the reality on the ground. President Obama reveals, yet again, an underwhelming understanding of IS and its imperial goals, even admitting recently that he had not yet fully formed a strategy for opposing IS. There is little doubt a defense condominium of Egypt, Saudi Arabia, the UAE, Jordon and Kuwait should be mobilized to engage the enemy on the ground, but these nations are looking for American leadership. The recalcitrance shown by President Obama is not regarded as leadership. By limiting U.S. involvement in the war to three years and restricting ground troops, the president is scripting a war to suit his own ambitions. Unfortunately IS leaders don't accept his script.

Willing a set of conditions doesn't make them accurate. Even though the president is seemingly taking a cautious stance, it is actually reckless. Pinprick bombings have not adversely affected IS' ability to attack, despite a few military reversals in the last few weeks. It would appear that the president is far more interested in adhering to his philosophical position of scaling back on American military commitments than degrading and destroying the enemy.

As I see it, President Obama's strategy—if I can generously call it that—is bound to fail. Airstrikes alone rarely win wars. The use of military trainers only needlessly puts U.S. soldiers in a vulnerable position. We are not in and we are not out. President Obama assumes the threats are overstated and we are being "alarmed" by events media panjandrums exaggerate. For him, expansive presidential war authority should be curtailed. Alas, on this point, he may be correct. But he is asking Congress to be as irresolute as he is, to move inexorably to a position that restricts all combat missions. Defining war in a manner consistent with philosophical assumptions doesn't make it true.

While the essence of his proposal is for a strict limit on warfighting capability, the president did note, "If we had actionable intelligence about a gathering of IS leaders, and our partners didn't have the capacity to get them, I would be prepared to order our Special Forces to take action, because I will not allow these terrorists to have a safe haven." If the president's initial comments closed the door, this statement seemingly leaves it ajar. Apparently some ground operations are acceptable, but the terms for their use remain ambiguous.

Representative Adam Schiff, a Democrat on the House Intelligence Committee, told reporters, "I think [the president's proposal] is carte blanche." Surely it is half-hearted, displaying the attitude of a man who doesn't want to fight but finds himself in the position of yielding to the need for some engagement. Hence a resolution that is irresolute, a direction that is unclear, a restriction intended to limit future presidents and a position that must bring a smile to our enemies' faces everywhere.

Airstrikes Alone by Obama Will Not Snuff Out ISIS (2014)
Originally published on Newsmax

President Obama finally delivered a presidential address in his strategy view of the war against ISIS. As a speech, it was admirable; as a strategy, it is questionable.

The president noted that he would rely on airstrikes, support for Syrian resistance forces, intelligence operations, Special Forces and the assistance of allies in the region. What the president actually enunciated were tactics, not a strategy, since ISIS is the latest and by no means the only radical group to emerge in the Middle East.

Moreover, the president insisted that Islam does not encourage the taking of innocent lives, a statement that overlooks the way infidels are to be treated according to Korani doctrine. An unwillingness to recognize the problem we as a nation are encountering makes it extremely difficult to deal with it.

Similarly, air power can degrade an enemy but not defeat him. If our goal is victory, air power alone won't do it and the performance of the Iraqi army indicates it cannot do it. In 2004 the U.S. had complete control of the air over Iraq and flew 700 sorties, yet it took 13,500 U.S. and British troops over seven weeks to ferret out the insurgents.

It was apparent when ISIS forces were on the march that the Iraqi army could not stand up to a ragtag force of 4,000 troops. Rather than confront the enemy, it fled. Could this same army be trained to take and hold ground?

Complicating matters for the president is the U.S. commitment to support the rebel forces in Syria, now seen as a surrogate for U.S. boots on the ground. The Free Syrian Army might have been a candidate for support two years ago, but now it is part of a rebel force that includes al Qaeda and al Nustra—clearly radicals themselves. Should the U.S. supply radical groups that we have vowed to defeat? The implications are startling.

Clearly the president has taken a tentative first step, but his commitment—by his own admission—is tentative. Politically he cannot admit that he was wrong about his precipitous withdrawal from Iraq. He noted after that last presidential campaign that he was elected "to end wars, not to start them." The naïve view that if U.S. troops withdraw from a battle zone then war ends has come home to roost. The president may not want war, but war wants him. And now he has no escape.

He is in the crosshairs of history, bound by forces he cannot completely control and unsure about possible outcomes. His instincts have been challenged. Events on the ground have altered his rhetoric and modified his position, but he seems incapable of recognizing the reality of a growing radical Islamic threat that will not go away even if ISIS is degraded.

The Middle East is aflame and we need more than firefighters. We need those who recognize and can come to grips with root causes and have a genuine strategy for attacking them. At this point the nation appears ready for leadership, notwithstanding so-called war fatigue. Can President Obama rise to the occasion? What will he do if his tactics are unsuccessful? Will his coalition hold? Can air power do the job that is necessary? The jury awaits an answer to these questions, and there is a lot at stake in the unfolding.

Obama's Cobbler Strategy (2014)
Originally published on Townhall

Since 9/11/01 the United States has been engaged in a struggle against radical Islam. The enemies have a variety of names, from the Islamic State to al Qaeda, from Boko Haram to the Muslim Brotherhood, from Hamas to Hezbollah, but they are all active in the name of Islam and all have an imperial goal of creating a caliphate. Tactics may vary, yet they consistently maintain an extreme level of violence as a source of intimidation.

Accepting these conditions as a given on the world stage for a decade and a half and accepting as well the fact that President Obama has had to confront this issue for the more than six years he has been in office, it is startling, alas mind-boggling, that the president admitted, "We don't have a strategy yet" for dealing with the Islamic State in Syria and Iraq. There are many comments the president has made that I consider questionable and some quite objectionable, but none have left me as confounded as this statement.

"Limited" airstrikes to protect the Yazidis and Christian groups is not a strategy; nor is rhetorical support for the Kurdish peshmerga soldiers. A coalition of "partners," as the president is proposing, is also problematic since the allies we once counted on are suspicious of the president's motives and competence.

Clearly the Islamic State is among the worst of a very horrible composite of Islamists, as the slaughter of James Foley amply revealed. However, we have the world's most skilled and seasoned military force ready and willing to take on these fanatics. All the diplomatic verbiage cannot substitute for a Marine given his orders to "take out" the enemy. The first and essential element of a strategy is clarity of purpose and a willingness to act. President Obama's statement that he will work "to cobble together…a coalition" displays diplomatic correctness but not leadership. The words "cobble together" reveal much more than the president intended.

Can one imagine President Jefferson saying we will "cobble together a coalition" to retrieve Americans kidnapped by the Barbary pirates? Or FDR saying after the attack on Pearl Harbor, there is an action plan to be developed?

The savagery of the Islamic State is a combination of the Barbary pirates and the Pearl Harbor invasion and then some. There is only one way to respond: fierce, determined action that ignores the new standard rules of engagement. The president must overcome his reflexive desire to keep his proverbial gun in his holster and unleash the full force of our military might.

In this instance the rationalization that U.S. intervention invariably yields chaos is without substance. Morality and common decency warrant a response, a response that even a war-weary America is likely to embrace.

This war has emerged as a civilizational struggle. Americans have been put in the crosshairs of history. Either fight today or we fight tomorrow. Our way of life is being threatened. The enemy does not care about life; he cares about goals. The question is whether we as a people can rise to the occasion.

It is also a question of whether this president can rouse himself from misguided beliefs about Islam to meet the international challenge. Will the office ultimately shape the man? Thus far, the opposite position prevails. Now, however, bodies callously killed and beheaded must leave a chill on the soul of every sentient human being. Those who have seen the action of the enemy know full well what our strategy must be. It doesn't require that much planning.

Mr. President, get your thoughts in gear. Every day of procrastination is another victory for the barbarians. A desire to avoid bloodshed is admirable, but what one avoids now will haunt you tomorrow. It is not whether we support the Christians, Kurds and Yazidis; it is question of whether we can defend our civilization.

The Debacle in Anbar Province (2015)
Originally published on Accuracy in Media

The Islamic State dealt a crushing blow to the Iraqi army in Iraq's largest province (Ambar), including the city of Ramadi—once home to nearly half a million people. What this victory revealed is the fragility of the Iraqi army, despite vigorous U.S. efforts to train it.

The deterioration in Ramadi was so rapid, Prime Minister Haider al-Abadi was left flat-footed. He immediately called in the Shiite paramilitary force to recapture lost territory, but altering the situation on the ground seems fruitless.

President Obama—in his "What, me, worry?" stance—indicated this setback will not change the tempo of U.S. operations—i.e., large-scale response by American troops is unlikely. Nonetheless, the White House signaled last month that it is coordinating a plan to reclaim Mosul, Iraq's second-largest city. Certainly that plan would have to be reevaluated on the basis of current events.

So complete was the Islamic State victory that Iraqi police and security forces were ordered to withdraw completely in order to prevent massive casualties. Naseer Nouri, head of the defense ministry's media office, suggested that deeper U.S. involvement is the only way to save Iraqi sovereignty. At the moment, there are 3,040 U.S. personnel in Iraq.

Colonel Steve Warren, speaking on behalf of the Pentagon and obviously the present administration, said, "ISIL seems to have the advantage. They will use this for their own propaganda purposes, but it doesn't give them a significant tactical advantage." Yet most of the support for ISIL terrorists comes through Ambar.

This overwhelming defeat put Prime Minister al-Abadi in a ticklish position: he could have either called the Shia militia forces that were critical to stability elsewhere in the country, or he could have reinforced Ramadi with regular forces. He chose to do the former, which may undermine his hold on significant parts of the country and even control of the government.

What this situation reveals is that despite the White House assertion that the Islamic State is being pushed back and the situation is improving incrementally, there is scant evidence to back up the claims. Airstrikes targeting extremist positions have been ineffective, in large part because there are relatively few sorties and, in most instances, ISIL forces are notified when U.S. plans are about to take off.

U.S. Special Forces have engaged in successful raids, such as the one that killed Abu Sayyef, the Islamic State's finance leader. But as talented as our forces have proven to be, they are hampered by constrained rules of engagement and by fighting against an army of more than 100,000.

While most field officers contend a dramatic increase in Special Forces is the only way to win, President Obama is reluctant to get "bogged down" in another Middle East war, to use the vernacular of the president's spokespeople. There is the hope that with the president's accommodative position on Iran's nuclear weapons program, Iran will land major support to the Iraqi cause, thereby stabilizing the region.

Of course an Iran more deeply involved in Iraq than is presently the case also means Iraq will be converted into a full-blown pawn in the Shia empire. Sometimes it is best to not get what you wish for. But there are very few options if President Obama retains his recalcitrant position. There is also little doubt that Iraqi officials wish openly for real U.S. engagement in their dissembling nation.

Iraq may turn out to be a troubling example of what happens to hundreds of thousands of victims slaughtered by terrorists when the U.S. turns its back on a nation that was once an ally. Abraham Lincoln once said, "If destruction be our lot, we must be its author and finisher." Lincoln could not have imagined a present situation where we are neither author nor finisher, but rather observer from the sidelines.

ISIS in the Driver's Seat (2015)
Originally published in The Washington Times

It has been argued by many analysts of the Middle East that the Islamic State is less of a threat to American interests in the region than Iran. Alas, that point may be true, but what is also true is that the Islamic State has imperial ambitions of its own. Its influence in Syria and Iraq has been established, as its army of young recruits and hardened Sunni militia veterans march across the desert sands causing chaos and devastation in their wake.

Surely these are sanguinic nihilists. Some would say means and ends are the same for them. However, there is a strategic strain in ISIL thinking. Libya is a divided nation; perhaps even the word "nation" may not apply. Qaddafi held it together with force and mercenaries who brutalized the indigenous population. Today Libya has disassembled. There are two governments, neither having effective control. There is the presence of several terrorist organizations, including al Qaeda. Most significantly, there is the major influence of the Islamic State.

For the Islamic State, Libya is a launch pad. Its members can enter Europe via Italy. At the moment, Italy is besieged by immigrants eager to flee the depredations in North Africa. Once in Europe, terror cells can operate to instill fear and panic. It is also a pathway for further recruitment.

ISIL not only has its own strategy, it is inadvertently an instrument of Iranian strategy. Some might contend this is not inadvertent. Nonetheless, the terrifying movement of its forces has secured the position of President al-Assad in Syria. How can the U.S. call for his ouster, when the only semblance of order in the country is found in the Damascus area he controls? Moreover, Syria, as Iran's vassal state, is the conduit for missile delivery to Hezbollah in Lebanon.

The notion that Iranian forces are united with the Iraqi army in the fight against the Islamic State is mind-boggling. But that is incidental compared to the military role U.S. Special Forces are playing in providing logistics for this combined Shia armed force. It is fair to say, nothing in the Middle East is predictable.

Presumably Iranian troops represent our boots on the ground in the war against the Islamic State. The Obama administration has made it clear that the Islamic State is our target and we will employ unsavory allies to achieve our goal of destroying it. What President Obama has given insufficient attention to is the distinct possibility the Islamic State's chaos works to the advantage of Iran in the halls of Congress as well as the Middle East battlefield.

ISIL is at the center of this complicated equation. As a Sunni militia, it can make the argument that it opposes the imperial goals of Shia capitals. It can create fear and engage in atrocities because the so-called allies do not have a clear, definable strategy for victory. I would contend that any strategy determined by Iranian forces does not bode well for U.S. strategic interests.

So we are at an impasse. We need Iran's military assistance to thwart the Islamic State's goals, but in the process we are unleashing powerful religious and ideological forces that may come back to haunt us. In fact, we cannot even be sure Iran is a reliable partner that wants to defeat the Islamic State.

The ship of state moves unsteadily, aware of some of the dangers that lie ahead but trapped by unpredictable conditions in a turbulent sea. the Islamic State, by contrast, knows what it wants and seemingly has few impediments in its way.

Hamas, Fatah and Palestine

Fatah is the majority government that controls the Palestinian Authority in the West Bank. They have been in power since the 1967 Six-Day War with Israel. Hamas is an internationally recognized terror group that controls the Gaza Strip, a portion of land on the Mediterranean that was voluntarily abdicated by Israel in 2005 in an effort for peace. Since 2005, over 10,000 rockets have been fired at Israel (including cities and Israeli civilians) by Hamas from the Gaza Strip. In 2014, Hamas and Fatah tried a yearlong arrangement of a "unity government." However, the two still remain at odds over leadership of the Palestinian political entity. Hamas, like many terror groups in the region, has called for the complete destruction of the state of Israel, one of America's closest allies.

The Hamas-Fatah Unity Government (2014)
Originally published on the Daily Caller

While there is much consternation over the Palestinian Authority (PA) unity government, there is nothing new on the policy front. Fatah, the so-called moderate in the alliance, has been an intractable enemy of Israel that speaks in peaceful tones for international organizations and promotes violence for its Arab sponsors. Hamas is and has always been a terrorist organization that believes the Palestinian state should include all of the territory from the Jordan to the Mediterranean. Hamas has been responsible for the murder of over 1,000 innocent Israelis and the firing of thousands of missiles at Israeli cities.

Recently Congressman Trent Franks and Congresswoman Michele Bachmann sponsored a resolution to withhold U.S. funding for this PA unity government. In the interest of full disclosure, the London Center for Policy Research is also a sponsor of this resolution.

As soon as the unity government was formed, Hamas reiterated its commitment to terrorism and the elimination of the State of Israel. By agreeing to the alliance, Abu Mazen revealed his hand as a partner in terrorist activity. Clearly, Israel should not conduct diplomatic negotiations with any organization that calls for the destruction of the Jewish state.

In fact, this should be the position of the Obama administration. The foolhardy peace overture by Secretary of State Kerry reflected a complete misunderstanding of Fatah and its motives. For Abu Mazen, there could never be a recognition of the Jewish state of Israel. All of the dancing around this central issue illustrated his intentions.

Outgoing Hamas leader Ismail Haniyeh, in praising the new Palestinian unity government that brings the PLO and Hamas together, boasted of the "advanced resistance" capabilities of the terror organization.

For Hamas, June 2, 2014, was a historic day, as reconciliation between Fatah and Hamas was accomplished. Hamas is recognized as a terrorist organization across the globe, never modifying its position that the Jewish state of Israel must be destroyed. Both parties assume greater solidarity than was recently the case, with Gaza and the West Bank coordinating their anti-Israel campaign.

Prime Minister Benjamin Netanyahu organized an emergency cabinet meeting in which he called for the suspension of peace negotiations with the Palestinian Authority because of its affiliation with Hamas, and a reduction in assistance given to the Palestinian Authority. Despite Prime Minister Netanyahu's exhortations to refrain from recognition of the new Palestinian government, European leaders and even the Obama administration applauded the unity arrangement, a somewhat strange response when compared with the widespread revulsion over the murders of Jews at the Brussels Jewish Museum—an event that Hamas usually praises.

Now Israel has to prepare for the onslaught of a new round of rocket attacks launched form Gaza and possibly the West Bank. The Israel Defense Forces understand what they face. Iron Dome and David's Sling (anti-missile technologies) will help. But ultimately the resilience of the Israeli people will be tested again, as it has been over the last seven decades.

The determination to withstand the threat will prevail, I am confident in asserting. What I am not confident about is the support of the United States and European nations. Unfortunately many on both sides of the Atlantic do not appreciate the fact that Israel is a battleground in the war against radical Islam, the same war we are fighting in other venues. That is a tragedy for Israel and a potential tragedy for us, since many Americans believe that a withdrawal from the Middle East will reduce hostility toward the United States. Unfortunately vacuums are always filled. Americans may not want war, but war has a strange way of wanting us.

Middle East Scorpions (2014)
Originally published by WAMC Northeast Public Radio

The old story of the scorpion and the frog is pertinent yet again. A scorpion says to a frog, "Will you escort me across the Red Sea? The frog replies, "Are you crazy? You will bite me and I will drown." The scorpion notes, "If I bite you and you drown I will drown as well, since I cannot swim." The frog, persuaded by the logic, reconsiders and asks the scorpion to hop on his back as he starts to swim across the sea. Halfway to his destination, the scorpion bites him. As the frog descends, he says to the scorpion, "Why would you do this? Now we will both die." The scorpion replies: "Because this is the Middle East."

Alas, this war between Hamas and Israel reflects the moral of this story. Hamas must realize it cannot win this war. In fact, it is isolated from its Arab allies. Egypt may be more inclined to see Hamas decimated than to achieve victories. Yet Hamas persists in firing missile after missile in a relentless effort to intimidate Israel into vague concessions—e.g., improve the condition of the Palestinians. A refusal to consider a ceasefire clearly suggests Hamas leadership has lost touch with reality. In fact, there is a question that looms over the horizon: How do you cope with a nation state intent on suicidal impulses? It cannot be ignored and it cannot be accepted.

This is an Israeli dilemma made even more extreme when the so-called moderate Palestinian president for life Abbas discusses his alliance and emotional ties with Hamas and its attendant murderous ways. What possible negotiation can occur when an adversary has only one goal: your annihilation?

The curious matter, of course, is that Hamas still has supporters. European nations still pour funds into both the West Bank and Gaza, and the United States does so as well. Lip service is still given to a two-state solution despite the fact that it is evident a Palestinian state would be converted into a chemical-Katyusha terror nation like Gaza. Any other expectation would be utterly unrealistic.

Yet there are many who deny reality. Left-wing Israeli politicians still hold on to the fantasy that Palestinians will live in peace with Israeli neighbors. The Obama administration still embraces the absurd idea that a negotiated settlement is possible, notwithstanding Kerry's failure at the negotiating table. Don't Secretary Kerry and President Obama realize this is the Middle East?

Here, terror reigns. It is in the culture that surrounds Arab life. Surely there are exceptions, people who insulate themselves from hateful propaganda. But words of hate are ubiquitous. They are in the markets, movie theaters, TV programs, even crossword puzzles. In my opinion, it would take a cultural revolution to undo the hateful mindset. That isn't to suggest the situation is hopeless. Time may indeed be on the side of an ironic disposition, but it will take at least one generation for this to unfold.

In the meantime Israel should remain resolute. The only way to deal with those who want to destroy you is to demonstrate that you cannot be destroyed. Now that troops have been deployed in Gaza, every effort will made to ferret out the rocket caches and destroy them. The Army will try to contain collateral damage, but there aren't any guarantees on that front. Many of the members of the chattering class will raise the issue of proportionality. Of course what really counts is the impression that Israel will not be intimidated or terrorized. This military occupation will succeed. Although this might appear as wishful thinking, sometimes the scorpions destroy themselves.

Regarding Islam

At the beginning of his term, President Obama made remarks at the University of Cairo in which he stated, "Islam has a proud tradition of tolerance." Refusing to acknowledge aspects of political Islam that inspire, even wrongly, extremism and violence has crippled the American response to worldwide terror threats.

Facing the Reality of a Religion of Peace (2010)
Originally published on Family Security Matters

Ignorant opinion is unquestionably on the rise and, from my perspective, there are dozens of examples daily that prove my claim. However, the most absurd of these examples, the one employed by government officials, academics and political candidates, is, "Islam is a religion of peace."

Let me parse this remarkable statement. It is agreed by people who know nothing about Islam that most Muslims do not commit violent or terrorist acts, ergo the religion is peaceful. But that is a classic non sequitur. Most Germans in the 1930s did not embrace the excesses of Nazism. Most Chinese did not subscribe to the slaughter of millions during Mao's Long March. Most Russians did not support Stalin's purges.

It usually takes a minority to start a revolution or "killing fields." The key feature of radicalization in any religion or political movement is the silence or seeming acquiescence of the majority, who are mainly moderate.

When the moderates say, "I didn't realize what was happening" or, "It is not any of my business," problems result. A minority controls a majority when the minority acts and the majority waits. It may indeed be true that the majority wants to go about its business without resort to extremism, but that is irrelevant. It is the meaningless fluff that makes us feel better and is meant to diminish a vision of fanatics rampaging across the globe in the name of Islam.

The fact is the fanatics influence history more than the moderates and, at the moment, the fanatics rule Islam. Invariably, well-meaning critics of Islam argue the religion needs an enlightenment, a reformation, a period of reevaluation. But overlooked by these critics is that Islam had this moment a century ago and it resulted in the ascendency of Wahhabism, an orthodox interpretation of the most extreme elements of the religion.

There is little doubt the Verse of the Sword and other Medina-related suras in the Koran promote violence in order to promote the religion. Many Muslims do not read those passages or take them seriously or regard them as a call to action. However, many do. And these are the fanatics who engage in suicide bombings, beheadings and honor killings. Moreover, because these are the activists in the Islamic faith, they take over mosque after mosque and spread their noxious views.

As I see it, the peaceful majority, the moderates the press representatives invariably reference, are cowed and extraneous. In Rwanda, where bloodshed and butchery reigned for a decade, one could argue Rwandans were basically peace-loving people. But the peace-loving are made irrelevant through silence. That is the incontrovertible lesson of history.

The group that counts, the group that launches historical trends, is the extremist that threatens everything we hold dear. To deny that is to deny a reality that allows the fanatic to control our very existence.

Needless to say, it is difficult to come to grips with this condition. The comforting notion that most Muslims are just like us won't fly when one considers who those moving historical forces are. What this adds up to may be difficult to contemplate, but, as I see it, it is better to confront that reality now than at a time when it is too late to resist. Claude Bernard once noted in a somewhat different but useful context that "the secret of function is apparent to us if we look hard enough."

My guess is we've been spending more time on delusional ideas, what we would like to believe, than on simply looking hard at Islam.

What We Think and the Arabs Believe (2010)
Originally published on Family Security Matters

In a 2010 Arab Public Opinion Poll conducted by Zogby International and the University of Maryland for the Brookings Institution, one can get a glimpse of Arab opinion in the so-called moderate countries of Egypt, Lebanon, Morocco, Saudi Arabia and the United Arab Emirates.

Included in the findings are the following points:

- Arabs hopeful about the Obama administration's policy in the Middle East declined from 51 to 16 percent between 2009 and 2010, while those discouraged rose from 15 to 63 percent.
- Those thinking Israel is a huge threat are at 88 percent (down slightly from 95 percent in 2008).
- The number of those believing the United States is the main threat to Arab countries and societies declined from 88 percent under President George W. Bush to 77 percent under President Obama.
- The number of those believing Iran is a threat grew from 7 percent in 2008 to 13 percent in 2009, and was 10 percent in 2010.
- Asked which foreign leader is most admired, almost 70 percent named an Islamist or a supporter of extremist forces. Turkish prime minister Recep Erdogan received endorsement

from 20 percent; Venezuelan president Hugo Chávez, 13 percent; Iranian president Mahmoud Ahmadinejad, 12 percent; Hezbollah's Hassan Nasrallah, 9 percent; Syrian president Bahar al-Assad, 7 percent; and Osama bin Laden, 6 percent.

Several conclusions can be drawn from this very interesting poll. First and foremost is the obvious conclusion that the adjective "moderate" hasn't any place in the Middle East, where one man's moderate is another man's radical. The assumption that President Obama's Cairo speech changed attitudes in the Arab world is certainly not borne out by the polling data.

Second, whatever change in tilt the present administration has given to the Israeli-Palestinian question, negative attitudes to Israel persist and it is unlikely this will change substantially as long as Israel exists.

Third, despite the rhetorical shift in Middle East policy reflected in President Obama's attitude and gestures, there is relatively little change in Arab attitude between President Obama and Bush. Considering the hoopla given to policy shifts, it is remarkable that the Arab man on the street retains essentially the same position toward the Unites States that he held two years ago—pre-Obama.

Fourth, despite the imperial aims of Iran and its threats against Sunni-dominated states, Arabs believe that the U.S. is a greater threat to their societies by a factor of 10.

Fifth, it is remarkable that not one moderate leader in the Arab world, alas even in the non-Arab world, made the list of most admired figures.

What this adds up to is an Arabic-speaking community where radicalism is ensconced; where despite foreign aid, diplomatic appeasement and attempts at cultural understanding, a passionate hatred of Israel and the West is unflagging. Judging from the data, conditions aren't improving. There is a lack of sympathy for democracy and liberalism and growing traction for Islamism, even when compared to Arab nationalism.

As a consequence, policy implications are apparent. The effort to appease, flatter and buy off has not worked. The notion that

President Obama represents a new chapter in Middle East history is regarded as mythology. And perhaps the most useless expression in the English language is "Middle East peace process." There cannot be a peace as long as Israel is regarded as a greater threat than Iran.

Apologias should be replaced by assertiveness. As long as the U.S. is regarded as "the weak horse" unwilling to restrain the advance of radical sentiments, American interests in the region will be imperiled. It is only when the radicals realize their revolutionary goals cannot be successful that transformation, or something approaching it, will be possible.

It is sometimes suggested that there is a huge divide between the realities in the Middle East, such as poverty, hatred, adventurism and internal competition, and the fantasies, such as the ultimate disappearance of Israel. And there is no doubt this divide exists and influences public opinion. But there is an even greater divide right here in Foggy Bottom, where the fantasists contend that all we have to do is have the Israelis make greater concessions to the Palestinians and Middle East peace will flourish, and the realists, recognizing the intractability of Arab beliefs, tell us that all the appeasement arabesques in the world are not likely to alter Arab attitudes to any appreciable degree.

Understanding the Radical Muslim Enemy (2009)

In the war of ideas in which the U.S. is engaged willy-nilly, any intelligence about our adversary—radical Islam—should take into account the social, cultural and religious dimensions of its behavior and psychology.

The need for such analysis is especially crucial when dealing with Islamic states that harbor the radical sensibility. One temptation in analysis is "mirror imaging," assuming that those in the Islamic world think and act as we do. But serious analysis must overcome this temptation by concentrating on Islamic jurisprudence, paradigms of leadership, the borrowing of Western ideas such as fascism and sect-specific characteristics.

At first glance modes of authority in the Muslim world include the following: prophetic authority based on the Prophet Mohammed, the Shiite Imamiyya doctrine or the Sunni Mahdism, all of which rely on the infallibility of the leader; scholarly authority that emerges from the belief that most Muslims lack the knowledge and acumen to understand the law of God and must therefore rely on scholars to interpret it; caliphate authority based on the traditions associated with the appointment of a leader; military authority such as the emir of the mujahideen; tribal authority of the sheikhs; consultative authority as exemplified by the Muslim Brotherhood; coalitional authority; hereditary authority; and popular authority of the kind enjoyed by Osama bin Laden.

At various times different authority models wax and wane and may even be coterminous. Some conditions based on ancient Islamic tradition remain largely unaltered. The *baya*, or oath of allegiance, is a pledge to maintain the sanctity of the faith, recognition of authority and reciprocity—translated as, an exchange with the prophet is an exchange with Allah (what might be called a spiritual transaction). The Hadith argues that if you do not accept the *baya*, you are not a true Muslim, a condition that helps to explain the psychology of the *shahada* (or suicide bombers).

While obedience is a factor, the *baya* recognizes that if a leader errs—i.e., strays from the faith—rebellion is possible, a condition that accounted for the rise of the Muslim Brotherhood in Egypt and the popularity of Sayyid Qutb and his writings.

The Wahhabist sentiment is also based on a body of knowledge— interpretation of the Koran—that suggests a leader may emerge who advises and guides based on his reading of the holy documents.

It is often said, perhaps as a contemporary cliché, that Islam needs an Enlightenment. But it is noteworthy that there have been several enlightenments, from the role of Wahhab to the Muslim Brotherhood to the position of Osama bin Laden, who by his own admission is not a religious leader yet commands religious attention.

These models indicate that Islam, despite a commitment to orthodoxy, can be altered and that authority can spring from various centers of influence, including the benign Sufi model based on the expectation that the guide (*murshid*) will lead disciples to spiritual perfection.

It is instructive that modes of authority in the Muslim world can be extracted from literature, history and a careful reading of texts. If we are to prevail in this war of ideas, we must understand what motivates our enemies, what inspires their judgment and what leads to their sacrifices. At the moment, our knowledge is deficient, but the road to understanding can be traversed through a return to diligent study and careful analysis of the texts Muslim scholars read and rely on.

Iran

The Need for Missile Defense (2009)
Originally published on Family Security Matters

The *London Times* recently reported that Iran has perfected the technology necessary to create and detonate a nuclear warhead. According to the report, which has been confirmed by others in our intelligence community, it would take approximately six months or less to enrich enough uranium for a nuclear bomb and another six months to assemble the warhead for possible deployment.

That means, in effect, that next year Iran will have the bomb and deployment capability. This may not shift the Obama administration from its present acquiescence, since it believes deterrence will work, but it will certainly send shivers down the spines of our European and Israeli allies.

Moreover, at the same time as the administration has seemingly averted its gaze from this impending nightmare, the Obama administration has scaled back the number of ground-based midcourse defense interceptors from 44 to 30. President Obama has also decided to freeze an additional 10 interceptors that were promised to Poland.

It would appear that at this critical juncture these budget cuts will seriously undermine American defenses against an Iranian threat. In fact, based on North Korean tests and the recorded range of Iranian missiles, it would seem that the U.S. should put additional effort into enhancing defenses against potential threats.

State Department officials assert that the nuclear force of the United States and the existing interceptors are sufficient to deter an attack from Iran or any other prospective enemy. Their statements of assurance, however, are not predicated on evidence. At the moment, the Iranian missile force cannot reach the United States, but it can hit every European capital and can certainly reach nearby Israel. What remains unknown is the condition that militates against a first strike.

Is the retaliatory capability of the United States enough to prevent a first strike by an enemy? Or is a theological state intent on national jihad resistant to rational countermeasures?

Moreover, even if deterrence works, or appears to work for a time, the existence of nuclear weapons in the hands of a rogue state like Iran is also a political weapon that can influence regional alliances and serve as cover for terrorist proxies such as Hamas and Hezbollah.

Since one cannot be certain about deterrence with an irrational enemy, that enemy cannot be certain about missile defense. The rogue state is unlikely to know how many of its missiles can penetrate missile defenses or whether any can do so. Hence, this nuclear weapons equation is filled with imponderables. The notion that we can deter is based entirely on past experience, but it has only a casual relationship to the future.

Therefore sensible policy is dependent on robust defenses, indeed even redundant defenses, that make the calculation of penetration more difficult for the prospective enemy attacker. As I see it, the intelligence reports on Iran should lead to the deployment of additional interceptors rather than fewer.

This retrenchment strategy is based on the view that our goodwill gestures will be reciprocated. But there isn't the slightest chance this will occur. The gains in Iranian prestige and influence from the possession of this weapon far exceed the pain we are prepared to impose on this rogue state. President Obama's strategic position appears to be "hope for the best and prepare for the best." Unfortunately history doesn't usually cooperate with unguarded optimists. Too bad our president doesn't read history.

★ ★ ★

Iran: An Ally, an Enemy, a Surrogate? (2014)
Originally published on Accuracy in Media

The Obama Middle East foreign policy lens is focused on one issue at the moment: the defeat of the Islamic State. In pursuing this goal, the Obama team is seeking allies including former enemies such as Iran, notwithstanding claims to the contrary. While the U.S. now sees Iran as a potential stabilizing force in Iraq and Syria, Tehran is chafing at what it considers the tough negotiating stance of the U.S. on its nuclear program.

No one at the moment—on either side of the negotiating table—has specifically referred to linkage, but the firm position of Ayatollah Ali Khameni is a sign Iran believes it has newfound leverage over Washington. A White House spokesman contends, "The United States will not be in a position of trading aspects of Iran's nuclear program to secure commitments to take on ISIS."

On the sidelines are allies of the U.S. apprehensive about the American position. Saudi Arabia, Jordan, Egypt and the UAE have vowed to assist the U.S. in the effort to destroy the Islamic State, but they are reluctant to use Iran as the instrument for doing so. The fear is that a stronger Iran, one with nuclear weapons, will become an imperial threat to the region. As Secretary of State John Kerry underscores the importance of Iran's role in the war against the Islamic state, Sunni leaders shudder.

Establishing a balance between a harnessed Iranian nuclear program and an Iranian army deployed as a regional balance wheel is a proposition emerging from the evolution of recent events. Already Iranian officials are calling the U.S. negotiating position "unreasonable." Iran's foreign minister, Jawad Zarif, said, "What do they, [the U.S.], want?...Iran has been...the first that came to the aid of the Iraqis in dealing with that problem."

What the Iranians cleverly avoid is the sectarian divide in the Middle East. With Iraq, Syria and Iran united as a powerful bloc of Shia-dominated governments, it poses a threat to their Sunni counterparts. In fact, the Sunni states accuse Baghdad of fueling the rise of the Islamic State by marginalizing Iraq's minority Sunni population, a stance adopted by the former al-Maliki government.

Israeli prime minister Netanyahu maintained that the nations of the world should not ignore the threat of Iranian nuclear weapons even if some officials "are saying that world powers should go easy on Iran's nuclear program so it will fight ISIS." This Netanyahu stance is consistent with the position of most European leaders.

However, the rise of the Islamic State and the barbaric beheadings have distracted policy analysts across the globe. The strategy, if there is one, is to put each of the Muslim threats in a "silo" as if one is different from the other. Admittedly tactics do vary at the margin, but the goals are extraordinarily similar. Whether it is the Islamic State or Khorasan or al Qaeda or the Muslim Brotherhood, the end game is a caliphate employing violence to achieve that point. As the United States stands as a Western superpower capable of thwarting that goal, it is "the great Satan."

Despite all the carping about former Vice President Cheney's comment that we must "clean out the swamp" in the Middle East, he is right and his view expresses a real strategy, one clearly avoided by the Obama administration. The question that President Obama will not ask is, why do Muslim radicals want to harm the U.S., and what can we do to preempt their destructive impulse? An unwillingness to fight is certainly not the answer, nor are conciliations at the negotiating table or a reliance on surrogates to fight this war for us.

This is a struggle for the survival of our civilization. Dropping bombs from 30,000 feet may scare and degrade our enemies, but it won't win this civilizational war. The message we deliver to the Iranians in Vienna is telling. If we concede on nuclear weapons roll-back so the Iranians do our bidding on the battlefield, we may degrade the Islamic State, but it will be a significant loss in the global war in which we are engaged.

The Iranian Empire Strikes (2015)
Originally published in The American Spectator

The clouds of evil surround the Middle East. For decades since 1979, Iran was and remains the leading state sponsor of terrorism. However, now Darth Vader has been converted into Luke Skywalker.

Qasem Soleimani, the head of Iran's Quds Force, is one of the covert operators undermining governments and promoting the imperial interests of his Islamic government. He has emerged as an international "hero" bolstering the morale of Iraqi troops and inserting his Revolutionary Guard agents into the struggle against the Islamic State. He stands in the vanguard of the empire Iran has created from the Mediterranean to the Red Sea and the Gulf of Aden. As Alaeddin Boroujerdi (an Iranian parliamentarian) noted: "Iran is more powerful than anytime in the past 30 years."

This has occurred with the tacit support of the United States. A hasty, and probably misguided, withdrawal of American troops from Iraq has created a vacuum filled by ISIL attacks and Iran's imperial ambitions. Cleverly, the Iranian regime is playing the role of regional stabilizer by leading the forces against Daesh, albeit the actual motive of regional hegemony should be apparent to anyone with even a cursory interest in the region.

For years, Iran preferred to work its goals behind the scenes by supplying missiles to Hezbollah in Lebanon and Hamas in the Palestinian territories. With its armed forces opposing the Islamic

State, however, Iran is out in the open, a "respectable" neighbor tackling the abuses and savagery of an extreme Sunni militia.

In Syria, Iranian Revolutionary Guard troops protect the al-Assad regime. In Lebanon Iranian troops resist any effort to oust Hezbollah control. And in Yemen, the Houthis have been supported from the outset by the Qud Force. There is little doubt Iranian militia groups are working across borders providing training, reinforcements and logistical assistance.

Commitments of this kind have placed a strain on the economy, but the trade-off of imperial—alas, empire—control versus immediate retrenchment at home is easily addressed, with the former taking precedence over the latter. One analyst maintained appropriately that "Iran is both the fire brigade and the arsonist." At the moment, the Obama administration sees only the brigade and is seemingly myopic to the arson.

Although the U.S. sacrificed blood and treasure to stabilize Iraq, that nation is a quagmire reliant on Iran to thwart the Islamic State. Even Iraqi leaders who once believed maintaining distance from Iran was in their best interest now cultivate close ties. The stage is set for the virtual union of Baghdad and Tehran as the center of Shia imperial ambitions.

Since the U.S. government seems to be intent on withdrawal from the region, Iran has become a surrogate for its military force. Putting Iran in this strategic position has alarmed Sunni neighbors like Turkey, Egypt and Saudi Arabia. In fact, a deal that accommodates an Iranian desire for nuclear weapons, or at least sufficient enriched uranium to produce these weapons, will land inexorably to proliferation. The Saudis will acquire nukes from Pakistan, and that will merely be the commencement of what I have called "the nuclear slide."

It is ironic that President Barack Obama received his Nobel Prize in part for his opposition to nuclear weapons. Yet it is precisely the policies that he has pursued that have brought the region to the brink of nuclear proliferation. History does have a sense of humor, arguably a tragic sense at that.

And while the Dark Empire of Iran is in ascendency, American interests in the area are in decline. Here again irony strikes. As a nation, the U.S. did all it could to thwart Iranian goals; now the arc has changed, as the Obama administration supports and encourages Iran's interest. Yes, the Iranian empire strikes and the U.S. is in the background nodding approvingly.

With the so-called deadline approaching, questions regarding the P5+1 framework abound. Perhaps several answers will be available when the details are hammered out at the end of June, but, from all accounts, that is unlikely.

There has been much discussion about the so-called breakout— i.e., that moment when Iran can produce the bomb. The problem with the idea is that incremental enrichment continuing at the present rate or an accelerated pace makes it difficult, if not impossible, to determine the moment when Iran will be ready to deploy.

Then there is the issue of tolerance. Supposedly there are penalties attached to non-compliance. But how can anyone be sure if Iran is violating the agreement? After all, the bureaucratic process for detection is obscure, and IAEA investigators must make appointments for surveillance. Surprise visits have been disallowed.

It is useful to recall that the IAEA recorded the lack of Iranian cooperation in the past as well as hidden facilities unmentioned in prior negotiations. Moreover, the agreement permits research and development at nuclear facilities in Fordow, where advanced centrifuges are located.

Amir Taheri recently pointed out that what we think this agreement means is different from interpretations by Iranian leaders. In the last week several Iranians have contended that the deal is a victory that recognizes Iran's path to nuclear weapons. By contrast, President Obama indicates the arrangement forestalls Iranian nukes.

Left out of the negotiated equation is the Iranian tie to North Korea. Nuclear technology has been transferred from Pyongyang to Tehran, and Iranian scientists have been present at every North Korean test.

It is also instructive that limits on uranium enrichment are easily overcome, since inspection does not seem to include "scientific examination" of the enriched uranium. Here too, incremental shifts might occur without any clear signal. Even the export of uranium beyond a certain level is dubious, since the determination of that level is in the hands of Iranians.

Verification in any such deal should not depend on trust or goodwill. Clearly the Iranians want the burden of sanctions removed; yet they are far more intent on acquiring nuclear weapons as a political club to be used against Middle East adversaries. That understanding should be at the forefront of all negotiations, but isn't.

Last, say for the sake of argument that Iran violates the accord. What do we do? First, there is the usual hand-wringing and UN debate. Second, there is yet another round of sanctions discussion. However, once sanctions are removed, they are virtually impossible to reinstall. Russia, China and Turkey are salivating at the prospect of Iranian trade and investment. In fact, without a military option, the West hasn't any way to tame Iranian impulses. Despite all of the talk about restrictions on the Iranian nuclear program, the reality is there aren't any.

In a recent conversation President Obama admitted that Iran's breakout time to the bomb will be "zero" in the near future.

What then can we know? Obviously we know that Iran has been provided a pathway to nuclear weapons, notwithstanding President Obama's assertions to the contrary. We know that verification processes are ambiguous, inexact and subject to modification by the Iranians. We know that Iran has violated one accord after another in the past and is hardly a reliable partner. And these are conditions we know now, even without details.

The major issue Americans face is whether they can accept the assurances of President Obama or whether they are more inclined to accept the "victory" address of Iranian leadership that Iran will not be prevented from pursuing its goal of nuclear weapons.

The Sunni Coalition Strikes Back (2015)
Originally published on Family Security Matters

It was merely a question of time before Sunni brethren struck back. The recent attacks in Yemen by the Saudi air force in conjunction with Egypt, Qatar, the UAE, Bahrain, Kuwait, Jordan, Morocco, Turkey and Sudan were united in delivering a message with devastating clarity to Iran. The presumptive target? Houthi militants that overran the government with the active involvement of the Iranian Revolutionary Guard. In forging this joint Sunni military force, the Saudis were saying there will be systematic opposition to the Iranian plan for hegemonic status in the region. Yemen's fall was the final straw.

The attack was also a repudiation of the U.S. rapproachement with Iran. In effect, the Sunni states were saying a Persian empire will not be tolerated even if it has American approval. The Obama administration's decision to withdraw military presence from the Middle East has led to a vacuum filled until now by Iranian special forces. This Saudi-led strike in Yemen is a new chapter in this ongoing saga. Sunni nations that may have had their differences in the past are now seemingly united for the security of the region and purposely poised to challenge Iranian imperial ambitions.

For the past seven months the Houthi minority seized control of the capital and the government, deposing president Abed Rabbo Mansour Hadi, an ally of Saudi Arabia. The Houthis were assisted by—probably led by—the Iranian Revolutionary Guard. By seizing control, Iran surrounded Saudi Arabia at key sea choke points, the portals to the Red Sea and the Strait of Hormuz. The Saudi ambassador to the U.S., Adel al-Jubeir, said, "The endgame is to remove the threat to Yemen and the threat to Saudi Arabia."

It is also an endgame to pool Sunni military assets to fight extremism in Syria, Iraq and Libya, dissolving states dependent on Iran in one way or another. The summit of 21 Arab League members will concentrate on drafting a resolution to create a permanent military force for the region, what might emerge as the NATO of the Middle East.

The airstrikes on Yemen do put the U.S. in an awkward position, since the easing of sanctions and an accommodative posture on nuclear weapons depend on an Iran that will live up to an accord. That level of confidence is certainly not shared by the Sunni nations.

Relying on rehearsed talking points, Secretary of State John Kerry commended the coalition, even going as far as mentioning American logistical support. However, he did not mention the withdrawal of all American troops from Yemen, nor was there any comment about President Obama's assertion that "counterinsurgency is working well in Yemen." And Secretary Kerry did not refer to the priority the U.S. attaches to nuclear talks with Iran.

For most in the Middle East, the claim is, if the U.S. will not protect us, the gulf states must protect themselves. This alliance is not only a military condominium, it is an arrangement fostered by fear and finance. Egypt's food needs must be imported. Turkey's economy declined precipitously after 2008 when foreign direct investments dried up. It is now a nation dependent on Saudi and UAE investment. The Sudan is an African basket case unable to recover from decades of civil war. Gulf state funds help to keep it afloat.

In this case, he who has the cash calls the tune. The Saudis and UAE have the cash and the concern about Iranian threats. What this military coalition suggests is that Iranian hegemony—which is what the U.S. relied on as a stabilizing regional factor—is now being called into question. A genuine counterweight to Iran is emerging, and this may be one of the few positive signs in a region wracked by chaos.

From the Barbary Pirates to the Seizure of U.S. Naval Vessels (2016)
Originally published on Family Security Matters

Although they often disagreed, John Adams and Thomas Jefferson had a mutually agreeable conversation—when the mantle of authority was being transferred (1800)—over the impressment of American seamen by Muslim leaders in North Africa. As U.S. commercial interests in the Mediterranean increased at the beginning of the 19th century, our ships were seized and seamen were forced into imprisonment and slavery.

President Jefferson indicated that the extortion payment made for the release of our citizens was humiliating. It was this sentiment that led directly to the creation of the American navy, a navy that ultimately protected the freedom of the seas for more than two centuries.

Now, however, watching American sailors on their knees with hands behind their heads, the humiliation that this nation suffered in the past has seemingly reappeared in the present. Obviously the two events are not the same; no two events separated by centuries are.

The White House downplayed the incident, indicating our sailors were well treated, with Secretary Kerry even thanking Iranian leadership for the release of the sailors. Vice President Biden made reference to the critical role of diplomacy and said at no point did our sailors apologize. Yet the facts belie these assertions.

One video shows a U.S. service member speaking to a questioner, admitting wrongdoing and apologizing. In fact, as Vice President Biden and Secretary Kerry should know, the Geneva Conventions, which govern military conflicts, ban the practice of employing prisoners for propagandistic purposes. The Iranian government had the videos in question plastered all over national television screens.

Several U.S. lawmakers described the arrest and detention, including the seizure of arms, as unjustifiable. Senator John McCain assailed the White House praise of Iran. He said, "The administration is pretending as if nothing out of the ordinary occurred. By failing to affirm basic principles of international law, it places our Navy and Coast Guard vessels and the men and woman who sail them at increased risk in the future."

It has long been recognized that it is unlawful for governments to use photographs or videos of military detainees for propaganda purposes, as was done routinely by North Koreans and the North Vietnamese military in the past. Whether there was a technical violation of the Geneva Conventions is a matter to be determined by lawyers, but there is little doubt the spirit and intentions of the Convention were violated.

While there is some indication the two U.S. naval vessels entered Iranian waters en route from Kuwait to Bahrain, the Iranian navy could have pointed the vessels in the right direction and sent them on their way. By addressing the vessels at gunpoint and forcing the seamen to their knees, it would appear that the Iranian government had an ulterior motive.

This was an opportunity to suggest that Iran is the "strong horse" in the region and American power and influence are in decline. President Obama would object to the characterization, as he did in his State of the Union address, but he seems to be oblivious to the way American power, or lack thereof, is regarded in the Middle East. Moreover, it would seem that the Iranian deal on nuclear questions has forced the U.S. to be self-deterred. There isn't any action that would put the Obama administration in the position of jeopardizing the P5+1 agreement with Iran. As a consequence, Iran tests U.S. mettle almost every day. It tests through U.S. citizens once held unlawfully, albeit recently released in a prisoner exchange. It tests with the flight of missiles that could carry mock nuclear weapons in violation of the accord. It tests by firing missiles near the USS *Harry S. Truman* in the Strait of Hormuz. It tests by seizing U.S. naval vessels.

Despite a lack of resources, President Jefferson vowed to build a flotilla that would force the Muslim leaders of North Africa to desist from acts of piracy. He did, which explains why the mast of the *Philadelphia*, a ship we intentionally scuttled in the war with the pirates, still stands in Tripoli. It explains why we sing, "From the halls of Montezuma to the shores of Tripoli."

Rarely in our past were presidents self-deterred. In fact President Lincoln captured the American spirit on December 1, 1862, when he said, "Fellow citizens, we cannot escape history. We of this

Congress and this administration will be remembered in spite of ourselves. No personal significance or insignificance can spare one or another of us. The fiery trial through which we pass will light us down, in honor or dishonor, to the latest generation." We are that latest generation and we might ask if we are lighted down with honor or dishonor. Yes, we cannot escape history.

Syria

Thinking About Syria (2013)

Among baseball's general managers it is often said that "the best trade is the one that was never made." Although it is an obvious stretch to international affairs, it might also be said that the best government action is the one that isn't taken.

For understandable reasons, the Obama administration wants to punish President al-Assad for the use of poison gas and the butchery of women and children. However, President Obama has passed that decision to Congress. But if it does decide to act, what do you do? The destruction of the Syrian air force, to cite one option, will embolden President al-Assad's supporters and demonstrate that the U.S. is a paper tiger unwilling to put boots on the ground. Deploying ground forces will certainly not be entertained, for this would be a quagmire not unlike Afghanistan that the American public will not accept. Massive missile attacks against al-Assad-backed troops will be an obvious aid to al Qaeda, now a military force among rebel troops and a fledging political entity eager to assert itself in a post-al-Assad government.

On top of those unpleasant options is a Russian presence supporting President al-Assad and investing billions of rubles in establishing a naval base on the Mediterranean. The displacement of President al-Assad is not in President Putin's interest, albeit the Syrian civil war has raised the world oil price to well over $100 a barrel—a clear boost for the Russian economy. In the U.S. military's calculations, what the Russians are likely to do after a military strike is one of several imponderables, arguably among the most dangerous.

Then there are the Iranians who regard President al-Assad as an ally and a surrogate in the promotion of Iran's imperial agenda. Hezbollah's rocket force is an extension of Iran's interest and a perpetual threat against Israel. With representatives in the Lebanon government and the use of local strong-armed tactics, Iran can shape the course of Lebanon's future and keep pressure on Israel simultaneously. Hence any U.S. action in Syria has to anticipate an Iranian response. Moving military chess pieces in this part of the world and at this time is very complicated.

Had the Obama administration carefully identified its interests and assets when the civil war broke out two years ago, there was a chance moderate rebel forces could have been assisted. That time has passed. In fact, U.S. passivity is one reason al Qaeda has been able to insinuate itself into the rebel mix. This example should demonstrate that "leading from behind" is really not leading at all.

Should the Syrian war reach some conclusion, even a semblance of stability, the U.S. might well promote geographic reallocation. Just as the British Foreign Office drew artificial boundaries in the 19th century—creating Syria—the U.S. and, yes, Russia, might conclude the three-state solution is in their mutual interest. Assume for the sake of argument an Alawite, a Kurdish and a Sunni state.

The Alawite state could promote Russia's desire for the maintenance of its naval base. The Kurdish state could generate entrepreneurial activity, including enhanced oil revenue for a decimated economy. Although regarded as a threat to Turkey, the Kurdish government would be obliged to renounce a Greater Kurdistan in return for its own state in former Syrian territory. The Sunni state would be embraced by Saudi Arabia and Turkey. Its very existence would be a counterweight to Iranian ambitions, even though Iran would most likely be recognized as an ally by the Alawite government.

Of course, this scheme is far too rational, especially in a part of the world activated by irrational impulses. At the moment, negotiations for stability cannot be considered. Bloodshed on both sides will continue, and the Syrian people will be battered and killed. The international community will wring its hands and gnash its teeth, but is unable to wrestle effectively with this problem.

Most significantly, the U.S. is damned if it does something and damned if it does nothing. The time for action has long passed, as the lessons of history reappear before the present naïve panjandrums of foreign policy.

The Syrian Negotiations (2015)
Originally published on the Manhattan Institute

The projection of power doesn't always solve problems. There are times when inaction is desirable. One might even make a case for U.S. withdrawal from the Middle East, albeit I do not make it and do not embrace it.

The problem is that when American interests are imperiled and U.S. allies are drifting into conflict, inaction is unacceptable. Perhaps what is even more unacceptable is actively adopting the position of presumptive enemies.

Without much fanfare, U.S. officials have agreed to Iran's participation in a multinational conference on the civil war in Syria, the first example of post-nuclear-deal "cooperation."

The talks will bring together diplomats from a dozen countries that have strikingly different positions on the Syrian War—and whose ties to Iran verge from warm to frigid.

In the frigid category is Saudi Arabia, a regional rival politically and religiously. Since 400 Iranian pilgrims died last month in Mina outside of Mecca during the Hajj, relations have regressed to icy.

Russia and Iran are backers of Syrian president Bashar al-Assad, while the U.S., Turkey and Saudi Arabia contend the only way to tamp down the civil war is by deposing President al-Assad. It may well be that the only long term multinational framework that could work is a Russian-Iranian-named successor who would continue to do their bidding, yet is someone who could give President Obama cover for a Pyrrhic victory.

Clearly, the motivation for the meeting and the apparent urgency is the wave of refugees that threaten to destabilize nations bordering Syria. António Guterres, the UN high commissioner for refugees, said, "Everyone understands the danger, not only to the region but to global security." As is the case with every crisis identified by UN officials, the answer is "more"—more money. What hasn't been addressed is why Saudi Arabia hasn't taken more refugees and refuses to consider this option.

The imponderable in these discussions will be President Putin's flexibility. It is already obvious that Russia is dictating policy to the United States. In crass terms, it has forced the U.S. to choose between President al-Assad and the Islamic State. If these negotiations mean anything to the secretary of state—who has been consistently outwitted—it is whether there is some concession he can get from Russia, even if it is the installation of a puppet government in Syria that gives President al-Assad the boot. That has been the Americans' stance until now. As a result of "negotiations," the U.S. has agreed to keep President al-Assad installed "for the foreseeable future."

All will agree the Islamic State is a regional threat, but the only nations with boots on the ground, Iran and Russia, are more interested in attacking the rebels opposing President al-Assad than Daesh forces. In fact, ISIL-created chaos works to the advantage of President Putin, since his aircraft clear the skies and his troops take positions. Middle East leaders do not have to be reminded about the regional "strong horse."

While the U.S. has a seat at the negotiating table, it hasn't any leverage, as the decision on al-Assad suggests. The Turks have the military means to degrade the Islamic State, but are far more interested in bombing Kurdish rebels who pose a threat to Erdogan's interests. The Saudis want to see al-Assad deposed— and are willing to support rebel troops to make that happen—but will not deploy their own forces in the effort. And the U.S. channels military equipment to the Peshmerga through Iraq, with most of it ending up on the Iranian black market. In fact, the Peshmerga forces rely on World War II vintage weapons when they can get them.

Hence Secretary Kerry is a recalcitrant puppet, but a puppet nevertheless, with Russian and Iranian puppeteers pulling the strings. Many contend talks are better than war. Of course, that is true, to a point. But when your interests are defined by others, when your bargaining leverage has been withdrawn, when you proceed to deepen your nation in a quandary of hopeless options, it might be better to avoid negotiations entirely.

The Gang of 51 (2015)

One can only wonder what is being served at the Foggy Bottom cafeteria. It was recently reported that 51 State Department officials, all of whom advise the Secretary of State on Syria, wrote a "dissent channel cable" arguing for military strikes against Bashar al-Assad's government and urging regime change as the stratagem for the defeat of the Islamic State.

By any standard, this is a remarkable statement. It's as if gravity is moving in reverse. The one question that stands out among many is, how did this gang of 51 come to this epiphany after eight years of mouthing the silly foreign policy nostrums of President Obama and Secretary Kerry?

It is also clear that CIA director John Brennan joined the dissent chorus. In fact, he may have been the inspiration for it when he testified that President Obama's war against the Islamic State is failing.

But what does this dissent cable actually mean? The answer is, not much. Despite a call for military strikes against President al-Assad, the U.S. has agreed he must stay in power for the foreseeable future, and U.S. policy, emanating from the nuclear deal with Iran, is that we will assist the Iranian Revolutionary Guard in the war against the Islamic State.

If extrapolated to its logical conclusion, strikes against President al-Assad are strikes against Iran and Russia. The war that has already resulted in 4 million refugees and 400,000 lives would be dramatically worse should the U.S. adopt the view of the "51." Hence, the question of what is being served in the State Department cafeteria.

On the one hand, these advisers are saying we cannot take it anymore. The Obama policy in Syria is a mistake at this time. Keep in mind President Obama in 2011 and 2012 maintained President al-Assad must go. So in a sense, these dissenters are reiterating the Obama originalist position.

On the other hand, this policy proposal is misguided. The U.S. is not prepared for a wider war, which these recommendations implicitly suggest. Nor is this government prepared to engage Russia in direct confrontation. It is, of course, true that the so-called peace negotiations over Syria cannot possibly yield peace, a point that has been obvious from the outset.

It is encouraging to know at long last someone in the administration is aware of the perverse direction of President Obama's foreign policy. Too bad, however, that the criticism is too late and ill considered. Moreover, neither Hillary Clinton nor Donald Trump has used this open rebellion to advantage. It is likely that the failure of the present, now recognized with the dissent cable, presages failure in the future.

Yemen

In September of 2014, a group of Shiite-backed rebels called the Houthis stormed the Yemeni capital and forced the government from power. The Houthis have ties to Iran: the U.S. intelligence community has uncovered covert operations of the Iranians providing arms to the Houthis to aid in the rebellion. U.S. Sunni allies in the region, such as Saudi Arabia and Egypt, view the Houthi coup as a power play by Iran.

Succession, Rivalry and Uncertainty (2015)

Originally published on The Hill

The deposition of Yemen's president by Houthi rebels supported by Iran Qud militiamen and the death of Saudi king Abdullah have opened a Pandora's box of unknown conditions in the Middle East. U.S. officials describe this confluence of events as leading to uncertainty in the region.

The Saudi kingdom has seen the United States as a protector, but the U.S. rapprochement with Iran has made the Saudi leadership uneasy. Overtures to Egypt and the UAE for defense cooperation are a symptom of emerging distrust with U.S. motives, leadership and alliance obligations.

A transition of Saudi leadership from King Abdullah to the former ruler's half brother Salman bin Abdulaziz may reduce the ability of the kingdom to move decisively if challenged by the Iranian-backed Houthi rebels that have taken over Yemen, on the southern border of Saudi Arabia.

The eastern provinces of Saudi Arabia, where the oil fields are located, have been the prize for Iran. In this region resides the nation's Shia minority, yet another justification for Iranian intervention. Talks between the U.S. and Iran over Tehran's nuclear program are viewed by Riyadh as a sign of a weakening American-Saudi alliance and circumstantial evidence the U.S. has been negotiating behind King Abdullah's back.

U.S. officials, speaking with diplomatic caution, assured the new leadership of support and a willingness to contain the civil war in Yemen. One overarching question looming in future discussions is whether the Saudi kingdom will continue pumping oil at extremely high levels, driving the price per barrel down and forcing competitors into an economic slide. With 20 percent of the global oil reserves, Saudi Arabia can tolerate this revenue downturn, but there is little doubt this strategy is having an adverse effect on its chief rival, Iran, and other nations dependent on oil for their hard currency.

Saudi Arabian rulers are likely to continue their present moderate course of action, perhaps even attempting to buy off the Houthis rather than confront them. What remains unknown is how the Houthi leadership will respond. If they see the Saudi rulers as hesitant or equivocal, they may use Yemen as a staging area for an attack. Another scenario has the Houthis aligning with the Islamic State to put additional pressure on the Saudi kingdom, notwithstanding the fact that Iran—the Houthis' benefactor—is fighting against the Islamic State in Syria and Iraq.

Uncertainly is the only way to characterize these unfolding events. They are made even more complicated by the fact that King Abdullah's younger brother who has succeeded him is 79 and the crown prince 69. As a consequence, a whole new line of succession must be established, a condition that is invariably disruptive. Moreover, no one really knows how this transition will play out and whether it will put Saudi Arabia in a vulnerable position. While it is unlikely the kingdom will face a popular revolution from within, this scenario cannot be discounted. Shifts in policy tend to be incremental. Nonetheless, close to half of the population is under 24, and many are jockeying for position and being raised with a sense of entitlement. Young people tend to be impatient.

The more immediate threat is exogenous. Iran's influence in Yemen is worrying. In addition, with virtual control of the Red Sea and the Strait of Hormuz, Iran dominates the sea lanes Saudi Arabia depends on for the exportation of its oil. In the recent past, Saudi Arabia could call on its American ally to protect its regional interests. That guarantee is no longer assured. If President Obama is intent on playing the Iran card to defeat the Islamic State and then being accommodative on the nuclear enrichment front, Saudi options will limited.

Will King Salman secure nuclear weapons if Iran is given a green light for fissile material in the P5+1 negotiations? Will the Houthis seize a moment of indecision to attack? Will Iran use its regional influence to broker a deal with Saudi Arabia, one that leaves the U.S. out of the diplomatic equation? These are questions that boggle the imagination; they also impinge on the future of the region.

Sunni and Israeli Concerns

As Iran continues to benefit from President Obama's favor, the Sunni allies of the United States and Israel are growing increasingly concerned. Complicating the situation are a war-torn neighboring Syria and the unchecked and violent behemoth of the Islamic State. President Obama's soft power provided little comfort to American friends in the region.

The Middle East Winter of Discontent (2014)
Originally published on Townhall

The Arab Spring has evolved fully into the Winter of Our Discontent. An American overture for negotiation with Iran over nuclear weapons and its apparent rapprochement have set in motion tectonic changes beyond the forecasting ability of any so-called analysts.

Let me cite two examples. Saudi Arabia was once an ally of the United States, notwithstanding its promotion of Wahabbist ideology around the globe. This nation of princes bought U.S. weapons, paid handsomely for visits by public officials and, most significantly, relied on a U.S. nuclear and defense umbrella for national security.

That is now virtually at an end. From the Saudi standpoint, the end of the sanctions regimen—they were effectively abrogated with the Iran negotiation agreement—and the tilt by the State Department away from the Egyptian military government have sent a powerful message to King Abdullah that Saudi and American interests are clearly at odds.

Public expression of President Obama's "political weakness" and "foreign policy incompetence" is unprecedented in Saudi circles. Yet this is commonly expressed today. There is the recurring belief that President Obama will allow Iran to possess nuclear weapons, or at least possess enough refined uranium to produce nuclear weapons, thereby putting at risk Saudi oil fields located in Shia areas of this Sunni nation.

From the Saudi point of view, the rise of Iran as a potential nuclear power is unacceptable. The combination of a political and military threat has precipitated a leap to Pakistan for the purchase of a Saudi nuclear weapon. Proliferation is accelerating.

Should the Saudis possess the bomb as a deterrent, Sunni friends in Turkey and Egypt will demand the same. The genie of self-abnegation is out of the bottle, and Sunni nations that may disagree on tactics are fully united in an anti-Iran strategy. Left out of this equation is the United States, even though the U.S. once had cordial ties to Turkey, Saudi Arabia and Egypt.

That, of course, brings me to the question of the U.S.-Egypt relationship. With the overthrow of Mohamed Morsi and the Muslim Brotherhood government, the United States has maintained a distinctly cold attitude toward the military leadership, contending that it is an illegitimate government underserving of diplomatic legitimacy. The uprising against President Morsi has been limned as a "military coup" preventing the dispatch of Apache helicopters to Egypt. These Apaches had been promised to fight the war in the Sinai against well-armed terrorists, including al Qaeda operatives. Now they are frozen in State Department bureaucratic files.

This tactic is a little like cutting off your nose to spite your face. If the terrorists are our enemy and the enemy of our friend Israel, the U.S. should do whatever is necessary to see them defeated. Yet remarkably we sit on the sidelines as Abdel Fattah al-Sisi, the likely next president, negotiates with Russia for the military assets Egypt requires. Willy-nilly, the U.S. has thrown Egypt into the willing arms of Russia, now fully ensconced in the Middle East, from which it was forced to withdraw in the 1980s. By any measure, the U.S. appears weak, unreliable and equivocal—characteristics one would not associate with a firm ally.

The challenges represented by these two national examples suggest a foreign policy that is uneven and, one might say, unusual. It appears as if the friends of yesteryear are easily overlooked in the eagerness to broker a deal with Iran. The implications of that policy are reverberating from Moscow to the Levant. Moreover,

Iran, recognizing the eagerness of the Obama team for a deal, has the U.S. over a barrel. The terms to be set are largely in the hands of the mullahs. Weakness begets aggression, as the lessons of history are revisited by an American administration residing in a fog of resignation.

Saudi Arabia at Odds with U.S. Over Iran (2016)
Originally published on Newsmax

From 2009 to the present, the Obama administration has been committed to the withdrawal of American forces from the Middle East, replaced by the management of regional state players. But this position is entirely ahistoric. From the Romans to the Crusaders, from the Mamelukes to the Ottomans, British and French, the Middle East *has never* ruled itself or managed stability through nation states.

Hence, the emergence of Saudi-Iranian hostility and the inability of these nations to reach an accord over Syria are a surprise to Secretary of State Kerry and the president, but to regional states this is merely the continuation of history.

Saudi Arabia at its core, and despite recent claims to the contrary, is a Wahhabist state that abhors Shiism as a perversion of the true Islamic creed. When the JCPOA accord was signed, Saudi leaders believed they had been sold out by the U.S. and Europeans, representatives that did not take into account Iranian imperial goals and the problem they cause for Saudi Arabia. As King Salman sees it, the United States cannot protect Saudi interests and cannot even secure its own interests.

As evidence, the Saudis cite the violation of the accord through Iran's advanced missile tests and an Iranian rocket fired close to the USS *Harry S. Truman* sailing in the Strait of Hormuz. In none of these instances did the U.S. issue more than a token protest. In fact,

Iran was invited to the Vienna peace talks on Syria's future, despite the incidents.

Saudi leaders now openly contest an American security umbrella, believing that the U.S. has tilted its allegiance to Iran and feeling it is unmoored from any alliance.

Complicating the Saudi position is the Shia minority that has demonstrated forcefully against the House of Saud. The execution of Nimr al-Nimr was an effort to challenge the fire-breathing rhetoric of Shia leaders and, as important, to demonstrate the hold Wahhabism maintains in the country.

It has not gone unnoticed that Saudi oil fields are located mainly in the eastern part of the nation, an area populated by minority Shia members. When Iranian leaders talk about ethnic unification, it sets off alarm bells in Riyadh. This sentiment is aggravated by President Obama's assertion that strategic balance is needed between Sunnis and Shiites. Saudi leaders read this as a pro-Shia statement.

Moreover, Saudi foreign minister Adel al-Jubeir, who is now heading the nation's diplomatic effort, was the target of an Iranian assassination attempt when he was the ambassador to Washington in 2011. Despite mild protests, this matter was ignored in the run-up to the so-called Iran deal. That, too, hasn't been forgotten by the Saudi leaders.

For leaders on both sides of the Islamic divide, it is clear that the withdrawal of the U.S. from regional influence has consequences unanticipated by American analysts. This is not a free-for-all, but the Saudis have adopted the mantle of authority for Sunni interests and Iran is the putative authority of Shiites. Although the U.S. has clearly played its once-dominant hand, maladroitly creating tension where it might have been avoided, it is also clear that there are pathologies in the Middle East that all the diplomacy in the world cannot resolve.

The muscular proactive Saudi foreign policy is coming into focus based on the beliefs that: the U.S. cannot be counted on, oil interests must be protected at all costs, internal dissention cannot be tolerated and Iran is an eternal enemy whose imperial goals must be stemmed.

If a U.S. president understands these concerns, a modus vivendi with the Saudis might be achieved. If not, the Saudis will act in a manner that challenges U.S. goals, particularly in Syria. The Saudi voice in Washington at the moment is largely mute, but since events in this tumultuous Middle East region are so dynamic, one cannot be sure about tomorrow's scenario.

Choosing Sides for World War IV (2014)
Originally published on Accuracy in Media

With the fall of Mosul to ISIS terrorists, the goal of a new state incorporating territory in northern Iraq and Syria may be a reality. As I see it, this is more than a Sunni-Shia conflict within the confines of one region. It has the potential to be the catalyst for World War IV, the Cold War being World War III.

All of the geographic suppositions of the past have been challenged. The lines defining Syria have been decimated. Syria will be dismantled along with Iraq. A Kurdish state is a distinct possibility even though Turkey will be vigorously opposed to it. Jordan's future is now in peril, forcing Israel to protect its eastern front. Iran will join its Shia allies in Iraq to realize as much of the country as possible and to oppose the Sunni Islamic State. Because of pressure from Congress, the U.S. is likely to provide support and logistical aid to the al-Maliki government in Iraq and assist Iranian efforts to stabilize the region, notwithstanding the rivalry between the U.S. and Iran on a host of other issues, including nuclear weapons development.

Waiting in the wings are the Sunni nations of Egypt, the UAE, Turkey and Saudi Arabia that fear Shia imperialistic impulses more than the Islamic State. Should Iran exploit this tumultuous situation to enhance its own position, those Sunni states would be obliged to act. Similarly, Prime Minster Netanyahu and other Israeli leaders cannot stand by and allow Jordan to be uprooted by ISIS radicals.

The peace with Jordan has preserved relative stability on Israel's eastern border for several decades.

Complicating matters is the nuclear weapons issue. In every escalation scenario, the possibility of nuclear exchange is the termination point. But with Iran on the cusp of development and Saudi Arabia consummating a deal for weapons acquisition with Pakistan, the genie is out of the bottle and the region is a powder keg.

Since Islam sometimes masquerades as a religion behind a political ideology, its politicized version promoted by Daesh, al Qaeda, the Khomeinists in Iran, the Taliban and Boko Haran is eager to establish a worldwide caliphate even if deprived of its theological mooring. The events, as they are unfolding in the Middle East, offer a scenario for a worldwide convulsion. While the caliphate project is unrealistic, at the moment it inspires radical aspirations leading to a recipe for conflict, terrorism and World War IV.

President Obama assumes the United States can remain immune from the horror. He decided to withdraw our forces precipitously from Iraq, even though the general staff warned him of the consequences. Now he has very few options, albeit war has a way of calling on you even if you are openly opposed to it. The declaration by President Obama that with the departure of our forces from Iraq, that nation will be free from war and a comment from Vice President Biden that Iraq is now stable and democratic were grossly unrealistic.

A foreign policy based on a denial of reality and a belief that U.S. intervention is always wrong have produced a world infinitely more dangerous than the one in the period before the Obama administration. If this government does not recover from its myopia, the U.S. will be dragged into the war whether we like it or not. Terrorism will be on the rise, and no American will be secure around the world or even within the confines of the United States.

The ISIS forces represent the front line in the Middle East's tectonic changes. Borders will be redrawn, tribal loyalties will energize full-blown as a motivation for geographic alteration and the revolutionary surge is likely to manifest itself on several fronts. This is not the end of the Arab Spring, but the commencement of the Middle East War, a war that has the capacity to enlist many non-Arab states.

The idea that Islam can resolve its political conflicts is a chimera. Iran's former president Khatami claims the Enlightenment is responsible for wars. His rational exegesis relies on Islamic tradition and protecting his people from Western political and cultural influences.

There isn't any turning back. The first, and arguably most important, consideration is the recognition of reality—what we as a nation can and cannot do and what we must prepare for. To do any less would be catastrophic. Time to engage in less texting, golf-playing and TV-watching and more strategic thinking. This is the challenge now facing Americans in the emergence of a potential World War.

Turkey

*In an interview with **Time** magazine in 2012, President Obama heralded Turkish prime minister Recep Erdogan as a trusted ally on the world stage. Since that time, President Obama has had to turn his head to some of the Erdogan government's worst offenses against Western Democratic values and the Turkish people.*

Misunderstanding History in the Middle East (2014)

President Obama is fond of saying his closest ally on the foreign stage is Prime Minister Recep Tayyip Erdogan. On almost any level this is a mistake of monumental proportions or a misguided judgment call or sheer ignorance.

Since taking office, Prime Minister Erdogan has moved his AKP party into a political movement that strives to oust and replace secular elites and traditional Turkish institutions that had bound the nation to Western values and American interests. Prior to the rise of the AKP, Turkey was rooted in NATO, had a friendly relationship with Israel and could be relied on to tilt to the West on key foreign policy issues.

That was yesteryear. Under Prime Minister Erdogan's leadership Turkey has emerged as a regional power claiming Ottoman Empire ambitions and, most notably, considers itself a leader in the Islamic world, particularly among Sunni Muslims. This sea change in attitude and policy has significant implications for the United States.

Some analysts in Washington still rely on a vision of Turkey as a bulwark against Soviet aggression. Still others rely on President Atatürk's modernization program. And then there are those who believe Turkey, despite the fear of Muslim emigration, can be a moderate addition to the European Union.

Prime Minister Erdogan obviously sees it differently. Based on his written and spoken commentary, the prime minister regards Turkey as *primus inter pares* among Muslim nations. Moreover, this desire for Muslim leadership has been accompanied by a distinctly anti-Western attitude, notwithstanding Turkey's role in protecting the southern flank of NATO. In part, I suspect, this attitude is a reflection of Europe's rejection of Turkey as an EU member. But this policy shift goes beyond retaliation.

On one matter, there isn't controversy: the United States has not resisted the Turkish strategic reorientation. In fact, President Obama still refers to Turkey as a Muslim "role model." This conciliatory viewpoint lacks a sense of reality and a contingency plan to curtail the AKP's neo-Ottoman ambitions.

Time after time Prime Minister Erdogan has challenged essential U.S. interests. For example, Turkey continues to trade with Iran in violation of UN sanctions. It is a sponsor of Hamas and engaged in, in fact has promoted, the attempted break of the Israeli Gaza blockade. Most significantly, he hasn't been penalized for these actions, in large part because the U.S. administration has not formulated a substantive strategy toward Turkey other than the personal friendship between the two leaders. Despite assurances to the contrary, personal ties are not a policy.

Moreover, the prime minister has recently shown his repressive side by denouncing and arresting peaceful demonstrators as "provocateurs and terrorists." The presumption is that a conspiracy, Ergenekon, is an underground ultra-nationalist group bent on destabilizing the country, albeit evidence to support this claim is slim. Nonetheless, Prime Minister Erdogan's vindictive side is on display, even giving supporters concern about his rule. Despite President Obama's often-cited rationalizations, Prime Minister Erdogan is creating an environment in which the future will be determined by his whims. This internal policy is consistent with Prime Minister Erdogan's foreign policy.

In 2009 Prime Minister Erdogan transparently proffered his anti-Western stance by describing sanctions against Iran's "peaceful" nuclear program as "arrogant." He even went so far as to contend that if the U.S. and Israel want Iran to give up nuclear weapons, they should be obliged to do the same. But Prime Minister Erdogan is also a policy schizophrenic. On the one hand, he does not envision Iran as an enemy, but on the other hand, he allowed NATO to install an anti-missile radar facility on his soil that was clearly designed to protect Europe from a potential Iranian missile threat. Some have argued this is a meaningless gesture designed to mollify his detractors in Europe and the U.S. but is not a transformative policy shift.

Turkey's goal appears to be evident based on most of its actions: a model oriented to Muslim domination with the immediate objective of binding Arab nations to a Turkish sphere of influence. If that is the case, which I believe conditions confirm, the U.S. must awaken itself from self-satisfied slumber and realize AKP regional influence dilutes U.S. influence. At the very least, a hard-headed assessment of Turkey's strategic position is called for with an emphasis on its regional ambitions and its internal schism with secular forces. Turkey could once again become a key ally of U.S. interests, but that is not likely to occur as long as President Obama confuses friendship with regional competition.

Turkey: Are We Giving Away the Store? (2010)
Originally published on the Gatestone Institute

The arrival of the USS *Harry S. Truman* strike group in the Persian Gulf and the Arabian Sea and its war games with France and Israel, as well as reinforcements for American forces in Azerbaijan (on the Iranian border) could be mere saber-rattling or a prelude to an attack on Iran's nuclear facilities. Whatever the motive, it is also clear that Turkey, as a NATO member, has access to a wide array of American military technology that could reveal our aims to adversaries in the Middle East. With a dramatic shift in its political orientation and increasingly close ties to Hamas, Hezbollah and Iran, Turkey has the potential to cause great damage to American regional interests and even forestall possible military action.

Yet the Obama administration has shown little interest in the radical reorientation with Turkey and its relationship to NATO according to a JINSA (Jewish Institute for National Security Affairs) report. The recent arrest of past and present military figures who are defenders of secularism should have prompted comment from the White House. Instead, there has been conspicuous silence. Similarly, the Turkish role with the Gaza flotilla and the inflammatory rhetoric that emanated from the Turkish corridors of power received very little attention from the State Department.

Clearly the Obama team does not want to jeopardize its alliance with Turkey, but it is also clear that Turkish intelligence services are working overtime to separate the military from Israel and former Western allies. From the U.S. perspective, a key concern is whether these moves lead to the sharing of information with our enemies, information that could undermine any action against Iran, Syria, Hamas and Hezbollah.

It should be noted that Turkey has the third-largest air force in NATO, with 230 F-16s. It has several refueling tankers, four AWACs to direct air battles and a navy with diesel submarines, and amphibious capability. Moreover, the United States has not taken any steps to reduce or eliminate the flow of military technology or systems to Turkey. On the contrary, because Turkey has a small contingent in Afghanistan, the U.S. regards this commitment as critical to its counterinsurgency program. But this commitment comes with serious risks. Turkey's growing closeness to Iran could complicate Afghanistan's future, particularly if ideological collaboration trumps all other strategic concerns.

That the U.S. appears to be dithering as Turkey moves away from its former friends is alarming to other nations in the region. It also foreshadows a U.S. withdrawal from the Middle East. General McChrystal said that in his meetings with President Obama, the president seemed disengaged and uninterested. It may be that this too was sign of America's emotional as well as physical disengagement from the region.

If that is true—and there is little reason to doubt it—it augurs for a dangerous period. A political vacuum is always filled. Iran is the emerging "strong horse" in this neighborhood, and everyone from Prime Minister al-Maliki to Prime Minister Erdogan realizes as much.

Can the U.S. recapture its influence after displaying a lack of interest? Will it allow Turkey to use its strategic association with NATO in order to advantage Iran? Will Turkey interfere directly or indirectly to thwart any military operation against Iran's nuclear facilities? These questions are not answerable at this time, but in the answers rests the fate of the Middle East and perhaps the world. As the French poet Charles Péguy noted: "Everything starts in mystery and ends in politics."

Returning Captured American Enemies to the Middle Eastern Battlefield

One of President Obama's priorities as president was to close the Guantanamo maximum security prison facility operated by the United States on the Cuban mainland. At this facility, the worst of America's foreign opponents, including many violent leaders of Middle Eastern terror groups, are housed. According to a 2014 report by the office of the Director of National Intelligence, 30%

of the detainees released from Guantanamo are suspected or confirmed as having returned to terror activities. Twelve of those released were confirmed to have killed Americans back on the battlefield.

The President's Prisoner Exchange (2014)
Originally published on Family Security Matters

For a considerable period I have argued that President Obama's foreign policy has been feckless, a function of inexperience and amateurish advisement. The overarching goal of removing the U.S. from harm's way seemed absurd, since even if you want to avoid war, it sometimes has a way of finding you. But there is logic in a foreign policy position that avoids overreaching.

However, I now believe I was wrong. Based on the diplomatic trade of one American, an apparent deserter and critic of national policy, for five terrorists who have killed Americans and have vowed to kill more, I now hold the view that this president is malevolent, that his hatred for the United States takes the form of "high crimes and misdemeanors."

Without providing Congress with the "required" 30 days' notice before releasing prisoners at Guantanamo Bay, the president acted, claiming "unique and exigent circumstances." The real story lies in a president who thinks of himself as being above the law. For him Congress is irrelevant.

The president's pursuit of Sergeant Bergdahl led directly to the loss of six Americans in Afghanistan, even though the president asserts, "We do not leave Americans on the battlefield." Do we retrieve deserters? This incident that now puts American lives at risk across the globe is worse than lawlessness; it is a violation of trust that imperils innocent life. If ever there was a time to consider the exquisitely made arguments in Andrew McCarthy's book *Faithless Execution: Building the Case for Obama's Impeachment*, it is now. This president does not abide by the rule of law. He is the law and a dangerous law at that.

This "deal" is seemingly timed to push the VA (Veterans Affairs) scandal off the front page. Better to have a new scandal rather than a developing old one. But it is becoming increasingly difficult for this administration to either admit to having made a mistake or avoid making new ones.

Republicans are ready to make their case to the American people, but so far they have treated the event as a commodity that needs funding to address. This is more than a fund-raising opportunity; it is a challenge to the Constitution and the basis for national legitimacy. The republic is at stake in more ways than John and Mary Q. Public realize.

Of course, any challenge by Republicans will immediately raise the specters of racism, a factor that usually stifles debate. In this case, the charge will have to be overlooked if we are to avoid a version of tyranny. America needs a popular outcry that says, "We have had enough, Mr. President."

As C.S. Lewis once noted in a different context, "There is light from behind the sun." This light is the glare of truth. Even those Americans brainwashed by media palliatives must be asking why the president would release terrorists who have vowed to kill Americans and, in at least two cases, have already done so. The question evokes a deep-seated emotional response.

Americans deserve answers; they also deserve a president who acts on behalf of the national welfare. At the moment, there are many who would question his motives and devotion to Constitutional principle.

"Catch and Release": Returning Terrorists to the Battlefield (2009)
Originally published on the Gatestone Institute

For several years human rights activists and defense attorneys have argued that the detainees at Guantanamo pose no security threat and should be released. President Obama, based on a campaign pledge, issued an executive order closing the controversial prison.

In a recent report, the Brookings Institution examined hundreds of pages of declassified military documents and arrived at the conclusion that many of the prisoners held without charges are innocent. The report concludes that only 87 of the 250 detainees have any relationship with al Qaeda, the Taliban or other armed groups hostile to the United States.

Several days later, however, the Pentagon released a report indicating that suspects who had been held but were subsequently released from the Guantanamo prison are increasingly returning to fight against the United States and its allies.

Sixty-one detainees released from the U.S. naval base prison in Cuba are believed to have rejoined the struggle against the United States. The total is up from the 37 reported in March 2008.

Pentagon spokesman Geoff Morrell indicated that "there clearly are people who are being held at Guantanamo who are still bent on doing harm to America, Americans and our allies. So there will have to be some solution for the likes of them, and that is among the thorny issues that the president and his new team are carefully considering." Furthermore Mr. Morrell said that the new numbers show a "substantial increase" in detainees returning to terrorist missions, from 7 to 11 percent. Presumably intelligence, photographs and forensic evidence such as fingerprints and DNA were used to tie the detainees to terrorist activity.

These contradictory reports raise important questions: is Brookings right, is the Pentagon's report on target or do both have valid positions, however different in orientation?

One thing is clear: the notion of 61 or even one released detainee trying to kill Americans is unacceptable. Moreover, the trend is in the wrong direction.

If the president ultimately closes Guantanamo, what will he do with the 250 detainees? Will they be released on the streets of the United States? Will they be sent abroad to fight against American forces in Iraq and Afghanistan?

Human rights attorneys representing the detainees often claim most are innocent of terrorism, but if that were true, they wouldn't return to the battlefield as soon as they are released.

It is instructive that most of the activists are persuaded the detainees pose no threat. That may even be the case with a few of them. Overlooked in their calculation is that these prisoners were apprehended on the battlefield. They aren't criminals who robbed a supermarket; they are trained as killers intent on mayhem. For most Americans, holding these terrorists is a good idea, and to assume they have the rights of American citizens, a very bad idea.

So despite all the declarations suggesting these detainees can be trusted, I demur. Let those go who have incontrovertible evidence they aren't a threat. The rest, however, should be kept in prison, weather it is Guantanamo or any other venue that will have them. Guantanamo made sense, but since it has been caricatured and denounced, alternatives must be found.

But the idea that all of these detainees should be released is absurd on every level, a point even President Obama has come to appreciate. Far better to deny the rights of terrorists than to have them on the battlefield attempting to kill American soldiers.

Who Lost the Middle East?

Who Lost the Middle East? (2015)
Originally published by WAMC Northeast Public Radio

Much has already been written about the feckless foreign policy of the Obama administration or, in some instances, the president's success in masterminding a global American retreat from foreign affairs. As events are unfolding, it is clear the U.S. has voluntarily ceded its interest in the Middle East. In fact, I can anticipate the title of a book a decade from now that reads *Who Lost the Middle East?* similar to the host of books in the 1950s entitled *Who Lost China?*

Perhaps the Middle East wasn't ours to lose. Yet one thing is clear: the Iran deal was proposed as a stabilizing influence in a region that is in disarray. What was not said, but is very much in the calculation, is a Russian, Iranian, Iraqi and Syrian intelligence arrangement that is supposedly the precursor to stability.

Despite presidential puzzlement about President Putin's intentions, that was clear when Iranian Quds commander Qasem Soleimani met with President Putin in Russia on July 24, despite a ban on Soleimani's international travel. President Putin struck a statesmanlike pose during the P5+1 deliberations on Iran, but all the signals indicated he intended to work with Iran to keep President al-Assad of Syria in power. Claims the State Department was blindsided aren't credible. With the Putin-Soleimani talks completed, there could not be any surprise for those who observe the political landscape.

Qasem Soleimani not only had links to terrorism, but he was on the battlefield in Syria defending President al-Assad's forces. Recognizing the assertive role Russia is now playing, President Obama said President Putin has entered a "quagmire," and Secretary of Defense Ashton Carter said we must commence "deconflicting negotiation." If this wasn't a deadly serious matter, one might consider these responses laughable.

The Russian buildup in Syria and the emerging ties with Iran occurred during the P5+1 meetings in Vienna. Not only was President Obama duped on the terms of Iran's nuclear weapons development, but he was myopic on the emerging ties among Russia, Iran, Iraq and Syria. So intent was he on a deal that he chose to ignore what was going on under his nose, without the slightest effort at concealment.

Iran will get the $150 billion when the sanctions are lifted, money that can be used to promote terrorism. The Russians have become the "strong horse" in the Middle East, the force that must be accommodated. And the U.S. sits on the sidelines, an observer unable to do more than express empty words for former allies. Who lost the Middle East? The answer is obvious now.

Charles Péguy, the noted philosopher, said, "Surrender is essentially an operation by means of which we set about explaining instead of acting." What this administration has refined is explanation. The Obama team argues we are degrading the Islamic State even when the intelligence reports are grossly exaggerated and the Islamic State is unrestrained by a modest U.S. bombing campaign. Ash Carter may believe in deconflicting rhetoric, but the Russians believe in deploying fighter jets and the Iranians believe in putting troops on the ground and bombing President al-Assad's opposition.

It is a cliché to contend "talk is cheap." In this case, talk is misleading. President Obama has lost the Middle East and there isn't any question about it.

The Future of the Middle East (2012)

In 1917 two members of the British and French foreign services (Mark Sykes and François-Georges Picot) drew lines in the sand of the Middle East, creating artificial states in place of the dismembered and defeated Ottoman Empire. These states were drawn to satisfy British oil interests and French imperial goals, with a bone thrown to Russian interests as well.

From the magic of map phantasmagoria emerged Lebanon, Syria and Iraq. While imperial interests prevailed, indigenous populations didn't recognize the imagined states. Warlords carved out their own spheres of influence, religious differences translated into tension and the outbreak of hostility, the precarious nature of national identity struggled to catch on and families close to British leadership became monarchs and potentates.

In 2012, more than a hundred years after World War I commenced, the Sykes and Picot plan for the region began to collapse. A civil war in Syria challenged the leadership of Bashar al-Assad. Moreover, with President al-Assad dependent on the Iranian Revolutionary Guard for the survival of his Alawite regime, sides were drawn, with Egypt, the UAE and Saudi Arabia eager to see him deposed and Iran and Russia his defenders.

Since the United States was uninvolved, notwithstanding its former presence in Iraq and Afghanistan, President Obama's "red line" over the use of poison gas by President al-Assad was subcontracted to Russian adjudication. Not only does Russia maintain a base in Syria, but it has reestablished influence in the eastern Mediterranean. Having once been ousted by U.S. forces decades ago, it has now been invited back in by a U.S. government eager for disengagement.

With the precipitous withdrawal of American troops from Iraq, sectarian squabbles led to open warfare. ISIL troops, formerly part of the Sunni brigades organized as a counterweight to Shia militias, overran an Iraqi military ill-equipped to compete. Huge swaths of Syria and Iraq were incorporated into the first formal global caliphate. In effect, Iraq's future as a nation was imperiled. The only relatively stable area in northern Iraq was controlled by the Kurds.

Teetering as the country is, Iraqi leaders turned to its Shia neighbor as a stabilizing influence against ISIL incursions. As a consequence, Iraq has become a vassal state of Iran, an ironic joke that history has played on once-warring enemies.

And then there is Lebanon—no longer a nation but a staging area for Syrian and Iranian objectives. Hezbollah, as a proxy for Iran, controls the military and political infrastructure. The minority Christian population, having been terrorized, emigrated in droves.

By the end of 2015 the Sykes-Picot plan will be effectively eradicated, a prediction borne out by the present unfolding of events. What then becomes of this region bristling with weapons and hatred?

Prediction is a dangerous exercise, particularly over a region with earth-shaking changes from day to day. A Pandora's box has been opened, and the aftermath is fraught with problems. However questionable U.S. actions might have been, the presence of American troops in the Middle East maintained an uneasy equilibrium, but an equilibrium that avoided a Hobbesian world of "each against all." Just as nature cannot tolerate a vacuum, neither can international affairs. The U.S.' departure from Iraq without a standing army agreement and the imminent departure of forces from Afghanistan have led to a dizzying array of events with Iraq, the Islamic State, Russia and terrorist organizations like al Nustra and al Qaeda all competing for control of one kind or another.

The Iranian plan for a Shia Crescent in the Middle East has been gaining ground literally and figuratively. Iran has access to and influence over Beirut, Damascus, Baghdad and Sana'a. It surrounds Saudi Arabia with its control of the entrance to the Red Sea and the Strait of Hormuz. It can now employ Yemen as a staging area for attacks against Saudi Arabia. And with a compliant P5+1 negotiating team, it is likely Iran will possess nuclear weapons or, at least, the fissile material to build them at a date of its choosing.

Without actually saying so, the Obama administration has tilted to the Iranian side. It is believed by President Obama's advisers that Iran can be a stabilizing influence in the Middle East. State department officials note that Iranian troops represent a significant part of an anti-ISIL contingent, a condition that may be responsible for the U.S.' accommodative stance on Iranian nuclear weapons.

As the P5+1 negotiations proceed, "roll-back," or what was once a firm position against Iranian nukes, has receded. Most of the discussion revolves around technical issues—i.e., the number of centrifuges permitted and the degree of uranium enrichment. Hence the belief a pathway for the Iranian bomb has been established.

For Iran "the bomb" has both military and political implications. In any escalation scenario, the fear of nuclear use invites a limited response, lest these weapons of mass destruction are employed. "The bomb" also offers Iran prestige and influence as a nation that can stand up to any other state, including the most powerful on the globe. It is often asked why Iran persists in this pursuit despite sanctions that have adversely affected the economy. The answer lies in a simple cost-benefit analysis: Iran has more to gain with nuclear weapons than it has to lose with sanctions imposed against it.

What this means for the region is apparent. Iran appears as the "strong horse." Its goal of controlling Saudi's oil assets in the eastern, Shia part of Saudi Arabia is realizable. Should Iran be nuclearized, as seems inevitable, a cascade of events is likely. The Sunni nations of Egypt, Saudi Arabia, Bahrain, the UAE, Kuwait and Jordan will create a defense condominium as a counterweight to Iranian aspirations. The pooling of military assets and logistical support is already in place. But it is only a question of time before Saudi Arabia acquires its own nukes from Pakistan, setting in motion the proliferation the U.S. and its allies have worked so hard to contain.

This scenario also puts in play the Israeli enigma. Israel has not attacked Iran because its U.S. benefactor disapproves. Faced with the existential choice of survival or invasion, the president— whether it is Prime Minister Netanyahu or a left-wing successor— has only one choice. This is what Prime Minister Netanyahu will say when he addresses a joint meeting of Congress on May 24. Israel must act or face the prospect of annihilation. Keep in mind that last month during the Vienna negotiations the supreme leader of Iran said, "There is no cure for Israel, only annihilation."

While the Sunni nations may not accept Israel's role with Palestinians, they are likely to avert their gaze should an attack against Iran be launched. In fact, Saudi Arabia has even agreed to refueling arrangements for Israeli aircraft. What this attack will set in motion is regional war.

Iran through its proxies, Hezbollah and Hamas, has stockpiled thousands of missiles—at least 100,000 in Lebanon alone—and has surrounded Israel with this potential threat in the West Bank, Gaza, Syria and Lebanon. Should an attack against Iran occur, however successful in setting back the nuclear program, war would be imminent and terror attacks around the globe would be initiated. Whether President Obama wants to remain on the sidelines or not, these events will force his hand.

Recognizing this grim unfolding, a bipartisan coalition in Congress is demanding a role in the Iranian nuke question. However, it is interesting to note that no one on the Obama team refers to possible resolution as a "treaty," for a treaty constitutionally requires Senate approval. As a consequence, the words "deal" and "arrangement" are used as a masquerade for the actual treaty resolution. Eighty-seven senators led by Senator Menendez, a Democrat, have called for Senate participation in the process as well as sanctions should the talks fail. But President Obama, arguing that the talks must remain on track, has vowed to veto legislation of this kind.

Clearly the status of the Obama presidency lies in the balance. The president regards these talks as his legacy. If he can extract a deal that delays weaponization of Iranian missiles, he will—amid great fanfare—describe it as a peaceful result of artful negotiation, something his predecessors could not achieve. Will Israel buy this line? That is unlikely.

While these political and military conditions are at center stage, there are other forces affecting the unfolding of historical events in the region. Iran has one of the lowest birth rates on the globe, a condition due to a high rate of sexually transmitted disease and a loss of hope about the future. The mullahs rule with an iron fist, but public discontent is still evident in every corner of the country. Will this lead to a revolution, a change in government? Many have predicted regime change over the last few decades and it hasn't occurred. Is the time ripe for it now?

Egypt, the traditional leader of the Arab world and the most populous Arab state, has had two revolutions in three years. When President Mubarak fell and elections were held, the Muslim Brotherhood—as the only well-organized political entity— was elected. But Mohamed Morsi overreached, with Muslim fanaticism and uneconomic programs leading to a public uprising with 33 million Egyptians taking to the streets for his ouster. His replacement, President al-Sisi, the former field general of the military, is regarded as a national hero…for now. But he has to find a way to feed 90 million Egyptians. At the moment more than half of his food is imported, with the Saudis paying that bill. How long can that continue?

Saudi Arabia and the UAE are the proverbial moneybags in the region. In an effort to punish Iran for its imperial surge in Yemen and the Russians for their support of President al-Assad and elsewhere, it is rumored the Saudis increased production of oil in order to lower the price per barrel. Since oil is the major source of hard currency in Iran and Russia, both nations have felt the adverse effects of this strategy. Despite the exaggerated influence of wind and solar power on energy production, oil will remain dominant for at least another decade. However, it will not be as dominant as it once was. The U.S., which only several years ago imported more than a third of its oil needs from the Middle East, is now largely independent due to the success of fracking. It is only a question of time before Saudi Arabia starts to feel the effect of a transition to alternatives. What will happen when Saudi Arabia is unable to pay the bills for the region?

While a radical, alas fanatical, sensibility dominates sectors of the Muslim world, it is instructive that President al-Sisi, speaking recently before imams at Al Azhar University—the center of Islamic scholarship—said there is inherent in Islam a violence that must be addressed. He had the courage to say, "We need a revolution from within." While President al-Sisi has a bull's-eye on his back, he, as a pious Muslim, may be leading a movement to moderate some of the extremist pressures that motivate Wahhabist theologians. Could this lead to a force for reform within Islam, a force that subdues much of the global violence?

Questions abound. There are signs of dismay and despair, and yet a few hopeful signs in the midst of confusion. Surely we must hope for the best, accept what is real, struggle against violence and be prepared for the worst. For even the best of predictions is usually wrong in part. As the distinguished French philosopher Paul Valéry put it, "The future isn't what it used to be."

The Indefensible Obama Policies (2016)
Originally published in The Washington Times

On December 6, President Barack Obama defended his strategy for combating terrorism, a strategy—if one can call it that—based on restraint and withdrawal. Without mentioning Donald Trump's name, the president went on to contrast his ideas with those enunciated by the president-elect. He clearly attempted to make the case for why his successor should adhere to his approach.

That approach includes scaling back U.S. military presence abroad, a ban on torture and the closing of the detention facility in Guantanamo. President Obama referred to his approach as "smart policy" and noted with pride that "no foreign terrorist organization has successfully planned and executed an attack on our homeland, and it's not because they didn't try." He argued, as well, for using diplomacy before military power, pointing to the Iran deal as the way to restrain a nuclear program.

While President Obama is keen on securing his legacy, the claims about "smart policy" are questionable. Alas, the scaling back of U.S. military presence has occurred with the precipitous withdrawal from Iraq, a symbol of misguided policy directives. The rise of the Islamic State is due in no small part to the departure of the U.S. military from the region. Similarly, the announcement that there will be a dramatic force reduction in Afghanistan on an announced date led directly to enhanced field operations by the Taliban.

The emptying of Guantanamo, with detainees sent to various locations abroad, has resulted in at least a third of them returning to the battlefield to foment terror. But the inaccurate claim about the closure of Guantanamo's being "smart policy" is small potatoes compared to the assertion that "no terrorist organization has successfully planned and executed an attack on our homeland." While a 9/11-size attack has not occurred, "the tree of terrorism" has used splinter groups in the form of ISIS-inspired terrorists to promote death from San Bernardino to Orlando. A change in tactics by terror organizations does not represent a change in purpose.

Clearly, as Churchill noted, "Jaw-jaw is better than war-war." Diplomacy should precede military action, as President Obama noted. But soft power without the requisite hard power behind it is a negotiated void. The ceasefire talks over Syria are a case in point. U.S. presence is subordinate to Russian and Iranian troops. As a consequence, Turkish officials have described the U.S. position as "irrelevant."

Last, the president, by his own admission, said Iran will be in a breakout phase—having sufficient fissile material for the development of nuclear weapons—in 10 years. Hence the much-heralded Iran deal does not restrain Iran from a nuclear program, it merely forestalls it. The real question is not whether Iran will possess weapons of mass destruction, but when it will have them. Moreover, President Obama has conspicuously overlooked violations of the deal and certainly the spirit of the negotiations. Voiced disapproval in the UN, sotto voce, by UN ambassador Samantha Powers, has certainly not moved the Iranian leadership. Hence, the vow made by the president to avoid nuclear proliferation in the region has been renounced by regional nations eager for a deterrent to counter the potential Iranian nuclear weapon.

U.S.-Israeli Relations

Since the formation of the Jewish state after World War II, the U.S. and Israel have shared a strong, significant alliance. Since the '80s, the U.S. has supplied Israel with funding, technology, military assets and training of the Israeli Defense Forces (IDF), to defend itself from those neighbors who would like to see Israel destroyed. Both Iran, to the east, and Hamas, to the west, have publicly called for the destruction of the state of Israel and death to its Jewish people. The Islamic State, Hezbollah and a host of other terror groups operate in close proximity to Israel. Hezbollah and Hamas regularly launch rockets and mortars at Israeli civilians— indiscriminately killing whomever they can reach. Former Iranian ayatollah Khomeini has called Israel the "little Satan" and the U.S. "the great Satan." For the U.S., Israel is an important ally on the front lines of a battle between the West and radical ideologies that seek to wage war against the West.

President Obama's reluctant and at times utter lack of support for Israel has been perplexing to observers and Israel alike. When Israel has been at its most vulnerable, America has always had its back. The same could not be said of the Obama administration. The following columns each tell part of the story of a strained and weakened U.S.-Israeli relationship under President Obama.

The Evolving Drama in the Middle East (2009)
Originally published on Family Security Matters

The world is now witnessing the reappearing drama of the Israeli-Palestinian conflict, with each of the parties playing their assigned role. In the background are the contemporary Sirens, the media organs who have only one lyric in their musical composition: proportionality. The United Nations stands in high dudgeon as it sends thunderbolts at Israel that reflect its considerable bias.

Hamas is the true villain, who in Orwellian fashion has become the victim. One certainly gets the impression in this drama that no one has read *Othello*. The vicious acts perpetrated against civilian population in Israel are a direct violation of the UN Principle of Distinction (attacking civilian populations intentionally instead of military targets). Hamas started this war as if it were Iago and now begs for international sympathy.

Israel has the right that every nation possesses, to defend itself. It doesn't have to rationalize or prevaricate. All the nation has to do is destroy the threat that challenges its very existence. It should be tone-deaf to the ludicrous protestations of Navi Pillay, the UN high commissioner for human rights, who condemned Israel's disproportionate use of force. (There is that word again. What, after all, is proportionate force?)

One of the leading characters in this drama is the two-faced Mahmoud Abbas, the self-proclaimed moderate who for months has been urging the Israeli government to take action against Hamas, and when it did, he issued a statement condemning Israel. Presumably he still has to mollify the militants in his Fatah camp.

The other actors in the Middle East read from their scripts with monotonous repetition. Egypt is publicly upset, even though conversations in back channels suggest it is very happy with Israeli actions. Saudi Arabia is appalled, yet can barely conceal its exuberance at the prospect of defeat for one of Iran's proxies.

Leftists of various stripes on both sides of the Atlantic play their role as useful dupes. If they had the capacity to examine conditions dispassionately, they might realize that Hamas represents a fascist and totalitarian ideology. But instead they can be found in Union Square Park or on the Champs-Élysées handing out literature that targets "Israeli aggression" and the "ventriloquist" United States that has sold sophisticated weaponry to the aggressors.

Remarkably the so-called aggressor is treating wounded Palestinians in its own hospitals. Moreover, Israel has allowed a convoy of trucks into Gaza so that food and medical supplies can be delivered. And Israel has permitted electricity to be continued so that Gazan lights can stay on. What other nation at war has treated its enemies with this kind of humanitarian concern? Yet Israel gets no credit. In fact, the more it does to prevent collateral damage, the more risks it takes in mitigating unnecessary bloodshed, the more media Sirens sing of disproportionate violence.

By contrast, Hamas has placed its rocket launchers directly in population centers. It has gone into hospitals and shot those suspected of giving intelligence to the IDF. It has refused to treat wounded Gazans. And it has used the termination of the ceasefire to fire dozens of rockets into Israeli population centers in an effort to trigger a response. Yet Hamas is the victim, alas even the martyr as far as the UN and world press are concerned.

How does one explain this casuistry? For one thing Israel is seen as an ally of the United States, and in the warped view of Western intellectuals Israel, ipso facto, is wrong. Facts need not stand in the way of an ideological judgment.

Second, there are many in the Middle East who will never countenance the existence of the Jewish state. Despite Israel's democracy, successful economy, rule of law and remarkable spirit, it is anathema to Arabs who live in tyranny, privation and backwardness.

And last, despite a reluctance to raise the issue of sheer bigotry and racism, it cannot be denied. Generation after generation of Arab and Persian children read in their textbooks and hear in sermons at their mosques and madrassas that Jews are the persecutors and exploiters. Even worse, they are told that Jews are the progeny of monkeys and pigs, that they are less than human.

At some point these lies, this blood libel, has had an effect. There are literally millions in the Middle East who believe it is appropriate to kill Jews, and those at the UN and media panjandrums are complicit in these crimes as they avert their gaze to the criminal acts against Israel.

If this is Act II in this latest drama, my hope is that the IDF will avoid the usual prevarication, will destroy every rocket site in the Gaza Strip and will say that self-defense has nothing to do with proportionality, but has everything to do with survival.

Beyond Appeasement (2009)
Originally published on Reflections

When Neville Chamberlain returned from Munich in 1936, he noted that based on his appeasement stance with Hitler, "peace was at hand." Alas, Prime Minister Chamberlain was duped and, as might have been expected, history has not treated him kindly. But, however false the concessions made by Hitler, Prime Minister Chamberlain believed he had obtained a concession—restraint on Nazi imperial ambitions.

In 2009 America's own Chamberlain, President Obama, has adopted a stance beyond appeasement; he engages in preemptive conciliation without any expectation of a quid pro quo. President Obama doesn't wait to be double-crossed; he is a concession man who gives before he is asked and remarkably puts American interests at risk in order to enhance his international standing.

Without securing any benefit from the withdrawal of missile sites and radars in Poland and the Czech Republic, President Obama blithely gave up what had been negotiated and settled with our allies. This move was heralded by the Russians, as might be expected. But Russian leaders immediately noted that they would not use this gesture to put pressure on Iran's ambition to obtain nuclear weapons. After all, a Russian spokesman noted, "why should we make a concession when you've decided to correct a mistake?"

On September 23 President Obama addressed the United Nations, and in the midst of negotiations between Israel and the Palestinians, he embraced the Palestinian position for a two-state solution based on the '67 borders, a divided Jerusalem, a cessation of new settlements in the West Bank and a "contiguous" Palestinian state. This was said without the slightest concession from the Palestinian side. There wasn't any demand that the state of Israel must be recognized. There wasn't the slightest recognition of defensible borders. There wasn't a hint that Palestinian violence would be arrested. And most significantly, there did not seem to be the slightest recognition of geographic realities: a contiguous Palestinian state of Gaza and the West Bank means Israel would have to be divided in half.

Israel, America's only real ally in the Middle East, was being dismembered in front of the General Assembly amid thunderous applause from the ranks of tyrannical states. It was as if President Ahmadinejad wrote President Obama's speech.

President Obama also suggested that he stands for the oppressed people of the world—a truly noble sentiment. Yet in the next breath he alluded to the electoral victory of President Ahmadinejad in Iran. In that nation the oppressed were on the streets, beaten by the Revolutionary Guard, harassed in their homes, murdered by government thugs and raped in prison. Yet these oppressed people were ignored by our president. Here again an emotional concession was made without the slightest reciprocal gesture from the Iranian leadership.

And why should they or any of our enemies concede anything when President Obama does their bidding? General Qaddafi thinks Obama should be president for life. The only problem with this idea from General Qaddafi's perspective is that the president will soon run out of things to concede.

This plunge into the UN quagmire has made the president and, to an unprecedented degree, the nation look weak and ineffectual. It appears as if the United States is in decline and cannot marshal the fortitude to defend its own interests. When Hugo Chávez, Fidel Castro, President Ahmadinejad and Colonel Qaddafi applaud the action of an American president, something must be wrong.

What is wrong, of course, is that the concession man in his pursuit of a transnational agenda no longer represents the will of the American people. He is, in his own eyes, president of the world, a world in which national sovereignty is subordinated to global concerns. From global warming to the zero option on nuclear weapons, President Obama is employing these policy instruments to foster his global goals.

Where this will end is anyone's guess. But on one point I am sure: should President Obama's policies be pursued, the world of the future will see an America in decline and instability rampant on the world stage. Welcome to the second Dark Age.

Obama and Benjamin "Bibi" Netanyahu

Nearly every U.S. president in the modern era has maintained a strong friendship with Israeli leadership. Yet Obama's presidency was one of a lackluster U.S.-Israeli relationship. President Obama frequently took jabs at Israeli prime minister Benjamin Netanyahu, both at the United Nations and on the world stage. President Obama's 2014 and 2015 nuclear negotiations and subsequent deal with Iran were all done under protest from the Israeli government. In 2015, nearly $350,000 was used by the Obama State Department to fund a political group in Israel to influence Israelis to vote against Prime Minister Netanyahu in his reelection bid. In a parting shot in 2016, President Obama failed to veto a UN resolution that condemned Israel as "occupiers" of, among other places, the Temple Mount, the holiest site in Judaism, which sits in the middle of Israel's capital of Jerusalem and has been a part of the nation of Israel since the Six-Day War of 1967.

The Obama-Netanyahu Rift (2010)

The authorization of 1,600 new housing units in north Jerusalem seemingly caught Prime Minister Benjamin "Bibi" Netanyahu by surprise. Needless to say, as newspaper accounts suggest, the timing turned out to be an embarrassment to Vice President Biden, who was in Israel at the time of the announcement.

However, when the vice president was departing from Israel, Prime Minister Netanyahu apologized and whatever tension existed appeared to wane. When Vice President Biden returned to the United States, a calculated campaign against the housing units commenced. Secretary of State Hillary Clinton engaged in a vitriolic attack against Israel. David Axelrod, representing the administration, raised the ante by describing Israel's action as "irresponsible."

Although hard evidence to support an anti-Israeli plan has not surfaced, it would appear that the administration used the incident to fan the flames of dissatisfaction with Israel and send a message to Arab and Muslim nations that the Obama team is not reflexively on Israel's side.

However, one wonders why what on the surface seems to be a pettifogging issue should have been elevated to a state-to-state schism. For one thing, President Obama has signaled President Abbas of the Palestinian territory that the United States will be an honest broker in peace deliberations rather than tilting to Israel's will. In addition, the Obama administration is attempting to influence Israel's domestic political alignment by encouraging overtures to Tzipi Livni as a coalition partner and perhaps removing Minister of Foreign Affairs Lieberman, who represents a right-wing perspective anathema to the Obama administration.

President Obama contends that it is incumbent on Israel to make concessions to the Palestinians, in the process overlooking a history in several Israeli administrations of extraordinary concessions, including Prime Minster Barak's willingness to give up more than 90 percent of the West Bank. Prime Minister Netanyahu believes progress in negotiations is not possible, given the split between the Palestinian Authority (Fatah) and Hamas. The Palestinian red lines are unacceptable to Prime Minister Netanyahu, and the credible concessions he appears to be offering are unacceptable to Abbas. A stalemate is the likely outcome, whatever anyone in the Oval Office assumes.

Another sticking point is that President Obama has virtually conceded nuclear weapons to Iran, notwithstanding formal rhetoric to the contrary. The president assumes deterrence can work and the situation can be managed. On the other hand, Prime Minister Netanyahu understands that his choices are limited. An Iran with nuclear weapons can threaten Israel directly and through proxies like Hamas and Hezbollah. The prime minister wants the U.S. to be active in curtailing the Iranian nuclear program; at the same time, he acknowledges that assurances about the future offered by Biden and others are hardly dispositive.

Once Iran goes nuclear it can control the supply of gulf oil and influence the price. An entirely dependent Europe and Japan will not only experience an even greater transfer of wealth than has already occurred, but likely political concessions will leave Israel in an even more vulnerable position than it is in at the moment. Faced with this strategic threat, Israel relies on cooperation with the United States, a cooperation that is now fading.

It is clear that President Obama has absolved the Palestinian side from blame for the instability in the region. Hence the diplomatic issue between Israel and the United States is a manufactured one that President Obama chose to exploit. What this has done is further weakened President Obama's standing on the Israeli streets, where his status was already plummeting. Additionally, President Obama's naiveté was evident, since his move to checkmate Israel through diplomatic pressure only hardened Prime Minister Netanyahu's resolve and resistance. And last, this move opened the floodgates for Israel-bashing across Europe as the press flaunts the apparent rift between Prime Minister Netanyahu and President Obama.

Explaining the Obama strategic vision in the Middle East is increasingly difficult to do. His maladroit moves undermine the conditions he is trying to promote, and his peculiar indecisiveness and vacillation are a source of woe to allies in the region and a source of derision for our enemies.

Obama: Churchill or Chamberlain or Both? (2011)
Originally published on the Gatestone Institute

President Obama's 5/19/11 speech on the Middle East was one part Winston Churchill and one part the echo of Neville Chamberlain. At long last the president revealed his secret George W. Bush hiding out in his soul with his version of the Freedom Agenda. He noted that promoting individual freedom, democracy and economic opportunity was America's "top priority that must be translated into concrete action." How this is to be achieved remains obscure, but it appears as if the president has decided he no longer wants "to lead from behind."

In some respects his language was Churchillian, since he was tough on the tyrannies in Syria and Iran, the areas' principal malefactors. He implied that the road to stability can only be discovered with a democratic map. This was a significant departure from his Cairo 2009 speech, which emphasized engagement and conspicuously avoided democratic impulses.

However, while there is much to applaud in his speech, there is another side, a dark and menacing side. In his dream of peace between Israel and the Palestinian territory, he made clear his Islamophilic instincts. His perception that Israel return to the 1967 border is right out of the Saudi Arabian playbook and would, in essence, jeopardize the very existence of the Israeli state.

Yes, President Obama did explicitly discuss the recognition of a Jewish state and he did note that a future Palestinian nation should be demilitarized, but he did not explore the security vulnerability rendered by the return to '67 lines.

President Obama's argument had to be heartening to Arab extremists everywhere, for now all negotiations will begin with this premise. The president went beyond what previous presidents have said publicly on the subject, and he did so hours before a meeting with Prime Minister Benjamin Netanyahu designed to explore negotiation tactics.

This statement by President Obama has the odor of Munich about it. Just as the Sudetenland was sacrificed to Hitler "for peace in our time," the contention that Israel return to the '67 borders may have the same toxic effect. An Israel with a width of nine miles would not be in a position of defending itself. Preemption would be its only option. A Hamas terrorist with a Stinger over his shoulder can shoot down any commercial aircraft landing at the Tel Aviv airport.

Prime Minister Netanyahu responded by noting, "Israel believes that for peace to endure between Israel and Palestinians, the viability of a Palestinian state cannot come at the expense of the viability of the one and only Jewish state." Alas, the echo of the 1930s fills the corridors of contemporary history.

It is difficult to know if President Obama is serious about his proposal. After all, he did engage in subsequent backpedaling at the AIPAC meeting. But even so, it seems as though he either doesn't understand what Israel is up against or doesn't care. He may think this is a historic opportunity to do what his predecessors could not. However, just as Prime Minister Chamberlain overreached in his desire for peace through appeasement, President Obama is overreaching in his plan for peace by sacrificing Israeli security.

There must be rejoicing at the United Nations, where the 57 Muslim nations seeking to impose a Palestinian state on the region have an ally in their quest for territorial gains. President Obama did admonish against the looming UN effort to delegitimize Israel, but that is a pettifogging matter compared to President Obama's stance on the rearrangement of borders.

There is an Orwellian quality to the speech, since freedom is embraced on the one hand and crushing imposition on the other hand. President Obama has found his voice on the Freedom Agenda, but there is the nagging Chamberlain apparition that haunts his perspective. Since the president has oscillated all over the policy screen in the last few years, from vigorous opposition to the war in Iraq to what is now an enthusiastic embrace, it is worth recalling George Orwell's statement that "in a time of universal deceit, telling the truth is a revolutionary act."

Sovereignty and Suzerainty in the Israeli-U.S. Relationship (2012)
Originally published on the Gatestone Institute

The recent Obama-Netanyahu conclave has evoked a jamboree of media speculation. Will Israel act unilaterally to attack Iran's nuclear facilities? Does the Obama administration really have Israel's back, as the president indicated? And where is that "red line," the point at which an attack must occur to prevent an Iran with "secure" nuclear weapons? Despite all the diplomatic bonhomie and announcements of solidarity, questions remain—questions fraught with uncomfortable implications.

U.S. officials made it clear that President Obama will not go beyond the broad policy enunciated in the past: that the United States is committed to preventing Iran from obtaining a nuclear weapon through diplomacy and sanctions and, as a last resort, force. Here too equivocation prevails. Secretary of Defense Panetta has indicated a reluctance to apply military force in this matter, and questioned the effectiveness of an Israeli strike, a position adopted by others in the administration.

By contrast, Prime Minister Netanyahu stated unequivocally that his primary responsibility as Israel's political leader is to ensure that this Jewish state survives and remains the master of its own fate. But the U.S. holds many high cards in this poker hand. Several officials already suggested that should an unauthorized attack occur, the U.S. would not replenish the ordnance and advanced military technology Israel needs to maintain its superior military position in the Middle East.

These strains in the relationship may not seem apparent at the moment, but the difference in perspective will emerge on the political front in the next few months, if not sooner.

Even the UN—notably hostile to Israel—voiced concern that Tehran "might" be developing nuclear weapons. The International Atomic Energy Agency recently restated its concern that Tehran has tested intercontinental ballistic missiles that could be weaponized.

However, hovering over the threat and the ominous effects of an air attack against Iran are the pull and tug of sovereignty versus suzerainty. Is Israel an independent nation free of American influence? Does the president of the U.S. have a veto over Israeli military actions? Or is Israel free of outside influences, a state enjoined by what it believes to be its self-interest?

At the moment, both sides hedge. Israel wants U.S. support, but if it launches an attack, the prime minister will provide only 24 hours of prior notice. The Obama administration seemingly fears an Israeli assault, particularly the blowback across the Arab world, but it is obvious that the United States cannot prevent this decision from being made. This is not a test of wills, but rather a test of interests and strategic perspective.

On at least one matter, there appears to be consensus: containment, of the kind that seemingly worked during the Cold War, is not applicable in this scenario, albeit that may be the United States' default position. But it is clear, even to the bureaucrats in Foggy Bottom, that an Iranian nuclear weapon has political as well as military consequences. U.S. interests across the Middle East would be imperiled by the Iranian bomb. Moreover, it is also clear that a "Japanese solution" in which Iran has enough fissionable material to produce several bombs and ICBMs to deliver them, but doesn't bring the two together is not acceptable. Presumably, with the right applications, the ICBMs could be weaponized in relatively short order. And, in fact, every nation in the Middle East will know what is in that Iranian tent.

Clearly it is better to see Israel and the U.S. move closer on this strategic issue than was previously the case. But there is a nagging feeling that President Obama will say whatever is necessary to forge ties to Jewish wealth and the Jewish Democratic voting bloc. Does he mean what he says? Based on past public commentary, many analysts in the Jewish community are agnostic about the president's commitment.

The next three months will yield an answer, one that could shape the future of global affairs for decades. In the backdrop of this decision is the tension between sovereignty and suzerainty. On this philosophical tension the fortunes of humanity may rest.

The Aftermath of Netanyahu's Victory (2015)
Originally published on Newsmax

The champagne bottles in the White House remain unopened. Despite the vigorous efforts of the Obama team to unseat Prime Minister Netanyahu in the recent Israeli elections, he prevailed. President Obama made clear that his vitriolic sentiments toward Bibi Netanyahu are undiminished.

In a stunning rebuke of a foreign head of state, President Obama dispatched his chief spokesman to criticize Prime Minister Netanyahu's campaign strategy, while anonymous administration officials hinted the U.S. could withdraw support for Israel at the United Nations. In an act of gratuitous pettiness, the president delayed the ritual call of congratulations.

President Obama contends that the rhetoric during the course of the campaign was deeply divisive, marginalizing Arab-Israeli citizens. The president neglected to mention the fact that his aides tried to encourage Arab voters even through the Arab party endorses Hamas, an avowed enemy of Israel. And this is the action and sentiment of a presumptive ally. "With friends like that…"

Despite the frosty nature of the relationship, there is bound to be some healing. Prime Minister Netanyahu has already modified his stance on the "two-state solution" from "not on my watch" to "under the right circumstances" a Palestinian state can be created.

Historic bonds between the two nations are not easily severed, even with a president whose hostility to Israel is palpable. The likehood of a shift in the U.S. position at the UN on a Palestinian state is, as I see it, an empty threat.

Steps that jeopardize Israel's future as a Palestinian state would invariably affect American interests in the region. The president may wish to punish Israel for what he regards as intransigence and resistance to his "deal" with Iran, but he is constrained by a Congress that has exhibited bipartisan support for Israel, even if that support is waning in the Democratic party.

There is another overlooked consideration. Even though Egypt, Jordan and Saudi Arabia will chastise Israel over the Palestinian question, they know that in their emerging struggle with Iran and its imperial Shia ambitions, Israel is an ally. All the negative votes in the UN cannot undo the cordial military-to-military communication and assistance between Israel and its Sunni neighbors.

Just as Israel is constrained by its reliance on United States support, the U.S. president is constrained as well. Should the president refuse to veto a Security Council mandate for the creation of a Palestinian state—a truly unlikely event notwithstanding press accounts to the contrary—the act would have little more than symbolic meaning. Israel would indeed be isolated but, in fact, no more isolated than it is at the moment. Prime Minister Netanyahu can play his diplomatic hand in China, India and Japan, as he increasingly does. Israel has much to offer the world through its technical expertise; the Palestinians offer nothing. What should be recognized is that a Palestinian state adjacent to Israel harboring hostility and the means to manifest its blood lust would only precipitate a regional war. There may be a Palestinian state in time, but it is unlikely to be in my lifetime.

It might also be recalled that after President Obama bids adieu to the White House, Prime Minister Netanyahu is still more than likely to be prime minister of Israel. The frost in the relationship will be melting. Perhaps this claim will be regarded as polyannaish to some, but even in this dark and pessimistic moment in history, there are occasional rays of light on the horizon.

State Department Supports Anti-Israel Activity (2015)
Originally published on Newsmax

Although it has received little public attention, recently the U.S. State Department granted the New Israel Fund and its social change and political lobbying organization known as SHATIL—$1 million under a program designed to promote political change and reform in the Middle East. This government program, the Middle East Partnership Initiative (MEPI), gives $600 million in grants to "social activists and reformers" in 18 Middle East nations. The list of nations includes Algeria, Libya, Lebanon and Yemen. MEPI's sphere of engagement curiously includes Israel, the only stable democracy in the region.

Since the New Israel Fund is devoted to the BDS (Boycott, Divestment and Sanctions) movement, the grant from the State Department presupposes sanctioning efforts to demonize and delegitimize the state of Israel. Knesset deputy speaker Yoni Chetboun said the New Israel Fund (NIF) is bent on "erasing the Jewish identity from the Jewish State." He added that NIF represents "the biggest left-wing lobby in Israel." Prime Minister Netanyahu and Naftali Bennett of the Jewish Home party both derided NIF as "anti-Zionist."

Needless to say, NIF denies the accusations, noting it is only interested in "internal change." However, the State Department grant willy-nilly vouchsafes NIF legitimacy for its political actions and seemingly approves of its interference in Israel's upcoming election. However one describes this State Department program, it is an attempt to interfere with the politics of Israel through strikes, protests and other forms of activism. While there may be justification for assisting grassroots organizations in their efforts to destabilize dictatorships like Iran, using American taxpayer money to influence Israeli politics is clearly unjustified.

The BDS movement against Israel, which NIF embodies, is an ideological war to demonize Israel as a racist "apartheid state." It has applied lies, misunderstanding and Orwellian logic as instruments in this war, whose sole purpose is to ostracize and isolate Israel as a state bereft of "social justice."

For those in this movement, social justice translates into a Palestinian state with Israel retreating behind 1967 borders. Yet the movement goes beyond this point. For BDS, Zionism is the essential evil; only dismantling the Jewish state can address it.

Many in this movement and in the NIF are idealists, dedicated radicals, either unaware or uncaring that they are being manipulated by Islamists and their sympathizers in the West. But the leaders of BDS know precisely what they are doing. In eliciting support from around the globe, they hope to make Israel into a state without allies, an outlier in the international community.

Unfortunately the American citizen most probably does not know how his tax money is being used. Some might contend the State Department grant to SHATIL is the continuation of President Obama's anti-Israel campaign, perhaps financial retaliation for Prime Minister Netanyahu's speech to Congress. Even if this isn't the case, it is odd that the State Department would apply grants to an organization that wants to disrupt a democratic nation. Isn't a stable democracy in the vicinity of a nest of vipers what we should be supporting?

NIF has confused many youthful Jews with its dissimulation. It is too bad these young people are unaware of Voltaire's admonition, "Those who can make you believe absurdities, can make you commit atrocities."

Revealing Israel's Nuclear Secrets (2015)
Originally published on The Hill

For years, Israel pursued a nuclear defense policy that might be described as intentional ambiguity. It was a position every American president since Dwight D. Eisenhower accepted. But in a recent decision adopted by the Department of Defense, a top-secret document detailing Israel's nuclear program was declassified.

By publishing the declassified document that specifies Israel's nuclear capabilities, the U.S. breached a silent, but well-understood, agreement. Moreover, the document the Pentagon saw fit to declassify redacted sections on Italy, France, West Germany and other NATO nations. The report also notes the existence of research laboratories in Israel that "are equivalent to Los Alamos, Lawrence Livermore and Oak Ridge National Laboratories."

It is, of course, quite interesting, perhaps revealing, that the declassification has occurred as the Obama administration has tilted away from Israel in written and spoken words. Some have said they have never seen an American document disclosing such extensive information about an ally's state secrets. With Iran's nuclear talks soon unfolding into an accord, the declassification will prove to be exceedingly awkward for Israel. It may well be that if monitoring of Iran's nuclear capability is called for, why not Israel's program? Is the Obama team trying to establish equivalency between Tehran and Jerusalem?

Although there isn't any equivalence between Israel and Iran morally or strategically, this position has gained traction among Obama adherents; one, because it suits U.S. negotiating strategy and two, because it punishes Prime Minister Netanyahu for what the administration considers his recalcitrance on the Palestinian question. Yet, remarkably, this story has received little attention in the press. President Obama has hinted he may endorse or absent the U.S. from a Security Council vote creating a Palestinian state. This "hint" and the declassified document are serious breaks in what has long been considered a "special relationship" between the U.S. and Israel.

It is instructive that political party positions on Israel have switched. An erstwhile Republican party influenced by former Secretary of State Jim Baker was equivocal on Israel, although the

Democratic party at the time was unanimously supportive. Today, a President Obama–led Democratic party is increasingly hostile to Israel, while Republicans are uniformly behind it. At the risk of overstatement, it appears that President Obama and company believe stability in the Middle East can be achieved through an alliance with Iran. If this means throwing Israel under the proverbial bus, that is a relatively small price to pay.

Believing that Iran will accede and live up to the demands of any agreement based on past history and recent comments from the supreme leader requires a suspension of disbelief. Nonetheless, Israel is in the crosshairs despite the longstanding ties with the United States. As a consequence, the declassification of Israeli nuclear secrets is hardly surprising. But for those who support Israel this Pentagon act is vindictive and dangerous—part and parcel of a dramatic alteration in U.S. foreign policy.

Palestinian Statehood

Much of the source of international consternation about Israel has been the question of Palestinian statehood. In a 1947 bid for its independence, Israel accepted a land deal offered as a compromise by the United Nations; neighboring Palestinians did not. In 1967, Israel engaged in a preemptive Six-Day War to defend itself from a massive buildup of military assets by the surrounding countries of Egypt, Syria and Jordan. Despite returning much of the land won in the war, Israel retained its traditional capital of Jerusalem and strategic defensive positions along its border.

To Israel's immediate west, the West Bank is home to the Palestinian Authority, led by its ruling party, Fatah. Despite several offers of land compromises and the recognition of an independent Palestinian state, the Palestinian leadership has accepted none of the offers, and it has never offered any of its own. In furtherance of peace, Israel removed itself from the Gaza Strip, a portion of land on the southwest of Israel abutting the Mediterranean Sea. It gave the land to Palestinians in an attempt at compromise. Hamas, an internationally recognized terror group, was elected as the governmental authority of the Gaza Strip.

Gaza has since launched over 10,000 rockets at the state of Israel, and continues to call for its complete destruction. A 2011 UN vote upped the status of the Palestinian territory from "observer entity" to "non-member observer state."

Fatah's True Objectives (2009)
Originally published on Family Security Matters

August 4 was not only the birthday of President Obama, it was also the opening date of the Fatah general conference in Bethlehem. Despite concerns, the Israeli government surrendered to U.S. pressure and allowed an influx of Palestinian hardliners and notorious terrorists to attend this meeting. According to reports, National Security Adviser James Jones offered a list of Palestinians the Obama administration wanted present at the Fatah event in order "to save the conference and Abu Mazen." One of those present was Khaled Abu Esba, who blew up an Israeli bus on the Tel Aviv highway in 1978, killing 35 Israelis.

What was saved at this conference is a matter of some conjecture. Although the Obama administration hoped that this Fatah conference would result in the emergence of moderate positions toward Israel, the obverse was the case. Not only was Israel routinely and ritualistically condemned, but there wasn't the slightest gesture in the direction of conciliation.

Fatah leaders argued they would continue their armed struggle against the state of Israel, engaging in whatever force is necessary to undermine the Jewish state. They made it clear that there wouldn't be any modification in their charter, thereby avoiding any possibility of recognizing Israel as a legitimate nation. To gild the lily, a number of spokespeople contended that Israel was responsible for the death of Yassir Arafat, a claim made without reference to any evidence.

While President Obama has adhered to what he would describe as an "even-handed policy," it is clear that his effort to employ Fatah as the moderate counterweight to radical Hamas will not work. The difference between Hamas and Fatah is that the former want to kill

Jews now and the latter want to kill Jews after concessions have been vouchsafed.

The conference comments should disabuse Obama administration officials of the dubious notion that settlements in the West Bank stand in the way of some accord between Israelis and Palestinians. There is little doubt the settlements argument is a ruse designed to make the Israeli government pliable. Moreover, the issue creates a separation between the Obama and Netanyahu governments that can be exploited by the Palestinian leadership. An illusion has been created over settlements that the Israelis are intractable and unwilling to come to the negotiating table in good faith.

Yet the conference in Bethlehem reveals an undisguised truth: it is Fatah that is unwilling to modify its hateful stance toward Israel. In an effort to compete with the sanguinic aims of Hamas, Fatah engages in rhetoric that is remarkably similar. Notwithstanding the words that are used, the Obama administration continues to search for a silver lining. This commitment to Abu Mazen, a man without any real influence or standing in the West Bank, would be comical were it not so tragic.

In the incandescent precincts in Washington, Israel is the problem and all evidence to the contrary, including the language and intent of Fatah, is either ignored or rationalized. According to Obama spokespeople, there is a policy in place for a two-state solution, and Israel's withdrawal from territory in much of the West Bank is its critical feature. That condition remains unaltered whatever the circumstances on the ground.

Peace, the much-abused word in these discussions, could be achieved overnight if Fatah would stop armed resistance against Israel and recognize Israel as a legitimate nation. If President Obama wants Israeli flexibility, this is the way to achieve it. All other negotiating points merely bypass the central issue. Whether Fatah can bring itself to adopt this argument seems unlikely since the coherence in the organization depends on armed aggression.

Prime Minister Netanyahu has tried to persuade President Obama of this Middle East reality, but obsessions and policy obduracy stand in the way. As a consequence, all of the talk in this multilateral negotiation, including Russia, the EU and the UN, can come to nothing productive. Should President Obama squeeze Israel, which he seems inclined to do, he will only increase the likelihood of future bloodshed that withdrawals from Gaza and southern Lebanon presaged.

If there is pressure to be applied, there is one side where the application makes sense. I doubt there will be a policy shift in the administration, but it would make sense for the president and his aides to read a transcript of the conference in Bethlehem. After doing so, I wonder if erstwhile General Jones could describe who he is saving and for what end.

Abbas Reveals His True Agenda (2011)
Originally published on the Gatestone Institute

In a recent discussion of the anticipated Palestinian state, Mahmoud Abbas, leader in the territory, said he "would not tolerate one single Jew in his new country, Palestine." Speaking before journalists in Ramallah, he clearly and unequivocally noted, "We have already said completely openly, and it will stay that way: If there is a Palestinian country with Jerusalem as its capital, we will not accept that even one single Jew will live there."

President Abbas rejected any suggestion that Jews in Judea and Samaria, who have lived in their homes for decades, could remain under Palestinian rule. Meanwhile in all negotiations, the Palestinian position is that "Palestinian refugees" have the right of return to Israel. Therefore, according to the Abbas proposition, Israel should open its borders for Arabs while Palestine closes its borders for Jews.

Here is the unvarnished truth. Arabs can live in Israel as full-fledged citizens with all the rights that status confers. They can have their own political parties, settle in their own communities and represent about 20 percent of the total Israeli population. But on the other side of the political ledger not one Jew, including those who reside on the West Bank, can remain once Palestine becomes an independent nation.

What more does one have to know about the Arab mentality? Sauce for the goose is not sauce for the gander. There is and will remain different standards for Arabs and Jews. Hence, what precisely is a two-state solution? An Arab state immediately becomes a threat to the very existence of Israel since Jews are recognized as the enemy and, by virtue of law, must be ostracized.

To make matters even more absurd, President Abbas is considered an ideological moderate. After all, he doesn't call for killing Jews, only for a form of apartheid, of absolute separation. Should such a Palestinian nation be created, how long would it take for open hostilities between the two states to break out? Can an Israeli government that encouraged its citizens to move into the West Bank after the culmination of the 1967 war now tell these residents that they must depart? Is the government prepared to extricate 250,000 people from this region?

These questions, and a host of others, will have to be addressed to meet the demands of a two-state solution. But even more fundamental is the attitude of the Palestinians themselves. If Jews aren't permitted there, then presumably Jewish tourist dollars and investment capital are not welcome either. Where does one draw the line?

Clearly modesty is in order. If President Abbas didn't have to mollify radical sentiment in the West Bank, these unmistakably racist comments would be an embarrassment and uttered only in private, if then. But his are the views of a radical sensing that the tide of world opinion is with him. Alas, he may be right, since condemnation from the media elite over his forthright apartheid stance has not been forthcoming.

If this Palestinian state is created, Israelis should not have any illusions about what it will mean. Further isolation, increased hostility, border tension and suicide bombers are all in the cards. In fact, the deck is stacked against Israel, and President Abbas has made that fact patently clear.

A Palestinian State Will Embolden Hamas (2011)
Originally published on Newsmax

With a vote on statehood about to come before the United Nations General Assembly in September, it is incumbent on those who will consider this proposal to examine several facts. A recent report by Itamar Marcus and Nan Jacques Zilberdik makes the following points:

- The Palestinian Authority pays monthly salaries to 5,500 prisoners in Israeli prisons, many of them known terrorists;
- The PA honors terrorists who have killed civilians, presenting them as heroes and role models;
- The PA glorifies terrorist attacks as heroic, including suicide bombings;
- Funding for these salaries and activities comes from the general budget, to which the U.S. contributes;
- U.S. law prohibits funding of any person who engages or engaged in terrorist activity.

At the moment, Hamas and Fatah terrorist prisoners are receiving monthly checks, a total of almost 18 million shekels ($5 million) monthly. In fact, it pays to be a terrorist, since these monthly stipends are more than the average salary of a PA civil servant or military officer.

While this practice is going on, Secretary of State Hillary Clinton stated that an additional grant to the PA will be made, bringing U.S. direct budget assistance to a total of $225 million annually. Of course, neither the American public nor most members of Congress are aware that a substantial portion of this foreign aid goes to support terrorists. My suspicion is that even Hillary Clinton does not know that a PA-sponsored summer camp for children is divided into three groups named after terrorists Dalal Mughrabi, Salah Khalaf and Abu Ali Mustafa, each of whom planned and executed murders against civilians. My suspicion is that the secretary of state does not know that Prime Minister Salam Fayyad, a man who she described as a moderate, routinely honors terrorist bombers on his radio broadcasts.

That these practices go on with U.S. subventions is outrageous. The PA is in direct violation of our laws, and all salaries to imprisoned terrorists and money that honors terrorists should cease immediately. But there is also another lesson in these revelations. Despite all of the rhetorical anodynes from the Obama administration, terrorism is the modus operandi of the PA. The creation of a Palestinian state is ipso facto the creation of a terrorist state with one goal, the destruction of Israel.

Despite all of the gamesmanship at the UN, despite President Obama's assurance about adjoining states living in peace, the PA and its Hamas partner will not repudiate their goal of destruction and will not recognize the legitimacy of the Jewish state. General Assembly members may be convinced that a newly created Arab state can live in peace with its Israeli neighbor; after all, petrodollars are very alluring. But the evidence that a narrative of violence is encouraged, alas funded, militates against an irenic scenario.

As I see it, the time has come for the United States to tell the truth about the West Bank and Gaza. We may not persuade Security Council members that this entire statehood enterprise is misguided, but at least we can state the American position clearly and unequivocally. As long as terrorism prevails, as long as it is cultivated by government authorities, there will not be, there cannot be, a Palestinian nation. If a day comes when Israel lays down its arms, destruction will follow; if there is a day when the Palestinians repudiate terrorism, peace will follow. The alternatives are clear. The question, of course, is whether anyone is listening.

Textbooks, Kids and the Question of Palestinian Statehood (2011)
Originally published on Fox News

The United States' Obama administration is trying to convince Congress that foreign aid to the Palestinian Authority (PA) is the key to peaceful coexistence with Israel. In keeping with this theme the U.S. has granted $4 billion in foreign aid. However, despite this remarkable allocation, a recent study of Abu Mazen and Salam Fayyad's school textbooks reveals how counterproductive this aid has been. Rather than promote peaceful coexistence, it has encouraged Palestinian terrorism.

The study in question confirms that Palestinian textbooks set the stage for the next wave of violence. These books encourage suicide bombing and martyrdom; idolize jihad and bloodshed; cite the 1967 borders of Israel as a "national goal"; define Israel as an illegitimate and immoral state; conspicuously omit any reference to peaceful coexistence; and call for the annihilation of Israel.

Our Beautiful Language, a seventh-grade text, notes: "We shall sow Palestine with [martyrs'] skeletons and skulls; we shall paint the face of Palestine with blood, but Palestine shall wash our face with heavenly water." The eighth-grade text says, "Our beloved Palestine is calling me, the orphaned cities yearn for me to return and rectify the blunder with storms and lightning."

At the same time children are being acculturated for war, President Obama speaks serenely and naïvely of peace. Palestinian education, media and mosques have been manufactured into lines of hatred, incitement, terrorism and suicide bombing. Yet the aid pours into the territory even though Congress is forbidden to appropriate funds that can be used to instill hatred.

It is instructive that Abu Mazen, a man many in the State Department call a moderate, was assigned the task of developing the Palestinian curriculum two decades ago. That curriculum is vehemently anti-Jewish, anti-Israel and anti-United States. Yet when it comes to aid, Congress blinds itself to the current reality. With this curriculum as a backdrop, it is not surprising that the thoroughly discredited and anti-Semitic *Protocols of the Elders of Zion* is a bestseller in the Palestinian Authority. Terrorists are idealized in schools, summer camps, tournaments and street names. And recent attacks on innocent Israeli children often led to street celebrations.

What then is meant by a two-state solution? By what standard should a Palestinian state exist when it encourages terror and promotes martyrdom among youthful adherents? How reliable can claims of peace be when thoughts of Israel's destruction are foremost in the minds of Palestinians?

If adjoining states are to live in harmony, violence must be contained and discouraged. If the U.S. is to play a helpful role on the pathway to coexistence, aid to the Palestinians should be suspended until it has demonstrated that terrorism is not a goal. Until that time all the discussion about statehood is absurd. Another state devoted to terror is not what the Middle East requires.

The hypocrisy in the United Nations belies an institution engaged in doing the bidding of the Islamic bloc. It appears that the General Assembly is prepared to deny reality and call for the establishment of a Palestinian state. But denial does not, cannot, obviate reality, and the reality is that an independent Palestine would invite terrorism in through Israel's back door.

Israel and the U.S. (2011)
Originally published on Family Security Matters

There is little doubt that Israel looks to the United States for support. It is somewhat like the picke-on younger brother eager to have his sibling come to his aid. In the case of the U.S. and Israel, that has usually been the case, albeit the 1956 war in the Suez was an exception.

Now something has gone sour. For reasons somewhat elusive, President Obama has arrived at the dubious conclusion that conditions in the Middle East might improve if Israel and the Palestinians could arrive at an understanding about a Palestinian state.

Never mind that President al-Assad kills his own Syrian citizens interested in regime change. Never mind that Egypt is unstable after

Hosni Mubarak's unceremonious ouster. Never mind that the civil war in the Sudan has led to the death of thousands. Never mind that the rebels in Libya may not be interested in a democratic republic. Never mind that Iraq is close to civil war as U.S. forces decline. Never mind that Afghanistan has a civil war with U.S. forces on the ground. Never mind that Pakistan is a friend by day and a foe by night. And never mind that Iran is about to acquire nuclear weapons. The issue for President Obama is organic population growth on the West Bank. Now that's an issue worth the president's attention.

What most people do not know, including President Obama, is that most settlements are a literal stone's throw from Jerusalem. The communities that the president complains about are the ones that allow Jerusalem to survive. They offer strategic depth or at least a little of it. Without Judea and Samaria, Israel's waist is eight and a half miles wide. Israel would simply become indefensible. In fact, in this scenario a terrorist firing a Stinger from the Judean hills could shoot every commercial plane taking off from and landing at Ben Gurion Airport.

While the president has referred to Israel's recalcitrance about a return to the so-called '67 borders, he overlooks the unwillingness of either Fatah or Hamas to recognize the state of Israel. On the contrary, even as they demand a state, they demonize Israel and launch weekly attacks against it.

Israeli opinion is divided. The left believes that since Israel cannot incorporate the nearly 4 million Arabs in the West Bank, the creation of a Palestinian state is a safety valve that avoids a demographic nightmare. The right contends a Palestinian state would be a sanctuary for terrorism, disrupting Israeli lives now and into the future.

Prime Minister Bibi Netanyahu contends a state can be created if the PA (Palestinian Authority) renounces violence, disarms and recognizes the state of Israel as a Jewish state. It is a reasonable stance politically, but one opposed by all parties in the Palestinian territory. Once again Palestinians seem to embrace the Abba Eban dictum in which "the Palestinians never miss an opportunity to miss an opportunity." However, in this case the opportunity may be seized by the General Assembly, seemingly eager to impose a Palestinian state on Israel without preconditions. Fortunately the U.S. is likely to veto any state proposal within the Security Council, halting at least for now any Palestinian national entity.

Within the White House there are very few divisions. President Obama is intent on mollifying Arab opinion. It is also much too complicated trying to sort out issues as political cultures in the region are roiling, but the Israeli-Palestinian issue can be addressed by simply putting more pressure on Israel. The only fly in the ointment is that President Obama is intent on reelection. For him to achieve this goal, he needs Jewish political and financial support. An active anti-Israeli agenda simply won't fly. So expect equivocation, appeasement and sounds of sweet harmony. It won't be sincere; then again it doesn't have to be since Jewish Americans are already inclined to support President Obama even if it isn't in their interest to do so.

Israel and Just-War Theory (2011)
Originally published on the Gatestone Institute

Now that a trade of more than a thousand convicted terrorists for one Israeli soldier has been transacted, it should be clear to any of the skeptics which side in the Middle East puts the greatest premium on life. Similarly, it should be noted from this trade which side adheres to the principles of a "just war."

Nevertheless, when Judge Richard Goldstone wrote his report about the conduct of the Israeli Defense Forces in the Gazan Cast Lead operation, he indicated in several places that the troops acted irresponsibly, leading to unnecessary deaths in the civilian population. Although Judge Goldstone later recanted, the damage was done. His report became a propaganda weapon against the Israeli government from Europe to Africa, from the groves of academe to the corridors of the United Nations.

The problem with the report is that Judge Goldstone relied on the reflections of officials in Gaza instead of films provided by the Israeli forces. Seeing isn't always believing, and doctored pictures have a notorious history. Nonetheless, I recently spent several hours viewing films that seem to offer incontrovertible evidence that Israeli troops did whatever they could to control collateral damage.

In fact, there were times when they put their own lives at risk in order to avoid killing an innocent person. Time after time a known terrorist hiding behind "human shields" in an apartment complex was spared in order to avoid the death of innocents. Rockets launched from a school roof remained untouched until children left the premises. In the heat of battle Israeli forces maintained a level of moral behavior that was exemplary. Were there civilians killed in the encounter? Of course; war is not volleyball. But that should not detract from the stance and behavior of the Israeli forces.

I recently had the occasion to ask a base commander about the behavior of his troops in battle. His response was revealing. "Our troops are trained to put life ahead of personal safety." The Israeli army officials contend that unnecessary shelling is not acceptable. Firepower is related directly to the force used against Israel.

Many commentators on this subject point to an Arab boy of about 10 crying as he approached a checkpoint. Soldiers on the scene went into high alert. It was obvious this deranged youngster had been recruited to be a suicide bomber. One Israeli soldier, recognizing the boy's agitation, called out to him, "Brother" in Arabic. It was not clear when or whether the youngster would set himself ablaze. Nonetheless, the IDF soldier continued to walk to the boy, took him in his arms and disarmed the explosive device around his waist. It is instructive that from that time on, the Palestinians began using a remote control device to explode suicide bombers. The episode also tells a great deal about the Israeli military psychology.

Arab attempts to paint a different picture of the IDF have been successful. Many in the Arab world see these well-trained and disciplined troops as amoral. That, however, is far from the truth. These Israeli 18- and 19-year-olds are told from the first day of national service that they carry the banner of a civilization that puts a premium on life. Their job is to protect and defend. They are given a green light to kill only when other methods to stop an enemy fail.

At a training session for IDF entrants at Ammunition Hill in Jerusalem, teenagers drafted into military service discuss the roots of war, the conflict in the Middle East, the history of this new nation. But most significantly, they study just-war theory and a moral stance for fighting those who rely on terror methods. Of course, no system is foolproof; occasionally a soldier will act improperly. This, however, is the exception. Israel is in a daily struggle. After all, 250 million Arabs want to destroy this nation. But Israeli leaders won't modify their moral code one iota. As the commander of this training center noted, "If we altered our approach, what effect would it have on soldiers when they leave military service?" One fights not only to save a nation, but to save basic civilizational values.

Israel's Existential Threat (2011)
Originally published on the Gatestone Institute

For a variety of reasons, including a misguided infatuation with soft power, neither the United States nor Israel has exercised the legitimate right of anticipatory self-defense against Iran. As a result, Iran's entry into the nuclear club is a virtual fait accompli. In Israel, a nation already targeted for annihilation, self-defense is limited to contingency plans, active defense and deterrence. However, each case is fallible.

Contingency plans make sense when preemption is an option. Should there be an attack on Israel, retaliation is the only option. Active defense is useful since it can confuse the planning of the enemy, but it is difficult, alas impossible, to know how many missiles will penetrate defenses in the mist of war. And last, deterrence is workable only if Iran is unwilling to risk the loss of life. If a theological scenario enters the nuclear equation, the prospective loss of innocent life may not deter.

In its latest report, 2011, the UN's International Atomic Energy Agency (IAEA) said it "remains concerned about the possible existence in Iran of past or current undisclosed nuclear related activities involving military-related organizations." However, when effective preemption or anticipatory self-deterrence is unstable, survival is largely dependent on missile defense from Arrow and Aegis destroyers. These systems in Israel are being perfected but they are not perfect. Hence Israel, as a way to enhance deterrence, might change its nuclear posture from "deliberate ambiguity" to counter city-targeting and cumulative penetration capability. As noted, this isn't a panacea, but it may well be that Iranian commentary about a nuclear conflagration as a prelude for the return of the Mahdi has rhetorical, not practical, applications.

Certainly Israel would like to avoid these contingencies, relying instead on the United States to deter, or if that fails, destroy the nuclear sites. At the moment, the U.S. seems to be resigned to an Iran with nuclear weapons. The Obama administration believes either that Iran is not a serious threat or that sanctions will at some point so damage the Iranian economy that deployment is rendered nugatory. With Germany, Switzerland, China and Russia violating the sanctions regimen, this hardly seems a viable course of action.

A nuclear Iran may be unthinkable, as every leader from President Obama to Nicolas Sarkozy has noted. But action doesn't necessarily follow a promise. President Bush argued that his presidency would be deemed a failure if he had left office and Iran had nuclear weapons.

Iran may be a threat to Europeans capitals and a long-term threat to the U.S., but it is a proximate threat to Israel now. It is the shadow that blocks Israeli sunlight. There are other issues in Israel, including the Palestinian question; yet there is only one existential issue: the Iranian nuclear threat. Whether it is six months, one year or several years away from completion, the Iran nuclear juggernaut is moving ahead, serving as a Damoclean sword over the heads of the Israeli people.

Israeli batteries at the Iron Dome and Arrow facilities remain confident. They have every reason to feel this way. The troops are strong and their devotion to the security of the Israeli people is unshakable. Still there are the unknowns—penetration ratios, effectiveness in battle, unpredictable conditions. Yet every commander I met in my recent trip to Israel expressed the belief that they will do whatever is necessary to protect the Israeli nation. In Israel, it often seems that God is nearby. Despite the destruction of the First Temple and the attempt by the Romans to destroy the Second Temple, the Jewish people managed to prevail. When I said to one officer that Iran could have the means to destroy Israel, he said, "Never again! Need I say more?"

The Israeli War with Gaza (2012)
Originally published on Family Security Matters

It is astonishing to see Ban-ki-Moon and Hillary Clinton, among others, clamoring for a truce between Israel and Hamas-led terrorists. One wonders where these diplomats were when more than a thousand missiles rained over Israel without retaliation.

Clearly the pressure on Prime Minister Benjamin Netanyahu to halt the bloodshed is intense. But the fact is, there are interests that keenly wish to pursue war. For Iran, this season of Hamas terror is a useful distraction, as it pursues its goal of nuclear weapons capability. For Egypt, this war offers Prime Minister Morsi an opportunity to rally his Sunni brothers in Saudi Arabia. For Turkey, the rockets fulfill Prime Minister Erdogan's dream of uniting the Muslim faithful. For Hamas, the fighting creates the imaginary belief that Israel is vulnerable and can be defeated in time.

Hamas has used the launching of rockets to convey the impression it is a political force to be reckoned with. Youthful adherents brutalize alleged spies on the streets of Gaza City, creating a belief that disloyalty will not be countenanced. And Hamas leaders demand that the blockade against the Gaza Strip be lifted before negotiations for a truce commence.

As I see it, all the talk about a truce, before every rocket is destroyed, is nonsensical. A truce at this stage only means Hamas can retreat to fight or launch rockets another day. It is useful for the Iranians to understand that the rockets it manufactures and sends to Gaza represent a diminishing asset, an investment without return. It is also important that Hamas realize the border it shares with Egypt is a target for military contraband.

Israel can certainly be threatened, but as this latest conflict shows, it cannot be defeated. The Iron Dome is 90 percent effective in thwarting incoming missiles, and the Israeli military has clear air superiority. However, these missile attacks are designed to sap the spirit of the nation. The sound of sirens in southern Israel awakens fear. Yet the global press ignores conditions that would be intolerable in any other nation. Israel is sui generis, a place where the blood of its citizens doesn't matter to the outside world.

Even as Hamas strengthens its grip on Gaza, U.S. secretary of state Hillary Clinton talks of reempowering Palestinian leader Abbas. Here is naiveté in full bloom. Hamas defeated Abbas' Fatah to gain control in Gaza. In fact, Abbas hasn't any standing in this den of terrorists; he has lost control over the West Bank as well. Extremism is in the air. Hamas smells it and whatever the outcome, this terrorist organization will claim victory. It is a false victory of pride born of what the terrorists desire, not what they are capable of achieving.

For Prime Minister Netanyahu, there is a way forward, since the peace he seeks is achievable only through war, a total war that emasculates Hamas' rocket force. Every other stratagem is either unworkable or subject to a succeeding chapter of warfare.

Whether the pressure from the international community for a ceasefire is irresistible remains to be seen. U.S. spokespeople contend that a truce is needed to prevent a larger, regional war. On several levels this contention is implausible. Egypt may have sympathy for Hamas, but an invasion of Egyptian forces would lead to an ignominious defeat, subjecting the Muslim Brotherhood to humiliation and possible electoral failure. Iran will provide missiles surreptitiously, but direct aid to Hamas could trigger an Israeli attack.

As a consequence, tension may be rising, but cooler heads are likely to prevail when Muslim faithful clamor for an all-out attack on Israel. As things stand, Israel's defense fortifications and the strength of its military forces stand as the bulwark for stability in the region. What Israel cannot forget is that the essential strength of the nation lies in the resilience of its people. They endure rocket attacks; they endure bloodshed. What can never be surrendered is the will of the Jewish people. Eretz Israel is the Jewish homeland; when Arabs learn this is a truth that cannot be overturned, peace will reign.

The Multipronged Attack on Israel (2014)
Originally published on Family Security Matters

In the international effort to undermine Israel, every avenue of attack from the military to the cultural is being employed. The Arab world is continually stirred to a frenzy pitch on imaginary or exaggerated threats. Palestinian Authority president Abbas (seemingly president for life) spread the unfounded incendiary rumor that Israeli settlers were "desecrating" Al-Aqsa Mosque and noting "we must stop them [the settlers] from entering by any means possible." But there isn't a scintilla of evidence that this claim is true.

When Mahmoud Abbas maintained that Jerusalem should be inundated with massive Muslim tourism in order "to preserve its Muslim nature," Sheikh Qaradawi repudiated this idea, arguing instead that visiting Jerusalem is forbidden so long as it is under Israeli occupation: "Jerusalem must be liberated by force and not by 'tourism.'" As al Qaeda sees it, "Jerusalem is the capital of the imminently approaching Islamic caliphate."

These threats and the ever-present hostile rhetoric create hateful responses. An intifada or the signs of it are breaking out in

Jerusalem. Hundreds of young Palestinians have been arrested for the use of "cold weaponry," such as stones, Molotov cocktails and light explosives. All of the assailants exhort the slogan of "popular resistance" preached to them by Palestinian Authority president Abbas, even though those in the Obama administration insist on calling him "a moderate."

None of these recent outbursts is surprising after President Abbas' speech in the United Nations in which he accused Israel of waging a "war of genocide" in the Gaza Strip. Needless to say, President Abbas did not mention the thousands of rockets fired into Israel before war commenced.

On October 22 Chaya Zissel Braun, a three-month-old infant, was killed when a Palestinian man slammed his vehicle into a crowd at a light rail stop in Jerusalem. Nine people were injured, three seriously, and one woman died from her injuries. Hamas took credit for this heinous act.

Forty-eight hours before the attack, President Abbas announced that any Palestinian who is involved in property transactions with "hostile countries" (read: Israel) would be punished by "life imprisonment with hard labor." Incitement is a way of life for the PA and Hamas, and unless it is curtailed there will be other terrorist attacks.

But this internal war and exogenous pressure is not the only way the enemies of Israel exert pressure.

An international movement to sever Israel from commercial activity and cultural exchange is well under way. The BDS (Boycott, Divestment and Sanctions) movement is a systematic effort to demonize and delegitimize the state of Israel. Front organizations for the Muslim Brotherhood such as CAIR and the Muslim Student Association have gained a foothold on many university campuses. In fact, they are often so successful that Jewish groups such as several Hillels have fallen for the rhetorical argument. This cultural assault continues unabated, with many faculty groups censuring Israel and refusing to engage in conferences or exchange with Israeli scholars.

In banning Israel from the normal intercourse of state and non-state activity, the Muslim activists are trying to create an environment in which Israel is regarded as a pariah, a state isolated from the international community.

Israel is clearly up against it, as has always been the case. Yet it maintains its resolve through a combination of military strength and unusual solidarity and morale, qualities attributed to military service. Truth is on Israel's side, a point many do not understand. It is a bastion of individual freedom in a sea of totalitarian control. Admittedly, as the quote usually attributed to Mark Twain goes, "a lie can travel halfway around the world while the truth is putting on its shoes." Israel must contend with lies daily, but its shoes are on and it faces the struggle with a stout heart.

Moral Equivalence in the Israeli War with Hamas? (2014)
Originally published on Family Security Matters

The winds of moral equivalence in the Middle East are persistent. As the war between terrorists in Gaza and the Israeli government escalates, the media resists the idea of taking sides. CNN contends there are valid positions on both sides of the divide. Ethan Bonner, a *New York Times* correspondent, contends the wall separating Gaza from Israel and Israel from the West Bank is the real impediment to peace.

But is this true? Israel has been attacked unmercifully, with 1,000 rockets fired indiscriminately at Israeli population centers. These rockets have only one purpose: instill panic. Israel has responded in the way any nation under siege would. It has fired back forcefully at all the launch sites in Gaza. This has led to collateral damage, with over 480 Palestinians killed. What hasn't been emphasized is that Gazan rockets have been fired from mosques, hospitals and schools. Human shields are the tactical defense for terrorism.

On the Israeli side, people are protected from rockets; on the Gazan side rockets are protected from people. There isn't an obvious moral equivalence between sides. Moreover, the Palestinian population rejoiced over the murder of three young Jewish students. The mother of one of the assailants said she admired her son's action. When a group of Israeli youths retaliated by apprehending a Palestinian boy and burning him to death, the Israeli officials were appalled and quickly brought the murderers to justice. Is Jewish blood worth less than the blood of Palestinians?

There isn't any world leader who can tolerate terror bombing on his people without a response. Prime Minister Netanyahu has been patient, but when he has spoken he has noted that Jews, whatever their political persuasion, are united in battling the terror and are prepared to respond with whatever force is necessary to eliminate the threat.

Children should not live their lives in fear that the sound of a siren might mean the end of life. This is the life of an Israeli today. Some contend that there are more deaths on the Gazan side, reflecting the use of disproportionate Israeli action. Clearly the loss of any innocent life is tragic. However, it is Hamas that has put its own people in jeopardy. The placement of its rockets reflects the barbarous view of Arab leadership.

This is not a war to end war, since the beating heart of bitterness and hatred is everywhere present in the Middle East. However, the immediate threat of Hamas, which has 100,000 missiles in its arsenal, goes to the very survival of Israel. Gaza must be disarmed. If occupation is necessary, so be it. The pockets of arms throughout this strip of land must be discovered and destroyed. There isn't any alternative.

Voltaire once contended that somewhere between differing views lies the truth. In the Middle East this contention is fundamentally flawed. There is one side that is right and one that is wrong. Unfortunately the side that is wrong has gambled the fate of its own population on a saturation bombing strategy.

Talleyrand argued, *"Surtout, pas trop de zele"* (above all, not too much zeal). Alas, this is the Arab problem. Zealousness dictates policy. A desire to destroy Israel by any means is an overarching theme. Violence has been romanticized by Hamas leaders. Rational discourse, compromise and negotiation have not and will not work. The romance must be eviscerated, revealed as the horror and misguided view it represents.

It starts in Gaza, but will not end there. Israel's enemies surround it, but if this nation under siege can remain strong on the military and emotional front, it will prosper. Determination is the antidote to enemy rockets overhead. Prime Minister Netanyahu understands that, and in the outpouring of public unity, the people of Israel understand it as well.

Israel and the United Nations

Will the U.S. Save Israel or Will Israel Save the U.S.? (2011)
Originally published on the Gatestone Institute

With a vote at the UN this week on Palestinian statehood, it is appropriate to ask if the United States will save Israel or if Israel will save the United States.

After my having spent 10 days visiting defense installations in Israel and talking to members of the general staff, my confidence about Israel's ability to defend itself has soared. This tiny nation of 7 million is a miracle of technical marvels and remarkable spirit. Every weapons system this nation buys is Israelized. The Israeli drone is a composite of parts from several nations and Israeli avionics. The F-15 is an American plane adapted for the unique conditions in the Middle East neighborhood.

While some sabras lament the decrease in national spirit, the IDF education program instills in each and every draftee a sense of national history and purpose. It is inspiring to meet teenagers of 18 and 19 who are prepared to make battlefield decisions. I almost fainted when I encountered a 21-year-old brigade commander in an elite unit who is an articulate warrior and at least as sophisticated as most officers 10 years his senior in the United States.

In their book *Start-Up Nation,* Dan Senor and Saul Singer point out that these soldiers with great responsibility become desirable candidates for corporate recruiters. One highly decorated communication's unit had three times the number of applicants as available billets. As one officer pointed out, these youngsters can secure some of the nation's most desirable jobs once the tour of duty is over.

Since Israel is not saddled with a hydra-headed bureaucracy expanding to meet regulations and oversight committees, Israel's military force is lean, adaptable and alert. Clearly incompetence at any point in the chain of command could be deadly.

The larger U.S. force structure and international missions militate against the adoption of an Israeli system. Nonetheless, there is much to be learned. The hair-trigger response to attacks of any kind, the ability to move ground troops quickly and the surveillance tools are unquestionably a source of security strength. Israel, despite having 7 million residing in a turbulent area of 250 million hostile Arabs, is a unique illustration of military preparedness.

There are those in the United States who believe Israel is a strategic liability. As long as we are committed to its survival, American forces will be obliged to be in harm's way. Of course, what these detractors overlook is that Israel is the *missus dominici* for the U.S., our eyes and ears in a region fraught with extremists. In a real sense, Israel is the first line of defense in the war against radical Islam, a war that promises to be long and bloody. Israel is not merely an ally, it is a democratic nation in a despotic wasteland.

This war is not only likely to be long, it is a civilizational battle in which liberalism—with its attendant values of individual rights, free markets, private property and the rule of law—is pitted against eighth-century adherence to conformity and opposition to personal liberty. Israel assumes the vanguard in this struggle, in part because of its location and in part because its very survival is dependent on prevailing against its adversaries.

To return to the question of whether the U.S. can save Israel or whether Israel can save the U.S. is to realize that the relationship is symbiotic. The U.S. needs Israel as a first line of defense, a barrier against the expansion of radical Islam; Israel needs the U.S. for technical advances and the assertion of international power. If the day comes when the U.S. believes Israel can be set adrift, international equilibrium will be permanently disrupted. Israel is the U.S. listening post in a world where intelligence is critical for security. As political currents are roiled by expressions of regional dismay and religious orthodoxy, U.S. interests are in a cauldron of uncertainty. That condition, perhaps more than any other, explains why the U.S. needs this extraordinary ally in the Kingdom of David.

Israel Deserves Fair Treatment by the UN (2014)
Originally published on Newsmax

While the anti-Zionists are busily scurrying about thinking of ways to yet again chastise Israel for defending itself, it seems to me important that the public understand what this Jewish nation faces.

Despite considerable success in eliminating rocket caches in Gaza, many remain and many can still be fired at Israeli population centers, despite the truce. The Iron Dome has been an extraordinary success as an anti-missile system for short-range rockets and as a deterrent for attacks. Yet even with a success rate of about 90 percent, a lot of damage and terror can be inflicted by the remaining 10 percent.

The Gaza arsenal controlled by Hamas and the rockets possessed by Hezbollah now can reach every area of Israel. Syrian-made M-302s have a range of 150 kilometers, or 93 miles. The Iranian-made FAJR-5 has a range of 75 kilometers, or 47 miles, and the Gazan-made Qassam has a range of 20 kilometers, or 12 miles.

The M-302, sometimes described as the Khaibar 1, is an anti-personnel and armor-piercing dual-purpose weapon. Its blasting head can be loaded with steel balls and prefabricated fragments. Most significantly, it is fuel-air capable—i.e., it can create a gas cloud fire burst yielding a vacuum that leads to suffocation and death. Some have described the M-302 as "the poor man's nuclear bomb."

In addition, on March 5, 2014, Iran tried to smuggle 40 M-302s, 180 mortar shells and 400,000 assault rifle rounds into the Gaza Strip, reinforcing an already well-stocked storehouse of weapons. This story of Iranian smuggling and capture was covered in the press, but it received scant attention and has not been mentioned during the course of the present war.

Although military experts sneer at the crudely made inaccurate Katyusha missiles, they often overlook the fact that this weapon can be equipped with chemical weapons, obviating the need for accuracy. An Israeli boy of about four years old was maimed and lost a leg from a Katyusha that was armed with ball bearings on the warhead, designed to destroy virtually anything in its path.

When the UN engages in debate on this Israel-Hamas war, it will invariably cite the "disproportionate" casualties in Gaza. What it won't do is examine the threat Hamas and its arsenal of weapons poses to every Israeli citizen. Nor will it consider a nation under perpetual siege and a Hamas charter devoted to the elimination of the Jewish state.

Two years ago in a conversation with Secretary General Ban-ki Moon, I asked why Israel cannot be treated as merely another state in the United Nations, not better or worse. His response was silence—a deafening silence.

Israel is regarded as sui generis. It is a nation expected to accept attack without retaliation. It is a place where every misdeed is magnified and excoriated. And it is a land in which vile slander and lies are supposed to be accepted.

Hamas terrorists (excuse the redundancy) assassinated 18 so-called collaborators on the streets of Gaza, an object lesson to others. Where is the outrage? What will the Human Rights Commission say about the matter? If history and common sense are guides, the answer is "nothing." If in some fantasy there were role reversals and Israeli troops shot suspected collaborators without a trial, world opinion would scorn the government.

Israel is different—it is a nation of Jews who understand individual rights and the rule of law in a region that neither knows nor cares about the perpetuation of life and liberty. Maybe the UN has a point, even if it is not the point intended.

The European Slide to Anti-Zionism (2014)
Originally published on The Algemeiner

Although it isn't binding, the British parliament voted in favor of recognizing a Palestinian state. British MPs voted 274 to 12 for a non-binding motion to "recognize the state of Palestine alongside the state of Israel as a contribution to securing a negotiated two-state solution." The remainder of the parliament's 650 MPs abstained.

Whatever one thinks of this vote, it is a sign of shifting public opinion in the United Kingdom and beyond. The debate in the House of Commons came after the Swedish government announced it would recognize a Palestinian state—the first European Union member in Western Europe to do so. Many contend that the war in Gaza influenced British public opinion against Israel, while others maintain the vote was merely the evolution of attitudes promoted by homegrown Muslims.

Britain's ambassador to Israel, Matthew Gould, said even though the vote isn't binding on the British government, it is "significant." Alas, it is. The resolution was welcomed by Palestinians and criticized by Israel.

The Israeli foreign ministry argues that the "premature international recognition sends a troubling message to the Palestinian leadership that they can evade the tough choices that both sides have to make and actually undermines the chances to reach a real peace." It is logical to ask why the Palestinians should negotiate at all when the end game has been established.

For years a two-state solution has been bandied about, but arriving at an understanding about the boundaries and security remains in limbo. Suppose there is a sovereign Palestinian state with rockets that can paralyze Ben Gurion Airport and reach every Israeli population center—is that a state Israel can countenance?

British parliamentarians may believe they are contributing to a negotiated peace, but in fact by suggesting a Palestinian state be imposed on Israel, they are bringing Israel to the brink of war.

This British vote is emblematic of a willful European tilt to the Palestinian position. There will undoubtedly be other symbolic gestures of this kind across the continent. Public opinion has been mobilized by Muslims, anti-Semites who no longer feel restrained by standards of public decency, left-wing activists and those influenced by news accounts in the Israeli war against Hamas.

European newspaper editorials invariably contend that anti-Israel sentiment is not related to anti-Semitism. Anti-Zionism masquerades as the pursuit of social justice, not bigotry. But for so many in Europe today, starting with the MPs, the question that remains is, whose justice?

If Zionism is perceived as the original sin, only dismantling the Jewish state can redress it. But for Jews with a memory, the main guarantor of Jewish security since the end of World War II has been the sovereign state of Israel. This state wasn't born on the ashes of the Holocaust, but it is the last fortress against its reenactment.

Votes in European parliaments may make politicians feel good, but the actual effect is pernicious, since a message is sent to the Palestinians that they don't have to reach ends through negotiation and concessions; the European parliaments will do that for them.

UN Unfairly Rages Against Israel (2015)
Originally published on Newsmax

It is axiomatic to suggest that if the UN issues a report, it will be anti-Israel. Last week a report was issued drawing a false moral equivalence between a terror group—Hamas—and a democracy in which Arabs are represented in the Knesset—Israel.

This libel that any Israeli response to violence, any retaliation for unprovoked rocket attacks, is reprehensible belongs in the book of shame. Nevertheless, the UN is shameless. The report blames Israel for war crimes despite a statement from military leaders from four continents that "Israel not only met a reasonable standard of observance of the laws of armed conflict, but in many cases significantly exceeded that standard" during last summer's war.

It was clear from the outset that Hamas was the aggressor, having launched thousands of rockets into Israel before there was any military response. But that is merely part of the story.

Hamas broke 11 separate ceasefire agreements during the war. It used civilians as human shields, a tactic employed in previous Middle East conflicts. And it fired rockets from schools, mosques and hospitals knowing that any retaliation at these sites would lead to casualties and international condemnation.

Israel is the only nation on the globe routinely criticized for defending itself. It is instructive that the UN charter specifically mentions self-defense as a necessity against aggression, but 57 Arab states, voting as a bloc, ignore the regulations in the body they personally sanction. Israel is by any measure an outlier—a nation with a set of conditions unmet and unneeded by any other nation.

There will be other wars fought in the Middle East, and like those in the past, reports will be written. The notorious Goldstone Report from the prior war, was ultimately repudiated by Judge Goldstone himself. But it doesn't matter. Recollection is selective. Those seeking to destroy the state of Israel will employ military and propagandistic tactics.

It is not surprising that the pressure now exerted on Israel for a negotiated settlement with Palestinians is coming from France, Germany, Sweden and other European nations. Rather than discuss terms directly with Israel, Hamas and PLO leaders will engage in forums in Europe to demonize Israel amid unsavory diplomatic and student audiences.

The latest UN report is in the arsenal of contemporary rhetoric. It is a useful and handy service that will aid in the public debate, however wrongheaded it may be. On the streets of Paris are protestors arguing that Israel must be censored, isolated, condemned. This echo returns to the corridors of the UN General Assembly. And this is what Israel is obliged to redress.

Some would argue—and I am among them—that truth will set you free. Needless to say, there is truth amid the miasmic propaganda. The question is how to release it and who will listen. So many minds have been made up about the Palestinian question that truth is a casualty of continued lies, and those lies become thought of as truth.

I have tried to debate detractors of Israel who are unwilling to hear evidence that challenges a mindset. This is not merely a closed mind; it is an environment intent on destruction of Israel. Hence any tactic is acceptable, any lie dismissed. Emotion rules.

The latest UN report that advertises itself as "evenhanded" is anything but fair. There is a moral gap between those that want to protect their people and those who intentionally put noncombatants in harm's way. For those who need additional fuel for their flame of indignation, this report delivers. For those who care about truth, this UN report is another in a long line of provocative and false allegations against the state of Israel.

Israel and Iran

The Unfolding Iranian Drama (2009)
Originally published in The American Spectator

Based on hints, feints, public pronouncements and off-the-record commentary, the administration's stance toward Iran is coming into focus. Without any question, military action against Iran is off the agenda. The Obama administration will do nothing to prevent the further enrichment of uranium by Iran's mullahs, notwithstanding who is elected in that nation's upcoming vote.

The negotiations with Iran are based on the premise that Iran can produce as much enriched uranium as it wants as long as a nuclear bomb isn't manufactured. In other words, President Obama seeks a "Japanese solution," the conditions for a bomb without actually making one.

For some, this is a distinction without a difference, since the bomb can be made in days if deployment is in the cards. If President Obama can get the Iranians to agree to this arrangement with adequate blandishments provided by our side, including the lifting of sanctions, he will announce with great fanfare that "peace" between Iran and the West has been achieved. For keen observers of the region, it will be regarded as a "Munich peace." For others, it will be seen as a significant diplomatic breakthrough.

In order to mollify Israeli leaders that this deal isn't threatening to that nation's survival, President Obama will argue that the United States stands committed to employ its nuclear umbrella to protect Israel against nuclear attack. Although this offer will be made with apparent sincerity, it is hard to believe that President Obama would be willing to risk the safety of New York in order to protect Tel Aviv. Moreover, it is also hard to believe any serious official in Israel will accept this proposal, albeit other options may not be available.

The Obama administration has made it clear that it will punish Israel if it decides to attack Iran unilaterally. Having failed to contain Iran, the United States is concentrating on restraining Israel. Administration contingency plans include a formal condemnation of Israel, support for a United Nations Security Council resolution that could include sanctions against Israel and suspending military aid to the Jewish state.

The big question is what the Obama administration will do if Israel determines that an Iran with the capacity to build nuclear weapons is an existential threat and, despite U.S. disapproval, attacks Iran in any case. Moreover, how will President Obama react if Iran retaliates against Israel as well as shutting down the 29-mile-wide Strait of Hormuz, through which 20 percent of the world's crude oil is transported? Would the U.S. fight back, would it blame

Israel for the preemptive attack on Iran, appealing to the "Muslim world" for understanding?

Iran, which has vowed "to wipe Israel off the map," and its Hezbollah and Hamas proxies would retaliate with missile launches on Tel Aviv and Haifa should any attack on Iran occur. For Israel to be even marginally successful, it must eliminate missile installations in Gaza, Lebanon and Iran—a truly formidable military objective.

Decades of appeasement and accommodations with Iran have led to the present impasse. These policy blunders cannot be attributed to President Obama. In fact, blame belongs on both sides of the political aisle. However, what distinguishes President Obama's diplomatic initiative from others is the "downgrading" of Israel in order to strike a "grand bargain" with Iran for regional "pacification." Whether Prime Minister Bibi Netanyahu wants it or not, Jerusalem is now on a collision course with Washington.

Israelis may be understandably stunned by the evolution of events. They are on the horns of a dilemma. Prime Minister Netanyahu has responded to the emerging U.S. position by noting that he will be accommodative on any argument with the Palestinians if President Obama can negate the Iranian threat. He is attempting to establish a nexus between a Palestinian accord and the elimination of this threat. After all, he contends, if Iran is in the position to build nuclear weapons, the weapons serve as a cover for Hamas missile attacks against the state of Israel, since escalation could lead to a nuclear exchange and should be avoided at all costs.

The Obama administration position is 180 degrees in a different direction. It appears to be arguing that an accommodative Israel that makes a deal with the Palestinians for a separate state will have American protection against a possible Iranian nuclear attack. But the first and overarching responsibility lies with Israel to arrange its negotiated settlement with Palestinian leaders.

President Obama believes time is on his side, since he has already conceded with his "engagement" drive that Iran will have the time to enrich enough uranium to build a nuclear weapon. Prime Minister Netanyahu, unable to accept the potential threat, feels time is of the essence. The closer Iran gets to the fateful "tipping point," the closer Israel is to survival issues.

Erstwhile president Jimmy Carter tried to assuage Israeli leaders in 1979 by noting that his craven concession to Iranian leaders did not pose a threat to Israel. Is President Obama preparing to go one step further in downgrading the importance of Israel in his attenuated negotiation with Iran? History is waiting impatiently for an answer, and the world waits with bated breath.

Russia's Presence a Bad Sign for Israel (2015)
Originally published on Newsmax

Recent reports have indicated that hundreds of Islamic Revolutionary Guard Corps troops entered Syria in early September. Moreover, the accord on intelligence among Russia, Iran, Iraq and Syria suggests Russian troops will be assisting the Iranians in the war against the Islamic State. That may not be all.

Israeli officials are appropriately concerned that Russian troops will be operating in the Golan Heights along with Hezbollah and al-Assad-led Syrian forces. Israel is faced with the additional challenge of the expanded Russian presence in Syria, especially in the Latakia region, where in the past IDF forces destroyed arms convoys intended for Hezbollah.

When Israeli forces returned fire on two Syrian positions near Quneitra, Russian president Vladimir Putin responded: "We respect Israel's interests related to the Syrian civil war, but we are concerned about its attacks on Syria." Clearly this statement is mutually contradictory; if you are concerned about Israel's interests, then it must be protected by defensive military action. Nonetheless, this response stands as a warning signal. Certain attacks may be justified as long as they do not jeopardize the position and security of Syrian president Bashar al-Assad.

In a recent trip to Moscow, Israeli prime minister Benjamin Netanyahu argued that Israel "will maintain its position of non-involvement in the Syrian civil war, but I would not allow Hezbollah and other terrorist groups to amass advanced weapons systems, nor would I tolerate attacks against the Golan Heights." This statement was obviously an effort to establish rules of engagement with Russian forces, rules that would be violated if Russia equips Hezbollah with sophisticated missiles. There is little doubt that the presence of Russian forces introduces a new and somewhat constraining variable in Israeli strategic thinking.

It is also instructive that Iran has agreed to purchase $21 billion of aircraft and satellite equipment from Russia, one of the largest military transactions in Russian history and a transaction made possible through the lifting of sanctions.

What this means is that Israel is not only surrounded by Muslim neighbors with evil intent, but Russia, directly or indirectly, could be in an adversarial position as well. From the defensive position Israel is in, there aren't easy answers. In the past the support of the United States served as a counterweight to the hostile intent of Israel's Arab neighbors. However, the Iran deal militates against active U.S. assistance. For the Obama team, Israel is a distraction standing in the way of a regional plan that includes U.S. withdrawal and Iranian hegemony.

Russia's enlarged military footprint in Syria has not even led to a whimper from President Obama, a silence that sends a clear and uncluttered message to Israel. As a consequence, Israel is on its own, unmoored from ties to the United States. This complicates military action, but it does not forestall what may be necessary.

Israelis realize what Evelyn Waugh once noted, that "barbarism is never finally defeated; given propitious circumstances, men and women who seem quite orderly will commit every conceivable atrocity." Israel has experienced those atrocities with knifings on the street, often from unexpected quarters. Now it is alone on a globe that seemingly does not care about the Jewish state. The questions that remain are: can Israel defend itself, and can it maintain the morale necessary to defeat its apparent and possible enemies? These are "big" questions.

Obama's Parting Shots at Israel

Obama Spurns Israel in Pursuit of Legacy (2016)
Originally published on Newsmax

The stabbing spree in Israel by Palestinian terrorists continues unabated. Even when an American citizen visiting Israel is killed, "What, me worry?" president Obama is unfazed. At this point in his presidency Obama has only one goal: burnishing his legacy.

To augment the chapters of a future history, I believe he intends to accomplish what none of his predecessors could—a Middle East settlement. And he intends to achieve this lofty goal through imposition. This president will not wander through the tall weeds of negotiation and give and take. Nor is he obliged to adhere to 242, the international law that requires an exchange between Israel and the Palestinian Authority before any settlement. He intends to propose a "two-state solution" to the UN Security Council, a body already predisposed to accept the idea.

President Obama is not likely to call on his Democratic colleagues in the House and Senate before he engages in this initiative. This is his call, yet another example of his imperial presidency. He is also likely to face almost no resistance in the United Nations, where many Arab states have recognized the Palestinian Authority (PA) as a legitimate state. The irony, of course, is that the PA is to a state what a meal is to a morsel of food.

Were it not for Israeli largess, international aid and U.S. support, the PA could not exist. The West Bank's so-called leader, Abu Abbas, has been serving as president for 12 years after a four-year term. Corruption is rampant in every area controlled by Arab leadership. The police function—to maintain a semblance of order—is underwritten by the United States. Hamas and the Islamic State have penetrated underground cells in Ramallah and other areas. While a tenuous relationship exists between Jews and Arabs in the region, Israeli businesses provide many of the job opportunities for Arabs, even the most disenchanted.

Into this morass enters President Obama, or so I believe. Recognizing the futility of attempting to secure congressional support, the president is a lone ranger using the agency of the United Nations for his agenda. Since the P5+1 deal over the Iranian nuclear program, it is clear the president has channeled foreign policy through the United Nations. It is also clear he assumes that his status as commander in chief gives him, ipso facto, authority for unilateral foreign policy decisions.

Since he has already alienated Israeli prime minister Netanyahu and, considering his lame-duck status, cannot experience any further political fallout from his UN posturing, this action will be widely admired in the Arab world, perhaps even altering a widely shared negative opinion of the president. And who knows, maybe it will result in deals and post-presidential speaking fees à la Bill Clinton.

The problem with this worthless effort is that Israel will be left holding the proverbial bag. PA officials, aka Hamas leadership, will claim a "legitimate" right for trade, transport and defense in the newly created state. The Organization of Islamic Cooperation, with all of its 57 states, will agree. As a consequence, Israel will be facing yet another hostile front, with the possibility a border will be created within a two-mile range of Ben Gurion Airport, the hub of commercial traffic.

In his delightful book *Alice's Adventures in Wonderland*, Lewis Carroll wrote:

> "He's dreaming now," said Tweedledee: "and what do you think he is dreaming about?"
> Alice said, "Nobody can guess that."
> "Why, about *you!*" Tweedledee exclaimed, clapping his hands triumphantly. "And if he left off dreaming about you, where do you suppose you'd be?"
> "Where I am now, of course," said Alice.

> "Not you!" Tweedledee retorted contemptuously. "You'd be nowhere. Why, you're only a sort of thing in his dream!"
> "If that there King was to wake," added Tweedledum, "you'd go out—bang!—just like a candle."

Alas, PA Arabs are obsessed with a dream about the elimination of Israel. They are nowhere without the dream, but in reality that dream can be blown away like a candle's flame. The only thing that keeps it burning is the misguided vision of a president who would like to be judged as the man who did what others couldn't. Too bad he hasn't read Lewis Carroll.

Barack Obama's Swan Song to Israel (2016)
Originally published by WAMC Northeast Public Radio

Now that the smoke has cleared at the United Nations, there is little question about President Obama's intentions; they are now crystal clear. Incontrovertible evidence exists that suggests the proposal for a return to the 1967 borders in Israel was orchestrated by the White House. By any measure that is a break from the historic ties between the U.S. and Israel and, as many commentators have noted, an act of betrayal.

It is also an act that cannot be trivialized. Of course, Israel will ignore the proposition. Prime Minister Netanyahu hasn't any alternative. President Trump will regard it as an openly hostile act and may repudiate it by naming Jerusalem the capital of Israel. But what must also be realized is that even a coat of paint in a Jewish settlement in the West Bank is technically illegal and a violation of international law, according to the International Court of Justice in the Hague. While the court doesn't have the ability to impose its will, as was demonstrated by Chinese president Xi Jinping's repudiating a decision on the Spratly Islands, it can bog down the Israeli government in legal harassment.

Most significantly, this proposal could be a casus belli. Suppose Palestinian activists decide to take matters into their own hands by arguing they have a legitimate claim to Samaria and Judea, thereby employing force to obtain the territory they have acquired through legal decree. What President Obama may not have thought through is how disruptive his proposal might be. Moreover, since the Sunni nations have put the Palestinian question behind them, it is odd that President Obama should insert it into the international equation as a front-burner issue. Now terrorist groups like Hamas, Hezbollah and Iranian Quds can claim a legitimate right to attack an Israeli government theoretically violating the law.

Even the insertion of a note into the Western Wall, a practice that has gone on as a Jewish religious ritual since 1967, can be declared an act violating the UN proposal. That President Obama chose this matter as his swan song is revealing. His hostility toward Israel has been manifest in many ways, but at no point in the past has an American president acted as President Obama has. This White House abstention and behind-the-scenes maneuvering with sponsoring states is unprecedented. The lies leading to the decision and rationalizations in the aftermath are also unprecedented.

In fact, this decision puts a slow burn on Donald Trump. Despite the number of global issues he will be obliged to digest setting foot in the White House, from Syria to NATO, from the South China Sea air perimeter to North Korea, he will now be saddled with a Palestinian state issue most officials thought was on hold for the foreseeable future.

President Obama has virtually destroyed any legacy he hoped to transmit to future historians about his eight years in office. He has left in ruins all he tried to manage.

The world is in disarray in large part because of his mismanagement or ignoring any management.

His ego won't allow a dispassionate assessment of the Obama presidency, but if one were to do so after this recent UN fiasco, Barack Obama would have to be considered among the worst presidents in American history.

Cultural Decline and Its Effect on Foreign Policy

American foreign policy requires the will of its people to persist, and generally mirrors the morality of the present. President Obama certainly came to the Oval Office with his own worldview, but his reelection indicated that at least half of the American electorate was satisfied with his job performance after four years. The following columns examine the context of the cultural trends that made room for American influence and moral clarity to wane abroad.

Post-Christian Europe and the Rise of Islam: A Strategy for Winning the War of Ideas (2010)

Great changes are afoot in Western culture. The world as we've known it is becoming a markedly different place, and a more dangerous one, where the very basis of our civilization is increasingly challenged. Let me begin by identifying some of the intellectual and moral factors that are altering our cultural landscape.

The first is multiculturalism, an attitude that proclaims the equality of all cultures but paradoxically assumes that non-Western cultures are somehow more equal, more worthy, than their Western counterparts. This Orwellian phenomenon preaches the gospel of equality, but proceeds as much from self-loathing as from egalitarianism. If women in America on average earn less than men, that is a form of oppression; but if an African culture indulges in ritual mutilation in the form of clitordectomy, that, for the multiculturalist, is simply an expression of cultural difference.

A second factor precipitating cultural change in the West is the decay of religion. European churches are now more museums than places of worship. And even the much-touted religiousness of Americans is often more a function of social activity than spiritual observance. In the precincts of elite culture, anyway, the moral and spiritual teachings of Christianity have been in large part interred and replaced by a tepid relativism or various "new age" or "spiritual" outlooks.

A third shift in attitude is that extreme form of liberalism in which the traditional liberal virtue of tolerance has degenerated into an unwillingness to discriminate. According to this anesthetic philosophy, right and wrong are archaic concepts that belong to the ash heap of history. What counts is "openness," that perversion of tolerance that, as Allan Bloom observed in *The Closing of the American Mind*, is indistinguishable from indifference.

Radical secularists nurture a hope that rationalism, now that it has supplanted religion, can solve all problems. If only people— or their more far-sighted representatives—are playing on the same field, then all the world's heretofore unsolvable problems can be solved. This is the fourth shift; a utopian delusion has led to the rise of transnationalism. In our time, the chief example of the trend is the effort to reduce or eliminate the national heritage of European states through continental harmonization. This effort has had the unintended consequence of making citizens rudderless, robbing them of their national identity and undermining their patriotism. In the United States, transnationalism has adherents who argue that the American experience should be recast as merely one species of world history. But such proposals invariably lose sight of American exceptionalism, suggesting that the United States is like all other nations.

The last factor in the West's cultural shift is a loss of existential confidence that is at the same time a failure of nerve. The retreat of apostolic teaching is a case in point. Catholicism, despite many new converts, is culturally in retreat, not only as a religion but as an authoritative voice of moral conviction. Pope Benedict XVI was utterly correct when he told a youthful audience, "The great challenge of our time is secularism," adding that "society creates the illusion that God does not exist, or that God can be restricted to the realm of purely private affairs. Christians cannot accept that attitude. This is the first necessity: that God becomes newly present in our lives."

Implicitly, the pope was arguing that the philosophic underpinnings of the West are under assault as much from the privatization of belief as from external enemies. If the vigorous liberalism cherished by America's founding fathers underwrites our political freedom, its degeneration into relativistic "openness" has left us prey to the blandishments of fanatics.

Of course, faith comes in many forms. Radical secularism itself is a kind of faith, as is the dogmatic commitment to scientific rationality, to which so many secularists appeal in the hopes of answering moral and ontological questions that were once answered by religion. Even what the sociologist Robert Bellah, and Rousseau before him, called "civil religion" involves faith in the achievements and existential vitality of our republican traditions, including its religious traditions.

For the secular humanist, the fact that the mass of humanity may be unable to live without religion is not dispositive. In considering this matter, however, the secularist disinters a "religious" canon of his own, one that has a distinct value system even as it rejects Christianity and Judaism. Of course, the secularist challenge to religion has been an important social force since the Enlightenment. What is different today is the unwitting collusion between some of the attitudes fostered by secularism and those promoted by the enemies of the West. As Bernard Lewis, a great scholar of Islam, and others have observed, democracies around the world face an imminent danger from elements within their own societies that often pose as pro peace and human rights. In the West, the leftist naiveté that exaggerates the imperfections in democracy has fueled the Islamic agenda that challenges the West.

Certainly part of the reason for the recent tumult is the belief circulating in the Islamic world that a secular West no longer has the will to resist Islamic jihad. The compromises and willingness to accommodate Islamic factions in European societies are interpreted as signs of weakness. The more open and liberal the society, the more likely it is a target for jihad. It was no accident, as the Marxists used to say, that Denmark and Holland, two of the most radically secular countries in Europe, should have been the site of some of the most violent Islamic outrages in recent years: in Denmark, the destructive riots that exploded in the aftermath of the publication of cartoon caricatures of Mohammed in the *Jyllands-Posten*; in Holland, the grisly murder of the filmmaker Theo van Gogh on the streets of Amsterdam.

For Islamists, the moment for a triumphalist campaign has arrived, a moment not unlike the jihad Mohammed launched against the three Jewish tribes in Arabia in the seventh century. That the West considers this Islamic fanaticism a form of acting out over deplorable conditions faced by Muslims within their own borders also plays to Islam's strength. Believing that there must be a rational explanation for seemingly irrational behavior, Western leaders and opinion makers bend over backward to contrive exculpatory explanations. Rarely do they come to the conclusion that the violence is fomented by religious zealotry no liberal concessions can possibly mitigate.

There is a civilizational fatwa metastasizing around the globe, from Hamburg to Tehran, from Nablus to Malmo, from Copenhagen to Islamabad. For Muslims, jihad is in the air, and the more it manifests itself in orchestrated street theater, the more it will highlight the weakness of the West. The confrontation between radical Islam and the West is fast becoming the defining test of our age. How that contest will unfold remains to be seen. But if the West cannot marshal the strength to defend its core values, these contemporary Crusades will assuredly end in disaster. Part—a large part, in fact—of that task is spiritual. It involves challenging the gospel of radical secularism, according to which the goal of human life is entirely defined by material well-being.

What the political philosopher James Burnham observed about the West's confrontation with Communism is even truer with respect to its confrontation with radical Islam. "No one," Mr. Burnham wrote, "is willing to sacrifice and die for progressive education, Medicare, humanity in the abstract, the United Nations, and a 10 percent rise in Social Security payments." And yet such "bloodless abstractions" essentially exhaust what secularism has on offer. "Things fall apart," Yeats wrote in his famous poem; "the centre cannot hold." It is not yet certain whether that dour vision is more a news report or a warning. I believe that we still command the resources to salvage the spiritual center of our civilization. But to accomplish this we must have the courage to challenge the seductive tenets of radical secularism and revivify the traditional values that informed and nourished America.

Decline and Revival of Western Civilization (2011)
Originally published on PJ Media

I used to assume that the decline of Western civilization was manifest in the unwillingness of elites to discriminate. The idea of the "discriminating man," the one who weighs concerns and assets, has been transmogrified into the "sensitive man," the one who resists criticism.

Of course arbitrary discrimination based on superficial concerns—e.g., skin color—should be opposed. But this is rarely the case. We live in an era in which any attempt at judgment is cause for arousal. A collapse of monumental proportions has been engineered and there is scarcely a word of protest across the land. Is that because almost everyone buys into the prevailing judgment, or is it because so many do not want to be the target of opprobrium?

Whatever the proposition, discrimination has suffered yet another blow. But while an unwillingness to take a stance is one dimension of civilizational decline, it does not compare in passion or intensity to preemptive capitulation, a desire to support the very movements that exist to undermine the West. If fact, the more extreme the movement, the more you find ardent defenders. For example, jihadists in the United States and Europe state without equivocation a desire to create caliphates across the globe and to introduce sharia as legal precedent.

Remarkably those on the left, who once renounced orthodoxies of any kind, now embrace the totalistic dimensions of Islam. They insist that the full panoply of civil rights be given to foreign combatants (read: terrorists). They contend that the Islamic faith promotes peace, even when every schoolboy knows Islam is designed to place the non-believer in a position of submission.

The Danish government that once stood up to Islamic intimidation has seemingly collapsed. Now one minister after another finds some justification for Islamic violence, a rationalization that makes commonsensical defense of Western traditions untenable. And this is rapidly becoming the European defense model, as many judicial officials opt to maintain order rather than confront extremists.

Can the West withstand this dual attack—one, a breakdown of judgmental standards and two, a capitulation to the most radical forces on center stage? My answer is yes, if the West awakens from its ideological slumber and attempts to slaughter the dragon of intimidation.

As Adam Smith noted, "There's a great deal of ruin in a nation," and I might add in a civilization. "The future is unknowable," as Winston Churchill pointed out in *A History of the English-Speaking Peoples*, "but the past should give us hope."

As I see it, overcoming war, poverty, tragedy, brutality and murder suggests that mankind possesses the instinct for self-preservation, even if it isn't immediately apparent. We root for self-realization even as we fail to see our failures. Can history resort to a turning back, a Dark Ages where standards of any kind are in disarray except the standard of might making right?

For a time, like the one we are in, it may seem that way, but recovery may be around the corner as an anti-toxin for what ails us. History has a way of being pliable and unpredictable, stretching out before us unimagined scenarios of replenishment just as the hour is darkest. That is the condition that offers hope amid the sundry examples of contemporary despair.

Multiculturalism in Retreat (2011)
Originally published on the Gatestone Institute

At long last a European politician, British prime minister David Cameron, has lifted the curtain on the pernicious dimensions of multiculturalism. After several decades of homegrown terrorism and an acceptance of separation by Muslim groups in the United Kingdom, the prime minister has said, "enough."

A new course will be charted that moves from accommodation to integration. There may be a risk of xenophobia with the Cameron approach, but it is a worthwhile trade-off if terrorist impulses are thwarted.

Prime Minister Cameron called his strategy "muscular liberalism," to wit: confronting extremist Islamic thought and challenging those efforts that attempt to undermine Western values. For example, the prime minister made special mention of zero tolerance for the subjugation of women, a practice permitted because of Islamic separation and application of sharia.

The notion that different groups within a society should be encouraged to pursue their own cultural paths is a formulation based on religious tolerance. But as George Santayana among others noted, the first duty of the tolerant man is to exercise intolerance for intolerance. In other words, a proverbial line in the sand must be drawn when religious groups use societal tolerance to promote intolerance.

For at least two generations Europeans have failed to integrate immigrants into their societies. These are recent immigrants who don't speak the language of the host country and have not accepted the basic historic and cultural background of the nation in which they now reside.

After observing the corrosive influence of multiculturalism, one can see that a consensus is beginning to emerge. In addition to Prime Minister Cameron's comments, German chancellor Angela Merkel declared multiculturalism a "total failure." Swiss voters approved a ban on the construction of new minarets on mosques. French authorities have issued a prohibition on burqas and other full-body robes worn by some Muslim women. And the Swedish Democratic party, which had almost no influence in the politics of the country, gained 5.7 percent of the vote in national elections after campaigning on a platform of anti-multiculturalism.

France, which has about 10 million Muslims, has introduced mandatory courses for all immigrants on "French values," women's rights and an overview of the national history. Whether national identity can be imbibed or transcend religious imperatives remains to be seen.

From a sociological perspective, integration represents a compromise between the traditions of the mother country and the host nation. Presumably one can be French, share the tradition of liberalism and at the same time be a Muslim. But is this compromise realistic? Will Islam allow sharia to coexist with liberal traditions?

On the other hand, assimilation demands the acceptance of the host nation's values and the shedding of the past. This is an all-or-nothing position that forces a stark and unalterable choice. Put bluntly, "If you want to join us, you will do so on our terms. After all, no one has forced you to enter our shores."

Clearly Europeans have a right, some would argue an obligation, to defend their Christian heritage against an onslaught from radical Muslim intrusion. The question is how best to defend those traditions. Prime Minister Cameron's well-stated diatribe against multiculturalism is the sound of national tocsin, a battle cry to preserve British culture. On this side of the Atlantic it is a welcome statement that sets the tone for the challenges the West now faces and will be facing in the decades ahead.

The Second Law of Thermodynamics and the Body Politic (2012)
Originally published on Newsmax

The Second Law of Thermodynamics, which suggests that physical forces are gravitating to entropy, is a perfect metaphor for the moment. European economies are cascading into the netherworld of insolvency even as governments deny the reality. President Obama seemingly defies the rule of law by issuing executive orders that bypass Congress. Unemployment in the U.S. remains at over 8 percent for the 42nd straight month. And unemployment in Spain for those under 25 is at 50 percent.

That isn't all. Iran, China and Russia have agreed to joint military maneuvers off the coast of Syria in an effort to bolster the al-Assad regime. The U.S. is on the sidelines issuing empty platitudes about the ongoing butchery. Iran is moving closer to refined fissile material for several nuclear weapons as futile talks continue on the disarmament front.

Missiles are being fired from Gaza into Israel on a regular basis, with more than 300 launched in the last two weeks. Evidence has been unearthed that Hugo Chávez, the president of Venezuela, has been underwriting the activities of narco-terrorists in Colombia and throughout the South American continent.

Extremist parties are gaining traction in Europe, a scenario reminiscent of the 1930s. The neo-Nazi party garnered 7 percent of the recent Greek vote. The Communist party is gaining adherents in France. Radical Islamists have safe houses all over Western Europe, from Malmo in Sweden to Hamburg in Germany and Antwerp in Belgium. To the astonishment of those who adhere to Christian traditions, sharia has been gaining ground as a legal defense in many quarters, including the office of the archbishop of Canterbury.

Educational attainment has been plummeting throughout the Western world, a form of international dumbing down, despite a widespread belief in self-esteem. Notwithstanding the economic miracle in China, that nation remains a police state capable of violating human rights routinely and, when the government considers it necessary, brutalizing is own people. But since the U.S. position is compromised by the assumption of debt in China, not a cross word about human rights violations is uttered.

The world is afloat in sovereign debt. Accumulated debt in the U.S. alone is more than 100 percent of the gross domestic product and climbing. A similar situation can be recorded in Japan and throughout the Western world. An entitlement psychology has brought financial markets to their knees, but few have the political will to tell electorates the truth.

A belief in the Judeo-Christian virtues is waning. Relativism has reared its head as a prevailing philosophical view, leaving its admirers subservient to those committed with a belief system. "Anything goes" is not merely a once-popular song, but a commitment to a way of life that rejects regulation, limits and tradition. The boundaries that defined normative behavior have been shattered by the relativist orthodoxy.

A *Wall Street Journal* editorial refers to a leaderless globe. Alas this is true as the U.S. withdraws from its role as the international "balance wheel" and there isn't an alternative anywhere in the G20. A world without leaders is a world on the brink of anarchy.

As Evelyn Waugh once noted, "Once the prisons of the mind have been opened, the orgy is on." Well those cell doors have been opened, and unleashed is a moral tsunami whose full effect we cannot yet detect. However, surrender to the forces of despair is at least partially evident. I often hear people say, "What can you do?" as they shrug in acquiescence. Perhaps it would be useful to recall that Charles Péguy argued, "Surrender is essentially an operation by means of which we set about explaining instead of acting." Indeed it is words we hear, more words from talking heads on television and Washington's leaders, but action is conspicuously avoided. The words are soothing as an astringent on a humid day, but ultimately they are delusional. The beast in the body politic has not been defeated and he is restless.

Why Do We Accept Our Enemies? (2010)

One of the curious conditions of modern democracies is the temptation to misunderstand their enemies. Time after time history parades political monsters across the world stage, from Hitler to Stalin, from Pol Pot to Bashar al-Assad. Remarkably the initial reaction to these leaders is to assume the "best." Che Guevara was widely regarded as a liberator; President al-Assad as a reformer. Why should this kind of misunderstanding reoccur?

First and foremost is the persistent unwillingness to recognize evil as more than a personality flaw. It is as if the Western world is composed of Pelagians who will not entertain human fallibility. As the British philosopher Walter T. Stace noted, "As a rule, only very learned and clever men deny what is obviously true." Evil exists beyond the dictator of the moment. Goethe's Mephistopheles says, "I am the spirit that denies! And justly so, for all that time creates, He does well who annihilates!" Yet interestingly, Western leaders transmogrify evil into narrowly focused personalities.

Secondly, there is romance attached to those who hate the West. Osama bin Laden T-shirts are sold in European flea markets. American students wear Che-festooned outfits, unaware of his killing ways. Chairman Mao is mentioned by an Obama official as her inspiration, despite his role in murdering millions of Chinese. As the author Evelyn Waugh wrote, "Barbarism is never finally defeated; given propitious circumstances, men and women who seem quite orderly will commit every conceivable atrocity." That atrocity may indeed be inadvertent as romanticism insinuates itself into the public's imagination. Killers become heroes in the percolating mindset of adolescents and their adult enablers.

And last is the intractable belief that if people say good things, all is permitted. Lenin noted that "if you want an omelet, you must break eggs." Unfortunately the eggs are metaphorical people reduced to insects in the minds of soi-disant do-gooders. For years Communist spokesmen such as Eric Hobsbawm tried to convince the public that Communist means were necessary in order to create a better world. Dupes in the West accepted this premise because they want to believe in utopia. Yet even when utopia morphed into dystopia, they refused to admit it. For the true believer, evidence is unnecessary; for them it is not as if "seeing is believing"; it is rather "believing is seeing."

What we experience in this form of mirror imaging that suggests the enemy is really like us—only more vehement than we are—is virtues gone mad. The idea of giving a foe the benefit of the doubt has been converted into accepting the belief that he is right and we are wrong. His "idealism" or fanaticism given him an advantage over our moderation. He knows what he wants; we are unsure, particularly in a universe of relativistic values.

The Noahide principles of civility that saved mankind from a state of nature that is nasty, brutish and short have been reversed. A civilization that created a social contract with God in return for a promise to avoid the catastrophe of another flood has become fraught with fear and uncertainty. Faith is going as well as the covenant that made judgment understandable.

As a result, the ability to distinguish between an ally and an enemy is obscure. The sense that dictators should not be embraced but opposed is mired in confusion. Just as lawlessness has dominated a significant portion of the globe, so has the ascendency of those who would destroy us.

Our need is a covenant with common sense. We must recapture a belief of who is with us and who would destroy us. At the risk of hyperbole, global leaders in the West must do so in order to survive. And the clock is ticking.

The Horror of Killing One's Own (2015)
Originally published on the St. Croix Review

Yemen's security forces have killed more than three dozen protestors in the last few days. Colonel Qaddafi has announced that allied efforts to destroy his anti-missile defenses are a form of terrorism and as a consequence, he is prepared to decimate the rebels in Libya. It seems to me that it is time to ask a question that haunts the history of our time: are there limits to dictatorial power?

Since the Holocaust, the international community has given lip service to the idea that mass murder by dictatorial leaders should never be tolerated. Yet remarkably there are instances in Africa and Asia where this is common practice. In the Arab world, where sharia prevails, the killing of apostates is a routine practice.

Based on recent events, it would appear that conditions across the globe are sliding back to a barbaric period in which murder of one's own people for the retention of power is permitted or at least ignored. The argument is that we cannot possibly intervene whenever atrocities occur. Or perhaps more logically, sovereignty trumps atrocity.

It is instructive that U.S. State Department officials employed the latter position for a time by suggesting we should not insinuate ourselves into a Libyan civil war. In other words, however sanguinic the attacks may have been and continue to be, there is not a justifiable role for the U.S. Needless to say, that position has been modified by our stance on the "no-fly zone."

As I see it the basic Obama foreign policy thrust is based on an incremental U.S. withdrawal from regional influence. The withdrawal, I should hastily note, is both emotional— an unwillingness to defend our interests and our allies—and physical—a draw-down of troops based on the belief we cannot afford these foreign ventures.

That strategic version, or lack thereof, has created a situation in which our enemies believe we are ineffectual and our allies believe we are untrustworthy. Instead of hastening to carve out a defensive stance for the U.S., one that recognizes our foreign interests, the administration has decided to channel our foreign policy through the United Nations. In doing so, the leverage that emerged in the past from the assertion of national power has been lost. We are at sea as one nation in an international armada that has lost its way.

The new concept of America opting out of unilateral action has implications for nations with imperial goals. Iran has become the "strong horse" in the Middle East neighborhood by default. Our emerging position encouraged its evolution. Ortega y Gasset once noted, "To create a concept is to leave reality behind." Our concept of multilateralism is a chimera surrounded by a fantasy.

Winston Churchill warned that when democracies triumphed in World War II, they "were able to resume the follies which had so nearly cost them their life." It seems we are at it yet again.

We watch with horror as power-hungry barbarians kill their own people. But we generally tolerate these actions. We are overcome by the magnitude of evil and the inversion of certitudes, but are helpless in their wake. We seek fresh creeds, but do not know how to deal with the revulsion in our collective gut. And all the while our leaders tell us this will pass and, after all, there is nothing we can do.

Is the world turning to savagery? Are the 1930s a scenario for the new century? Are we to allow shamefacedly the death and horror we have the capability to prevent? The derision of death lurks in our imagination, but the will to reverse it has not emerged. America cannot police the world, but the U.S. is still the only anchor that can assure international stability. It seems to me that role must be recognized and given the attention history has placed on it.

Culture Begets Foreign Policy (2016)

"Orlando" now bespeaks murder, bloodshed and savagery. It also suggests denial, blindness and ignorance. A nation fueled by reason has, in many quarters, behaved irrationally. There appears to be an unwillingness to call the murderer what he calls himself: a devoted follower of the Islamic State to whom he has pledged allegiance. How is it that so many in America are determined to refute the truth? This wasn't merely terror and violence, bigotry and hatred; it was the manifestation of a specific condition, militant Islam. Yet as obvious as this may be, some cannot speak its name. Why, it might be asked, has the culture produced such blindness? Why has a society as dynamic as the United States lost it way in foreign policy trenches? This is only partially explained by the odd verbal stance of President Obama. Yet President Obama expresses one man's point of view; the culture he represents is the arterial system of the U.S. and accounts, in large part, for foreign policy perceptions.

With the onset of the '60s, leftists embraced Jean-Paul Sartre's defense of Communism: "It should be judged by its intentions and not by its actions." Alas, so many are judged by their apparent goodwill, not by the reality they are obliged to confront.

Plato made the argument that he who controls the "chords" controls the state. What Plato meant is that culture determines the course of politics. For the U.S. circa 2016 this means a debased culture that is misogynistic, violent, pornographic and often intentionally dehumanizing, one that cannot pursue policies in the national interest. In most cases, people cannot even tell you what the national interest is.

Some might contend there isn't a relationship between national security and rap music. But, alas, that is not true. When the U.S. military created a radio station in Iraq, al Hura, to promote American culture, it routinely played rap music. That so-called music and its perverse lyrics became a powerful argument for militant Islamists, who argued if the Americans prevail, this is the culture you'll get.

Faust's dying words is Goethe's masterpiece were, "Only he deserves freedom as well as life who must conquer them every day!" This might be the motto for an America that understood its mission and defied entropy, living a life filled with energy and imagination. That America is on the wane. Signals of that enervation appear in labor participation rates and a dramatic increase in food stamp recipients. As significantly, the manifest signs of disinterest in foreign policy exist everywhere, notwithstanding the obvious fact that foreign policy reached our borders on 9/11 and in San Bernardino, California, and now in Orlando, Florida.

As my former colleague Neil Postman pointed out, "We are amusing ourselves to death." Images have penetrated our view of the world that rely on an invulnerable U.S., one protected by our collective Batman. Yet, despite the brave men and women who protect America from harm, this nation is vulnerable to attack. Whether we like it or not, the temper of the nation is another line of defense and foreign policy.

An aversion to risk is the first cousin of complacency. President Obama is so risk-aversive, he will not send a battle force of any magnitude to contest Chinese adventurism in the South China Sea, and popular opinion as seen through the polls appears to support the president. If risk aversion is the first priority in foreign policy judgments, then U.S. interests abroad cannot be protected. The U.S. as defender of open access to the seas becomes a footnote to history.

Most people ignore the ties between art and war. Thomas Mann wrote during the First World War: "Reliability, exactitude, discretion; boldness, steadfastness in confronting trials and defeat in contention with the resistance of the material; contempt for that which is called 'security' in bourgeois life: All of this is in fact at once military and artistic. When we ignore the qualities necessary for artistic expression, we inadvertently squander the state of mind needed for war fighting." How many Americans today would say, "I am willing to risk my neck to fight terrorism?" How many put their minds to work on genuine artistic expression?

In 2009 only 3 percent of Americans reported playing classical music in the preceding year as opposed to the 70 percent who listened to or played contemporary music that has neither exactitude nor discipline. It is as if Americans consume kumbaya liquids and then sing John Lennon's "Imagine," to wit, a world without nations and religions to divide us and each person is free to define his identity. This is the new age in the West, where there is nothing worth fighting for or against. Hedonism prevails and the terror threat is merely a fiction hoisted on the public by Washington legislators who have a stake in its promotion. But if there is nothing worth dying for, there is probably nothing worth living for, a cliché that has extraordinary resonance at the moment.

A culture of risk-taking—when appropriate—and of steadfastness suited the American sensibility and provided implicit direction for foreign policy. I yearn for the moment that sentiment can be recaptured, but until the U.S. regains its bearings, I can only lament the extent of our debasement.

What the World Sees in the U.S. (2016)
Originally published in The Washington Times

The secular religion of America is in disarray. Black Lives Matter disavows loyalty to the Constitution. Many Americans of various ethnicities have detached themselves from the bedrock beliefs that made this nation unique in the history of the world.

The director of national intelligence, James Clapper, recently gave Congress an assessment of threats around the globe that amounted to an indictment of President Obama's failed foreign policy. A "literary of doom" is on the lips of the candidates for president in both parties. Donald Trump refers to America as a "mess." "We don't win anymore." Bernie Sanders speaks of the unfairness in the political system, where billionaires control the outcome. Even Hillary Clinton, who walks a fine line between supporting and criticizing the Obama administration, notes that there are "mounting challenges that have to be addressed." Pessimism is on the rise.

The "shining city on the hill" that President Reagan exalted is enshrouded in fog. Despite many of the qualities it possesses, candidates and critics have conspired to tear down America in the eyes of the world.

Clearly the Obama foreign policy is interpreted by our enemies as a sign of weakness. Retreat and acquiescence are usually viewed that way. Now, however, perceptions run deeper. From Iran to China there is a belief that the culture—i.e., the sinews of civil society—is tearing. In conversations I have had with Chinese and Japanese nationals, there is a conviction that the U.S. is suicidal, a nation overdosing on metaphorical Valium.

This is a viewpoint buttressed by: a debt that has risen to $19 trillion; extremist political language; a breakdown in the educational system at all levels; families in distress; and a fundamental ignorance of the national past. The bread-and-circuses atmosphere has led to serious misgivings of America as a serious nation—one that misunderstands its own interests and those of its allies.

Traveling to the Middle East reinforced this opinion. Leave aside comments about President Obama's failed policies; there is a growing belief that there is a cultural cancer metastasizing throughout the American body politic. The fact that a campaign for president on both sides of the political spectrum deals almost exclusively with failure demonstrates this point. This is what many foreigners see in the United States today.

The land of opportunity, of hope and virtue, the beacon of light across the ages for liberty, has foundered on the shoals of self-doubt. A loss of confidence is palpable. Xi Jinping, Vladimir Putin and Ali Khamenei recognize this condition in addition to recognizing President Obama's strategy of withdrawal.

Our founders understood this danger. George Washington argued: "If in the revolution of ages, virtue should give way to a corruption of morals, profligacy of manners and listlessness for the preservations of the natural and unalienable rights of mankind, then usurpation may arise upon the ruins of liberty…against which no human prudence can effectively provide."

Here is the dilemma: we amuse ourselves into listlessness. And our enemies and friends sense it. The island of hope has become a nation of despair. We talk ourselves down and wonder why the U.S. isn't appreciated. Hope has not evaporated, but the ability to recall the romance and achievement in our history has gone out of favor. That is a shame that awakens a call to action. For those who remember what America was recall the virtue, the liberty and the confidence this nation gave as gifts to the world. It helps to cite what America has accomplished in addition to what it might accomplish.

Concluding Thoughts and Prescriptions for the Future

The School of Emergent Global Peace (2013)
Originally published by WAMC Northeast Public Radio

For meta-historians who take the long view—e.g., Arnold Toynbee—there is the emergence of a "looming global peace" that is gaining acceptance in the corridors of academe. It is predicated on the belief that we are nearing a point in history where war as we know it has disappeared. Presumably the world is becoming safe and secure, with few violent conflicts. Moreover, the United States faces no plausible existential threats or great power rivalry. This is the unvarnished theme at its most basic level.

There is evidence to support it. Since 1946 armed conflict across the globe, including deaths in battle, have declined precipitously. There are zones of peace, such as Europe, that throughout the last 400 years have known nothing but war. Most of the conflicts that do occur are intranational rather than an imperial desire for empire. Even China's view of the Middle Kingdom does not overlook the sovereignty of its Asian neighbors. And there is Francis Fukuyama's belief that we have reached the "end of history," a point at which the rivalry among nations is eliminated.

That this worldview is in the ascendency is not surprising. It is consistent with the Obama position that fewer forces than we now deploy will be required on the battlefield and, while military hardware is still necessary, being armed to the teeth is an unnecessary expenditure of scarce resources. This isn't Kellogg-Briand all over again, but it is a distant cousin of the proposition that war as we've known it will not be seen again.

While evidence for these claims cannot be casually dismissed, they are hardly dispositive. The Chinese are not likely to be satisfied with a military force about a fourth the size and strength of the United States'. Deployment of the Chinese navy in the South China Sea and the Sea of Japan has already raised alarms in Japan and the Philippines. Vladimir Putin's Russia has ambitions to reclaim areas lost with the fall of the Soviet empire and to reassert his influence in Eastern Europe.

Arguably the most serious challenge comes from the Islamic radicals intent on creating caliphates across the globe. Since these radical groups comprise many non-state actors, opposing and defeating them is increasingly complicated. Moreover, it is conceivable that nuclear weapons can be secured by these groups, disrupting any form of stability.

Then there are the Shia imams in Iran who believe nuclear weapons offer leverage over Sunni rivals in the region. The quest for nuclear capability is both a political and military weapon that could give Iran leverage as a Middle East power to be reckoned with.

Nuclear weapons themselves could alter the balance of power in any region of the globe. Since proliferation is likely to occur in both nuclear weapons and other forms of lethality, it isn't clear if nations with these weapons promote stability or the possibility that weapons of mass destruction will be employed.

The diffusion of technology and the influence of information available in real time alter the notion of international equilibrium. It is possible that uneven economic development, an aging workforce, widespread urbanization, unemployment and demographic perturbations could result in areas of instability and the rise of extremist political parties.

As a backdrop, the withdrawal of the U.S. from its post–World War II role as international balance wheel and frayed alliance resilience are opening vast unknowns on the world stage. Since political vacuums are always filled, there are many imponderables, including many dangerous outcomes that await us. Resource competition and socio-economic stress must be added to the scenario mix as potential sources of conflict, albeit innovations such as fracking could mitigate the resource concern.

Since the future is not foreseeable and human nature not predictable or linear, the only guide to the future is the past, and that too is not a reliable guide, since history does not repeat itself exactly. Even if emergent trends suggest zones of peace, they do not ensure order and stability. War has not stopped evolving and whether we like it or not, all forms of warfare, from terrorism to major combat, are possible. Therefore it is best to prepare for the worst and hope for the best. Recent history isn't a definitive guide for defense allocations. And the Obama administration's belief that the bulk of budget reductions through sequestration can be imposed on defense spending is potentially very dangerous.

Writing about his belief in God, Blaise Pascal made the point that if you believe in God, but He doesn't exist, all you've done is wasted time. But if there is a God and you do not believe in Him, you have sacrificed everything. Applying this notion to security, it is obvious if war is still a possibility and you do not believe in preparing for it, you will have sacrificed everything—your future, your liberty, your nation. Hence skepticism about the school of emergent global peace is a healthy response.

What We Are "Sure" We Know About Foreign Policy (2014)
Originally published on Family Security Matters

What do we know, or think we know, that just isn't true? There are myths, riddles and indeterminate conditions, but for many these factors are ignored in favor of what one believes to be true.

Let me cite several examples.

It has long been contended by foreign policy analysts that the security architecture of the Eastern Mediterranean was based on a preponderance of American power, specifically naval power. What was once undeniable is now subject to clear challenges. The withdrawal of American naval forces from the region has led to a vacuum in which a Russian naval presence has become more prevalent than was previously the case and radical Islamic influence has heightened. Moreover, it is not clear that the U.S. is aware of the possibility of losing the eastern part of the Mediterranean Sea to Russia or radical Islam, or is preparing to forestall such a scenario.

President Barack Obama has noted that the prime minister of Turkey, Recep Tayyip Erdogan, was his closest ally, someone on whom he can depend. However, it is clear Prime Minister Erdogan has not cooperated with U.S. military operations in the region, despite his stated opposition to the Islamic State. Turkey has also violated the sanctions regimen by continuing its trade with Iran. And it pursues a foreign policy that increasingly sides with the most extreme elements in the region.

State Department spokespeople continue to assert that the Arab Spring represents the efflorescence of democratic sentiment. And in Tunisia that may be true, but it certainly isn't anywhere else in the region. Libya, Syria and Iraq—to mention three examples—have been transformed from spring thaw into winter freeze.

It is an article of faith to contend that the U.S. is Israel's closest ally. Indeed since the creation of the state, Israel has been the beneficiary of American largess. With President Obama at the helm, however, a page has been turned in the relationship. President Obama is considering sanctions against Israel because of the construction of settlements in East Jerusalem; at the same time, he is relaxing sanctions against Iran in the hope that this will introduce flexibility into the talks on nuclear weapons in Vienna. For many Israelis, deciding on friend or foe isn't easy any longer.

It was a facile judgment to maintain "oil is king" in the Middle East neighborhood. Black gold in the ground paid the bills, gave Arab states leverage in the West and provided riches beyond the contemplation of Croesus. But with oil prices dropping into the neighborhood of $60 a barrel, or half of the price of two years ago, the oil-is-king scenario has lost its bite. Natural gas and fracking have altered the energy equation. With this shift, the need to deploy troops to protect the Middle East oil interest is less pressing.

It was axiomatic that U.S. military influence was a stabilizing influence on global affairs, a position that almost anyone at a foreign policy desk in Washington once accepted. President Obama has a different view, arguably a revolutionary position. He contends that our oversees commitments do not enhance global stability. It is his belief that in order for the U.S. to restore its standing in world affairs, it should channel foreign policy interests to global partners—i.e., "lead from behind."

Alas, the world turns and with it the assumptions of yesteryear—alas, yesterday—no longer apply. Hence the consistency needed to make foreign policy isn't evident. Those who think they know how the world works are often referring to a world that doesn't exist.

There will always be those who appropriately apply the lessons of the past, and yes, we must learn from them. But those lessons must be tested against an ever-shifting backdrop abroad and here at home. Demography, for example, may not be destiny, but it does influence politics and a foreign policy orientation, as does the changing cast of policy makers. What does this all mean? Just when you are sure you know, try reviewing your position again and again.

Recapturing Virtue: A Strategy for Opposing Radical Islam (2015)
Originally published by WAMC Northeast Public Radio

The contest on the world stage is not merely between Islam and the Judeo-Christian world, but between modernity and tradition.

Modern life has disrupted traditional values, creating a cultural environment in flux. Modernity has also ushered in a standard of living unprecedented in human history, transforming the way people live and think. Material benefits are at the forefront of this new era. They are accompanied by lassitude, enterprise, licentious behavior, envy and greed—i.e., a mix of emotions and actions.

The rise of secularization in conjunction with material welfare has resulted in a latitudinarian worldview in which limits, ostensibly moral limits, are to be shattered.

For many imams this moral laxity is what they often associate with the Western form of government. In their mind, there is a belief that moral turpitude found in popular culture is a reflection of democratic injunctions. Their argument to adherents is that the West has lost its virtue. Hence Islamic leaders regard themselves as the guardians of virtue. Needless to say, it is a perverse view of morality that permits the stoning of adulterers and other grotesque practices. However bizarre these sharia-imposed laws may be, they reinforce a Muslim perception that Islam is the last reservoir of moral strictures.

Western leaders can use a bullhorn to contend that advanced technology and free market applications can improve economic standards in Muslim nations relying on sharia, but it will not make the slightest difference. Islam and the West speak past one another. The West is driven by materialism—a view shared by many in Asia—and Islam is searching for virtue.

Wars are fought on many levels. We must defeat Islam on military fronts and avoid the establishment of caliphates that inspire young misguided youths searching for meaning in their lives. We must defeat Islam with ideas that challenge the violent dimensions in Koranic texts. But it is also necessary for the West to ask questions of itself. Most significantly, it must address the relationship between modernity and virtue.

As long as there are "wardrobe malfunctions" by Western celebrities, violent lyrics in rap music, internet pornography and so many other lascivious dimensions of culture, imams will balk at rapprochement with the West.

There is an uplifting, romantic story in Western history, but it is no longer imbibed. It is a virtuous tale of struggle and overcoming hardship and war. Surely there were errors made in the name of Western positions, but there are also sacrifice, honor and dedication, qualities universally admired. And these are qualities routinely overlooked in contemporary life.

The strategic outlook for the future is based on several factors: radical Islam should be resisted and rolled back on every front; reformers within Islam should be encouraged, recognized and honored; and the West should employ its educational resources to capture the qualities that set Western civilization apart from all others.

Radical Islam will be defeated when the West recaptures the spirit and confidence that resulted in its prodigious achievements. The guilt that surrounds Western thought today is choking the expression of accomplishment. It also prohibits an honest portrayal of radical forces and an accurate self-assessment.

Reason uninformed by faith is as inert as a faith uninformed by reason. The West is immersed in the former condition, with secularism on the ascendency. Radical Islam represents the latter condition, obsessed as it is with fanatical opinion unguided by the moderation of reasoned judgment.

For those in the West, it is time to realize that modernity has distinct benefits, but it fails to recognize the virtue in its history. Recapturing that sense of virtue not only empowers the Western perspectives, it answers the criticism leveled against the West by Islamic leaders.

Is War the Real Alternative? (2015)
Originally published on Accuracy in Media

Coursing through the bloodstream of American history are wars that devastated the young and plunged the nation into despair. In World War II millions lost their lives across the globe. Recently thousands were casualties of the attenuated war in Afghanistan and the conflict in Iraq. Bodies were broken, minds impaired, suggesting yet again that war is hell.

So moved by conditions in the recent past, the West will do whatever it can to avoid war. Appeasement is in the diplomatic air. Verbal arabesques are employed to avoid saying the obvious. Yet despite all the efforts at avoidance, war is encroaching. As Trotsky noted, you may not want war, but war may want you. Alas, war wants us.

It is axiomatic to contend that if you are unwilling to sacrifice in order to defend liberty, the enemy will sacrifice to tyrannize you. The choice we face is not war or peace or even war or conciliation. The real choice, the one we want to reject, is war or enslavement.

The radical Islamic forces may represent a small faction of the total Islamic population, but that claim is irrelevant. Small groups invariably dominate historical forces. Although tactics may vary, radical Islamists share basic principles: the desire for a global caliphate, the imposition of sharia and the use of violent jihad as an instrument for advancement. If we do not oppose these ideas directly in battle and on the ideological front, we will be dealing with them on our doorstep.

While the Islamic State at the moment does not have the capability of reaching our shores, Iran, the newly anointed ally of the United States, does. As Iran is the principal state sponsor of terrorism, whose tentacles have reached Argentina, Venezuela and European capitals, it is odd that the P5+1 has been so accommodative in nuclear negotiation. It appears that we have backtracked from our stance that Iran must not have nuclear weapons, to a position that supposedly delays their acquisition. This, of course, has been stated before and in many quarters, including in a letter written by Senator Tom Cotton and signed by 47 senators.

In the quiver of these senators are sanctions, alleged to be a factor in bringing Iran to the negotiating table. However, even with the sanctions of the past, Iran has never expressed a willingness to suspend its nuclear development activity. What most people will not say, what even I shudder at contemplating, is that only force will alter the direction of the Iranian threat.

No one knows precisely what this means or the logistics behind this claim. Yet it is time to consider present reality. An Iran with nuclear weapons represents a threat to Israel, every European capital and possibly the United States. Its missile force in Parchin is not open to negotiation. The IAEA indicated that there is much that is unknown about the Iranian nuclear program and probably much that will never be known.

Surely, war is not something anyone wants or desires. It is the last possible recourse. But in my judgment, we have reached that juncture.

To preserve the United States as a free society, sacrifices must be made, however unpleasant that may seem. Nicolas Chamfort, the writer and dramatist, said, "Nearly all people live in slavery for the reason the Spartans gave us as the cause of the slavery of the Persians: they are not able to utter the syllable 'no.'" We should say no to Iran and simultaneously be prepared to defend that decision.

National Will and Foreign Policy (2015)
Originally published on Newsmax

Despite the Marxist assertion that economic factors drive the forces of history, modernity offers a different response. Jacobins during the French Revolution argued that politics—understood as the quest for power—drives history. Here, too, history provides an equivocal response. It is in the warehouse of liberal dogma that if you have a democracy and a free market, the quest for historical justification is in the offing. Presumably these are the characteristics of a smoothly running machine of state.

While politics and economics are certainly undeniably important in historical assessment, they in themselves are not the dynamic force in history. At the core of historical movement is what people believe, cherish, worship. The real test of history is what a people are willing to sacrifice, on what are they willing to stake their lives.

In the tool kit of human aspirations is belief—what do you really care about? Some have written off culture, assuming that technology will replace it as virtual reality subsumes what we hear and see, bending all things to our service. But redemption through technology is a chimera.

A society that does not believe in anything but the latest Apple gadget is hostage to the totalitarian impulses of enemies. How does the United States—in the grip of relativism—defend itself against militant Islam, which has a fanatical devotion to what it does believe? Ancient Rome, despite its superior armies and worldwide empire, fell to barbarians because it could not sustain a belief system.

Foreign policy is partially a matter of moving metaphorical chess pieces on an international board. At times, it requires rational judgment and hardheaded assessment. As Lord Palmerston noted, what counts for states in "interest." That is true, as far as it goes. However, interest is determined by belief, by the will of national sentiment. The people must know why they are being asked to defend interests. They must have a stake in the outcome. They must be convinced the sacrifice is necessary.

After 9/11 President Bush said the nation is prepared to attack the perpetrators of this murderous attack on the United States. He also said, go about your business; shop in your malls; don't let the terrorists change your life. His comments—even though the intent was clear—are mutually contradictory. It is impossible to be at war and at peace simultaneously. On the one hand sacrifice is needed; on the other, sacrifice is unnecessary.

In *The Scarlet Letter* Nathaniel Hawthorne has his leading character say, "No man, for any considerable period, can wear one face to himself and another to the multitude, without finally getting bewildered as to which may be true." The face of disinterest and relativism struggles against fanatical Islam. It struggles against a past in which most Americans understood what they were obliged to defend. Interests were laid bare after the attack on Pearl Harbor. Today these interests remain obscure.

What should, perhaps must, be recaptured is the "will of the dead," of those who came before us and were united in building and sustaining a nation. British historian J.F.C. Harrison wrote: "The most enduring aspects of a social movement are not always its institutions, but the mental attitudes which inspire it and which are in turn generated by it." The ultimate foundation for historical judgment is the binding tie of cohesive sentiment. This sentiment emerges from tradition, gathering up to create a civilization that the larger public seeks to defend.

A foreign policy that does not recognize this condition is rendered nugatory by the confusion in public opinion. How do you mobilize a public to defend itself, to stand by its liberty, when there aren't any principles of national cohesion that have been imbibed? The barbarians stand at our gates and smile. We cannot define the enemy; we cannot ask for sacrifice, and our will to fight is withering away. Is it any wonder American foreign policy is in disarray?

Evaluating the Obama Foreign Policy (2015)
Originally published in The American Spectator

Now that we are entering the last chapter of President Obama's foreign policy tale, how might one judge his tenure? Writing in the pages of *Foreign Affairs*, Gideon Rose argues that due to the restrained and "clever" leadership provided by the president, "the United States today [2015] may be richer, stronger, safer than it has ever been; if not, it is certainly close to it....And it is at the center of an ever-expanding liberal order that has outwitted, outplayed, and outlasted every rival for three-quarters of a century."

While Mr. Rose is a gifted editor and writer, I find his conclusions mind-boggling. Admirers of President Obama's foreign policy often refer to the end of U.S participation in the Iraq and Afghan wars, but no one could argue that peace and stability reign. Nor can one point to a single nation anywhere in the Middle East and beyond whose fortunes improved during the Obama years. Needless to say, Mr. Rose will claim I am in the gloom-and-doom choir, but I think it is important to note that gloom is sometimes an accurate barometer of global conditions. Let me be somewhat more precise in my assessment.

The unprecedented migration of hundreds of thousands of North Africans into Europe and beyond is a reflection of the naïve belief that stability in Iraq could be achieved without U.S. military assistance. So profound is this population transfer that some have predicted it is a scenario akin to the fall of the Roman Empire, and others have argued it will undermine the already economically fragile nations of Italy, Greece, Spain, Portugal and even France. By any reasonable standard, this is a migration that could transform Europe into what Bat Ye'or has called "Eurabia." It is a foreign policy blunder that has given the Islamic State a metaphorical green light to engage in murder and rape as tactics for its imperial ambitions.

Second, the president, through his representatives at the P5+1 negotiations in Vienna and Geneva, has initiated a rapprochement with Iran that will allow it to develop enough fissile material to build nuclear weapons in eight to 10 years. That is if "cheating" does not occur earlier. Moreover, despite administration claims about verification, it is clear, based on "side deals" between Iran and the IAEA, that the Iranians are responsible for monitoring their own enrichment programs.

As a consequence, one likely outcome of this negotiation and deal is an uneasiness among Sunni states that is likely to result in the proliferation of nuclear weapons. As Saudi leaders have noted, what is good for Iran should be good for us. Alas, the lid of Pandora's box is open and ominous clouds for the future have emerged.

Third, sensing a withdrawal of American military force in the Pacific, the Chinese have established unilaterally an air perimeter zone in the South China Sea that incorporates a host of contested islands. Moreover, the Chinese have built airstrips on reefs that are capable of accommodating attack jets. In addition, a blue-water Chinese navy has been operating close to Alaskan territory with impunity.

By any stretch of the imagination, these are foreboding developments that have disrupted global equilibrium. It is hard to imagine the veracity of the suggestion that we have "outwitted, outplayed and outlasted every rival" when the conditions outlined indicate just the opposite.

President Obama has been an abject failure in foreign policy. He has been outwitted and outplayed by Iran, Russia, China and the Islamic State, among others. The once-heralded American military behemoth has lost its luster. Challenges that were once inconceivable occur routinely with an Obama team that seems weak and irresolute. The U.S. still has strength, leverage and extraordinary assets, but the government does not have the will to act when action is necessary.

Eliot Cohen and John Gooch in *Military Misfortunes* argue that "military failures can be attributed to three causes: failure to learn, failure to adapt and failure to anticipate."

In my judgment, President Obama failed to learn from history. Our military withdrawals only hastened the action of enemies. Power cannot tolerate a vacuum, a fundamental lesson of international affairs.

Once Russia seized on the opportunity to annex Crimea and insert itself into the Middle East as a defender of President al-Assad in Syria and an arms supplier to Egypt and Saudi Arabia, it was time for the U.S. to adapt to evolving conditions. But this government could not or would not reset the "reset."

And last, the Obama administration failed to anticipate next steps. Surely, someone in authority should have realized that the deal with Iran would have profound implications for military adjustment in rival Sunni states. Yet that person didn't speak out or was ignored, as anticipation of obvious effects was all but ignored.

It might be recalled that Prometheus stole the secret of fire from Olympus so that man might be enlightened. But the benefits of fire, at least for mankind, proved to be questionable. Nowhere is this clearer than in the arrival of Pandora, who was sent by Zeus— supposedly as a gift, but in fact as the price for man's acquisition of the stolen fire. In an obvious nod to the original deception by Prometheus, the gods disguised Pandora beneath an intoxicating layer of beauty and charm. In a quintessential act of curiosity Pandora's box is opened and with it is released illness, sorrow, toil and countless evils into the world. Fortunately the box was closed to prevent hope from escaping. Hope is still here as the potential harbinger of change, but countless evils are afflicting the globe, many precipitated by President Obama's decisions.

Civilizational Conflict (2016)
Originally published on Newsmax

The world is on edge. Tectonic change is occurring before our eyes. While the shifts are profound, it will require historical analysis in the future to sort it all out. However, there are things we know, conditions that are transforming global affairs.

For one thing we are witnessing a dramatic difference in civilizational outlooks. The West is inherently optimistic and eager to embrace the future. Islam, or at least significant elements of it, rejects modernity and wants to return to a simpler time when Islam was on the ascendency.

Because of advances in technology, global interactions have intensified. As a consequence, the awareness of differences, what might be described as a "civilizational consciousness," has emerged. One can live in a bubble, but it is a bubble brought about by real-time exchanges and limitless e-mailing.

The search for identity in a turbulent sea of change has led many in the West to fetishisms and cults of various kinds. And in Islam, it has fashioned a militant devotion to the most extreme interpretation of the religion. In the former, identity is fungible, like hair color; in the latter, it is immovable and often fanatical, with Wahhabism a classic example of the extreme.

A sense that the West has passed Islam economically, perhaps philosophically, has engendered anxiety among many Muslims. The response is a belief and desire to refashion the West, to tear down its "superior" institutions and foment uneasiness about its role in world affairs. This deep-seated hostility is embedded in militant Islam—a culture of schadenfreude.

Spokesmen for Islam contend the West is morally perverse and corrupt, with a culture that promotes debasement. The openness and pornographic displays are used by imams as an example of Western decay. By contrast, Islam allows for honor killings, stonings and the marginalization of women. Cultural investments are so hard and fast, there isn't any way to cross the divide.

Hence, what Samuel Huntington called the "clash of civilizations" is inevitable. A pulling back, a retreat, may occur episodically, but the basic differences are likely to be resolved through conflict.

Religious belief is not easily modified unless leading figures in Islam demand an examination of the Koran and Hadith with the possibility that hostile intent is purged or new interpretations are permitted. President al-Sisi attempted to unify Islamic thought under a banner of moderation. Yet remarkably his courageous remarks have received scant attention throughout the world.

The signs of increased tension, even war, are scattered throughout Europe. Rather than attempting to integrate immigrants, most Western European states said they will turn our collective backs on the issue and let hostile colonies of angry Muslims separate themselves from the rest of society. That this policy has failed is evident with the recent terror attacks in Paris, Brussels, Lahore and elsewhere. Europe is in a clash that will imperil the very cultural foundations of the continent. In fact, the Rubicon has been crossed; there isn't any turning back.

There are the rationalizers seeking a modus vivendi. There are others who attempt to isolate extremism, which is, of course, the right thing to do. But increasingly, violence is not perceived through the lens of distinction. Fear only encourages extremism and extremism reinforces the clash of civilizations in which we are already immersed.

90722648R00207

Made in the USA
Columbia, SC
07 March 2018